Never Good Enough

**How to break the cycle
of codependence and addiction
for the next generation.**

Carol Cannon, M.A., N.C.A.D.C.

Pacific Press® Publishing Association
Nampa, Idaho
Oshawa, Ontario, Canada

Edited by Marvin Moore
Designed by Tim Larson
Typeset in 10/12 New Century Schoolbook

Unless otherwise stated, all Scripture references
come from the New International Version.

Library of Congress Cataloging-in-Publication Data:

Cannon, Carol Agnes.
    Never good enough : growing up imperfect in a "perfect"
family : how to break the cycle of co-dependence and addiction
for the next generation / Carol Cannon.
        p.   cm.
    Includes bibliographical references.
    ISBN 0-8163-1145-5 (pbk.)
    1. Codependence (Psychology)—Religious aspects—Chris-
tianity. 2. Compulsive behavior—Religious aspects—Christianity. 3. Family—Religious life. 4. Religious addiction—
Christianity. I. Title.
BV4596.C57C36   1993
362.2—dc20   92-43283
                                                         CIP

    98 99 00 ● 9 8 7

Contents

Introduction 5

**Part 1: The Impact of Codependence
on Christian Families**

1. Will the Real Codependent Please Stand Up? 11
2. When "Knowing Better" Isn't Enough 20
3. Sin, the Ultimate Addiction 27
4. Anesthesia for Wounded Spirits 35
5. Addiction as a No-Fault Disease 42
6. Why Conservative Christians Are at High Risk
   for Addiction 52

Part 2: Hidden Addictions Among Christians

7. Officially Approved Addictions 61
8. The Abandonment of Self 73
9. Trying Too Hard to Do the Right Thing 82
10. Using Religion as a Mood Modulator 92
11. Confessions of a Churchaholic 101
12. The Hurry Disease 109
13. The Making of a Martyr 122

Part 3: The Anatomy of a Dysfunctional Family

14. Shattered Dreams, Wounded Hearts, Broken Toys 129
15. Shot Down by Friendly Fire 142

16. Robes of Righteousness, Coats of Shame 154
17. Who's in Control—You or Your Feelings? 168
18. Do Christians Have to Be Boundary-less
     to Be Selfless? 179
19. What We Didn't Learn in Kindergarten 186
20. Can the Church Be a Dysfunctional Family? 200

Part 4: Thrice Born: Recovery From Codependence

21. Pardon, Your Symptoms Are Showing 211
22. Sanctified White-Knuckling 218
23. Healing for Adult Children of Pharisees
     and Publicans 226
24. When the Holy Spirit Came to Akron 237
25. Rejoicing in the Lord *and* in Recovery 246

Introduction

Good Christians wonder why. *Why* do their children violate deeply held parental beliefs and values? Why do they get involved with drugs and alcohol? Why are they being eaten alive by anorexia? Why do they get hooked on abusive relationships? There are reasons, but probably not the ones we think.

"Many of the youth of this generation," says Ellen White, "in the midst of churches, religious institutions and professedly Christian homes, are choosing the path to destruction."[1] They get involved in intemperate habits; then they fall into dishonest practices to support them. Their parents' hearts are broken. Aliens from God, outcasts from society, these poor souls are without hope for this life or for the life to come.

"Men speak of these erring ones as hopeless," says Ellen White, "but not so does God regard them. He understands *all the circumstances* that have made them what they are and He looks upon them with pity." And then she adds, *"This is a class that demand help."*[2]

The problems that conservatively reared young people have with drugs and other druglike compulsions do not develop in a vacuum. Circumstances play a part. Our children's negative behavior is as much about our homes and churches as it is about them. It is as much or more about *our* impact on them as it is about *their* perversity!

We adults assume that the self-destructive behavior of our young people is attributable to lack of conversion, parental neglect, institutional failure, or the churches' inconsistency.

While these things may be implicated, there is another possibility that bears consideration: the presence of subtle addictions in ourselves, which, when transmitted to our children, grow silently like hidden tumors, unseen yet deadly. The development of such tumors into full-blown, overt addiction may require years. Throughout that time, the pathology may go virtually unnoticed. It may even take more than one generation to manifest itself, appearing subtly at first, not revealing itself in its most malignant form until the third or fourth generation.

Regardless of how silently and subtly the disease progresses, it will surface ultimately in some dramatic form: alcohol or drug dependence, anorexia, bulimia, sexaholism, etc. Or it will appear as a less dramatic but equally devastating dependence on a druglike process or activity whose destructive potential is as great as that of alcohol and other drugs.

It is commonly understood, for example, that workaholism has the same impact on the next generation that alcoholism does: children of alcoholics and children of workaholics are equally likely to develop crippling addictive disorders. If they were to be compared by their symptoms, they would be indistinguishable. And specialists suggest that the children of workaholics are harder to treat therapeutically than children of alcoholics.

Many rigid religious families unwittingly replicate the dysfunctional patterns of alcoholic homes, thus creating a high risk for addiction in the next generation. Parental preoccupation or *drivenness* of any kind has a negative effect on children. We need to explore these painful realities and come to grips with the presence of compulsivity and addiction in our homes and churches if we hope to prevent further suffering and loss.

This book will put our feet to the fire. It will examine why so many children from fundamentalistic families feel that they are never good enough—the psychological setup for compulsive behavior. It will explain why they find it necessary to medicate their emotions with chemicals and other addictive substances and activities.

Having shared in the recovery process of hundreds of young adult/children from conservative families, I have come to realize that perfectionistic homes are places where children find it almost impossible to feel OK. Parents who judge themselves without mercy tend to judge their children without mercy as well.

In an austere, disapproving environment, a child doesn't just develop low *self-esteem*. He develops no *self*. And then some well-meaning Christian comes along and warns him that his greatest battle is going to be with self! The battle is not with self. It's with *lack* of self!

I've watched the most precious young people, including my own sons, weep as they described feeling that they could never please their parents, that they could never live up to the expectations of the church, that they could never measure up to God's ideals. I found their sorrow and shame painful to behold because I knew I had contributed to it.

A child's environment has a tremendous impact on his addictive or nonaddictive potential. Every system of which he is a part—home, school, church, society as a whole—has the power to affect his sense of self. If serious doubts about his competence and value are instilled in a child by an individual or institution, he or she is deprived of vital resources for successful living. From this, the impulse toward escapism and dependency arises, according to Stanton Peele.[3]

The good news is that change is possible! For this reason, I would like to share some of the experience, strength, and hope I've been given in twenty-five years of struggling with my own unhealthy dependencies and working with other chemically dependent and codependent Christians. Perhaps I'm not the only one who didn't know what my problem was or how to go about "fixing" it. Of course, I tried to fix it anyway, and, thank God, I failed.

Looking at the issues of addiction and codependence within the church is difficult for me, because I am a fourth-generation Seventh-day Adventist. My identity is thoroughly bound up with my religious heritage. Addressing the hazards of growing up in a Christian home, admitting that perfectionistic parents can be toxic, and writing candidly about our weaknesses are threatening to me because I have been addicted to the belief that Christians must always be right and perfect. If you have believed this as well, I invite you to join me in asking God for courage and direction as we examine these unsettling issues together.

In the pages to follow, we will look at specific factors that sabotage the efforts of Christian parents to rear their children in the nurture and admonition of the Lord. We will consider why good Christian kids from good Christian homes hurt themselves and their families by falling into addictive behavior.

In Part 1, we will compare the chaotic alcoholic family and the religiously conservative family and note that either environment can predispose children to addiction. How do "looking good" families replicate the dysfunctional patterns of abusive, addictive families? Can Christian parents render themselves emotionally unavailable to their children the way alcoholic parents do? How do they unwittingly model addictive behavior?

We will describe addiction as an intrinsic part of the human condition, "the drama of the human spirit responding to the stress of life," as William Lenters puts it. We will discuss the fact that fundamentalistic families may be at higher-than-average risk for addiction, and we will discover that all of us are vulnerable to one form of addiction or another.

In Part 2, we will explore hidden addictions in conservative homes and show how these impact children. What happens when parents try *too* hard to do the right thing? How does this set children up for addiction? We will examine certain "officially approved" addictions and their effect on the social, emotional, and spiritual development of children.

Part 3 is devoted to specific aspects of recovery that create internal conflict for some Christians. Many question the appropriateness of psychotherapy. Does therapy encourage self-centeredness? Is it selfish to take care of yourself? Are emotions evil? And is it wrong to defend your rights? Healthy self-care, appropriate expression of feelings, and boundary setting are critical to recovery from codependence and other compulsions, but there is much misunderstanding in Christian circles regarding them.

Codependence is a complex problem. Codependent Christians have distinctive challenges. Their historical and theological biases can make recovery a frightening, difficult task. It is possible to rejoice in the Lord *and* in recovery. But it takes faith to stand on the bank of the Jordan and step into the current when there is so much skepticism in the church about the therapeutic process. Part 4 defines and describes this process and identifies viable sources of guidance and support.

Symptoms of codependent compulsivity and other hidden addictions have robbed many sincere Christians of the ability to be all that God meant them to be. They are unable to sustain healthy relationships. They don't feel close to God, family, or their fellow believers. They exist in a state of mild depression, not knowing what's wrong, wondering why they feel spiritually dead. They come home from church every week feeling vaguely dissatisfied and unfulfilled, and then feel guilty for feeling that way. They blame themselves for their spiritual malaise, not realizing that they are manifesting the symptoms of a "dis-ease" that originated long before they were born—a disease from which they can recover.

We have known for years that *alcoholism* is both a moral and physical disease,[5] the end of which is spiritual bankruptcy.[6] Now it is clear that *all* addictive/compulsive disorders end in spiritual bankruptcy, including those addictions that have been traditionally looked upon as "clean" addictions—workaholism, perfectionism, etc.

It is in our best interest as parents, teachers, pastors, church administrators, and lay members to recognize how addictive thinking and compulsive behavior have permeated every segment of our society and every corner of our homes and churches. Our children did not develop their drug problems in a vacuum. They learned addictive behavior from *us*!

And we can do something about it—if we are willing to take the necessary steps. Whether or not it is our fault is immaterial. I will argue in chapter 5 that it is *not*. What matters most is whether we are willing to accept the responsibility for individual and institutional change.

In all cases except personal references to myself and family, I have altered the names and identifying characteristics of the individuals mentioned in this book. In some cases I have created composite accounts based on my clinical experience. All of the examples to which I refer are accurate and real.

I am grateful to my husband and sons for standing by me in sickness and in health and for granting me permission to describe my symptoms in the context of our family experience. I am grateful to God for steadfastly refusing to "enable" me, even when I was most insistent. I am grateful to my delightful sponsor, who is truly an angel in disguise; to my esteemed colleague, who is a long-standing friend of Bill Wilson's and a blessing to many; and to hundreds of fellow sufferers who have shared their experience, strength, and hope with me. Thank you! You are loved.

1. Ellen White, *Testimonies to the Church* (Mountain View, Calif.: Pacific Press, 1948), 6:254.

2. Ellen White, *The Ministry of Healing* (Mountain View, Calif.: Pacific Press, 1942), 171, 172, emphasis supplied.

3. Stanton Peele and Archie Brodsky, *Love and Addiction* (New York: New American Library, 1976), 6.

4. William Lenters, *The Freedom We Crave* (Grand Rapids, Mich.: Eerdmans, 1985), viii.

5. *The Ministry of Healing*, 172.

6. *Twelve Steps and Twelve Traditions* (New York: Alcoholics Anonymous World Services, Inc., 1953), 21.

Chapter 1

Will the Real Codependent Please Stand Up?

During our junior year in academy, Gerri, Gloria, and I started a girls' trio. It was one of our first notable accomplishments, other than winning an occasional poster contest or spelling bee in elementary school. We sang for chapel, church services, and even the local Jaycees' Christmas banquet of 1957. I remember the first song we performed publicly:

Open my eyes, that I may see
Glimpses of truth Thou hast for me;
Place in my hands the wonderful key
That shall unclasp and set me free.

Silently now I wait for Thee,
Ready, my God, Thy will to see;
Open my eyes, illumine me,
Spirit divine![1]

We sang with feeling and fervency. It was more than a song to me—it was a sincere prayer. With all the intensity and idealism of an adolescent, I dedicated my life to Christ and Christian service. I had no idea then that my joy in serving the Lord would be compromised by a set of symptoms that didn't even have a name but would later come to be called *codependence*.

I still have copies of the music I transposed and arranged for our trio. The oval notes are impeccably penned. The words are meticulously written. Eventually I would recognize in those hand-written copies of music evidence of pathologically perfectionistic behavior. But I was to torture myself for years before that realization came.

As an eight-year-old, I recopied my arithmetic papers over and over until the rows of problems were in perfect alignment. In the sixth grade, I sat mute at my desk, blinking back tears because I didn't understand how to do my assignment but didn't *dare* ask the teacher for help because he humiliated anyone who didn't comprehend. I felt utterly alone and helpless. I had to do it right, and I had to do it by myself.

While I was learning my three R's, I was also learning the rudiments of codependence. Two core concepts were ingrained in me at an early age: (1) I must do everything perfectly, and (2) I must not ask for help. The day would come when I would be sitting in a therapist's office hearing her tell me to cut myself some slack. And I would heave my first real sigh of relief in over thirty years.

Painful family systems

Every child struggles to learn the rules, to find his or her identity, to be accepted. For most, the struggle is not easy. Growing up is painful. It is especially difficult for children whose families are crippled by dysfunction or addiction, which appears, unfortunately, to be the norm in this society.

Many Adventists assume that their irreproachable behavior and unimpeachable piety immunize them from the social problems other people have. They think "sinners" bring their problems on themselves. After all, people reap what they sow, don't they? I'm ashamed to say that this is the way *I* thought at one time. Maybe *other* Christians don't reason this way, but I did.

Melanie was a perfect example of my all-or-nothing thinking. Her home was a classic alcoholic home: unpredictable, chaotic, violent. My attitude toward parents like hers was, "What a shame that innocent children have to suffer for their parents' sins! If only they would get right with God and be a better example to their kids!" And I would pray most earnestly and condescendingly for the poor souls at prayer meeting (after describing their sins in detail so people would know exactly what to pray for).

Melanie's family *was* poor—so poor that her mother carried deep within her a sense of poverty that persisted even after they were obviously prosperous and living in a prestigious neighborhood. You can take the person out of poverty, but you can't take the feeling of deprivation and shame out of the person!

Melanie's mother was obsessed with appearances. Her children weren't allowed to bring friends home because their house wasn't nice enough. Every weekend, she loaded Melanie and her brother into their station wagon and drove through the wealthy suburbs, coveting the beautiful homes and luxurious cars they saw there. Her sense of inferiority and insecurity smothered the whole family with shame. The drinking only made matters worse, because what few luxuries they *could* afford were soon destroyed.

As her parents' drinking escalated, Mel took to the streets. On the rare occasions when she *did* come home, she found furniture broken, windows shattered, and her mom and dad passed out on the floor. They were physically absent at worst, emotionally absent at best. Sharon Wegschieder-Cruse describes this as an environment of high stress and low nurturance.

Mel survived by doing whatever she had to in order to get her needs met. As a schoolchild she "knowingly" sold sexual favors to her classmates to earn lunch money. She *paid* a great deal more than she *earned* in so doing, as time would tell. But at least she had a hot lunch!

Years later, Mel despised herself for her promiscuity. She had no idea that it was behavior without choice. When there is only one option on the ballot, there is no real choice! Mel simply considered herself "bad." She added this burden of guilt to the sense of family shame she had already absorbed, creating a core of pain that never stopped aching. Feelings of such magnitude demand medication!

By the time she was sixteen, Mel had been anesthetizing her emotions with alcohol and other drugs for years, beginning with nicotine at age five. She had committed petty larceny, vandalism, and strong-armed robbery to support her habits. She was placed in juvenile detention, jail, and rehabilitation centers scores of times. Within the next nine years, she would have two abortions, give up a child for adoption, become involved in numerous destructive relationships, and develop serious medical problems. She would run from the police, criss-cross the country trying to find a geographical cure for her problems, and finally end up living on skid row.

At age twenty-six, she put on her backpack and hitchhiked west one more time in a final, futile attempt to find sanity and serenity *somewhere*. Her parents—now sober and deeply concerned about their daughter—thought they would never see her alive again.

Hidden trauma

By contrast, Anne grew up in a conservative Adventist home. She was a conscientious child with a generous heart and a tender spiritual nature. She collected stray puppies and wounded animals. She was helpful and kind. But no matter how hard she tried, she could never quite gain her mother's approval. Nothing she did was ever good enough; her mother was never satisfied. When she did something well, her mother's automatic response was, "You can do better."

In her eagerness to please, Anne became hypervigilant, sensing her mother's moods, anticipating her needs and wants, begging for her blessing. By age ten, the child was a world-class care giver. No one recognized her care giving as a symptom of her own need for nurturance. She took care of herself by taking care of others. Anne's hunger for approval designated her role. She became the unofficial family social worker, fixing people, managing circumstances, and trying to make everything nice for everyone.

When she was nineteen, she met a young man who was exceedingly needy. This so appealed to her nurturing nature that she overlooked his liabilities. He was not a Christian. She would save him. He had a questionable past. She would forgive him. Her drive to rescue him took priority over everything she believed in. Although the church frowned upon marriage to unbelievers, she married him nonetheless.

Soon she gave birth to a baby daughter. Now she had *two* needy souls to care for. Because she believed her child's eternal welfare hinged on her own spiritual condition, Anne redoubled her efforts to be a good Christian. Her first challenge was that of getting her husband into the church. He wasn't the least bit interested! Because his wife's spiritual inclinations were incompatible with his carnal instincts, he left her.

Now it was just Anne and little Colleen against the world. Anne had to find a way to manage financially and at the same time be the best mother and best Christian possible. She remodeled her house to create rental apartments. She took in foster children. She started a small business downstairs. She worked night and day while her daughter stayed alone in their apartment, so scared that she hid in a closet much of the time.

Conquering the challenges of daily living wasn't enough for Anne. Being a mother wasn't enough—she needed more. Because taking care of other people had always given her a sense of satisfaction, she unconsciously sought relief from the loneliness and frustration of single parenthood in her old "care-giver" role.

Once again, her self-esteem flourished. Doing things for others made her feel worthwhile. Pleasing people made her feel good. She found the missing sense of meaning and identity in being a Good Samaritan. And her compulsion to rescue and repair people was fed by the sincere conviction that it was her Christian duty to do so.

She found one needy soul after another to occupy her time and attention. She rented her apartments to down-and-outers and was frequently victimized as a result. She opened her home to troubled children and ignored the dangers she was exposing her daughter to. Because she was so preoccupied with the people she was helping, she was oblivious to the fact that they were abusing her little girl. She was all things to all people, except her own daughter. Anne's insatiable need to be needed progressed into a full-blown addiction.

The child was physically abandoned by her father and emotionally abandoned by her mother. Often, as Anne was leaving home on another one of God's errands, she assured Colleen that she mattered more to her than anything else: "Remember, sweetheart, you're the most important thing in the world to me," she crooned as she walked out the door. "Bye-bye." How does a child feel when his parent's words and actions don't match?

Occasionally, Colleen's biological father came for a brief visit. He told her he loved her and plied her with gifts and promises of the wonderful things they would do together when she was older. Then he would disappear for months or even years. When "older" came, he wasn't there.

Like any normal child, Colleen longed for a daddy. When her mother made plans to remarry, she was ecstatic. The man Anne chose this time was a dedicated Christian who shared her goals and ideals. He and Anne were equally yoked—they were *both* workaholics!

They found positions teaching church school and immediately became obsessively involved in their work. The school became Colleen's home. Colleen felt like a piece of classroom furniture. She went to sleep at night under the desks with a pillow and blanket while her parents graded papers and made lesson plans. She cringed under the same desks while one of their students sexually molested her. She was left unattended and unprotected.

To make matters worse, Colleen and her stepfather didn't get along very well. They competed shamelessly for Anne's attention. Invariably, their worst fights took place on the way to church. But by the time they arrived, no one could tell they had been fighting. After all, they had to be a good example. Happy, happy home!

In their struggle, Colleen and her stepfather reached an impasse. What Colleen lacked in size and strength, she made up for in verbal skill. The more powerfully he dominated, the more subtly she manipulated. Eventually her mother was drawn into the fray, making the tug of war three-sided. Anne was alternately the proponent, the opponent, and the prize. *Triangulation* is what the experts call it. A *soap opera* is what I call it.

At age seventeen, Colleen found a way to escape the craziness at home: drugs and alcohol. Drinking made her feel better. She met people at bars who accepted her, who thought she was pretty, who treated her like someone special. She fell in love with a young man who gave her more attention and affection than she ever had been given before. His devotion gave her a sense of worth.

Colleen had no idea she was about to repeat a pattern that had occurred in the previous generation! Like her mother, she equated being needed with being loved. She made herself responsible for her boyfriend's happiness and him responsible for hers. As their mutual dependence grew, each was drained by the other's insatiable needs. He eventually betrayed her, and their relationship ended bitterly.

Undaunted, Colleen found another man. Before long, a pattern became obvious: she was attracted to men who were physically and emotionally abusive. She unwittingly chose lovers who would at first take her hostage (take control of her life) and eventually abandon her like everyone else had. Her next boyfriend "happened" to be an alcoholic, just like her biological father.

Where was God when I needed Him?

Where did Colleen go wrong? Why was she hurt again and again? Why didn't God answer her prayers? She prayed faithfully, even when she was drinking. Didn't God care about her? What kind of God would force her mother to serve Him so obsessively that she didn't have time and energy to nurture her own daughter? What kind of God would allow her to be abandoned and abused repeatedly? Why did He fail to meet her needs?

Mel screamed the same question at God: "Where were You when I needed You? I was hungry, and You didn't feed me. I had to earn lunch money prostituting!"

Colleen was reared in an apparently normal Christian home. Mel was not, but she found God through a group of loving Christians when she was twenty-six years old. Much to her disappointment, however, being born again didn't cure her or put an end to her suffering. Why not?

The best explanation I've seen was written by another wounded child who was also the product of a dysfunctional family. Like Colleen and Mel, she wondered if God had deserted her: "My dispute was not really with Him [God]," she said, "but with the wrong I could not comprehend." As a result of abuse and neglect in childhood, "a cavity of spirit began to form deep within my heart," she continued. And then she asked, "How many marriages [lives, relationships] go awry because of left-over, unresolved debits carried into adulthood like hobo packs on a stick from childhood? And when, over the sawdust floor, such 'sinners' are called to repentance, does Calvary automatically equalize all the hurt and damage sustained while living in this hostile world?"[2] Probably not.

Herein lies the error many Christians make: They assume that past hurt and damage will be automatically voided when they are born again. When it isn't, they're devastated. The effects of childhood trauma and pain are not necessarily negated, either by being born into a Christian home or by being "born again." Conversion does not automatically cancel the consequences of childhood abuse and restore all that has been lost.

Colleen was an emotional orphan. She was attracted to emotionally unavailable men. She expected to be abandoned. She was programmed to be a victim. She would be trapped in more than one disastrous relationship before she reached out for help. She would develop an eating disorder, alcoholism, and— perhaps most tragic of all—an addiction to abusive relation-ships.

Common denominators

While Mel's and Colleen's stories are very different, they have much in common. Mel's parents were alcoholics. Colleen's were compulsive do-gooders. Mel's parents were non-churchgoers. Colleen's were "looking-good" Christians. Mel's mother and father were preoccupied with alcohol. Colleen's were preoccu-pied with doing the Lord's work.

- They were both born into addictive family systems.
- Both suffered abuse and neglect.
- Both were physically and emotionally abandoned.
- Their surroundings were chaotic and unpredictable.

- They felt lonely, unloved, and afraid.
- They learned to be needless and wantless.
- They were forced to grow up and take care of themselves.
- They medicated their pain with addictive behavior.

If a parent is abusive in any way—if he overeats, overworks, or overdoes anything to the neglect of his family—that behavior will affect his children's lives for years to come. It will be a determining factor in the children being attracted to dysfunctional people, medicating their own emotions with compulsive behavior, or becoming addicts themselves. They will be seriously limited in their ability to have fun, to enjoy relationships, and to take care of their own basic needs. They will not be prepared to live happy lives or raise healthy families of their own.[3]

People bring all of the debits and liabilities incurred in childhood into their adult relationships and impose them on their mates and children, and the children pass them along to the next generation. Joining a church does not automatically reverse the intergenerational effects of addiction and family dysfunction. It is possible to be a committed Christian and still be dysfunctional (unable to function as God intended). And dysfunctional families produce children with dependent personalities.

When a child's physical and emotional needs are neglected, he is hurt. And that hurt is indelibly marked on his soul. Becoming a Christian does *not* negate the law of cause and effect. If a child is wounded, he will bear the scars. Which of the two young women is the real codependent? Obviously both.

---

1. Clara H. Scott, "Open My Eyes That I May See," *Seventh-day Adventist Hymnal* (Washington, D.C.: Review and Herald Publishing Assoc., 1985), no. 326.

2. Esther's Child, *Light Through the Dark Glass* (Nampa, Idaho: Pacific Press, 1990), 5.

3. Dennis Wholey, *Becoming Your Own Parent* (New York: Doubleday, 1988), 22, 23.

Chapter 2

When "Knowing Better" Isn't Enough

As an adult, Mel judged herself without mercy. She believed that she was fully aware of what she was doing when she first prostituted herself as a child and that she made a deliberate choice to act out sexually though she knew better.

Colleen also knew better. Although her mother's well-doing was addictive in nature, Colleen was reared in an Adventist home where strict abstinence was portrayed as an eternal value. She was taught that her body was the temple of God and that everything she did should be to His glory. Her mother did such a thorough job convincing her of the evils of alcohol that the child gave her first temperance oration when she was a mere three years old. She saw a man in the grocery store buying beer and announced in her big outdoor voice that he probably wouldn't get to go to heaven because he drank beer!

Home alone

At five years of age, Dianne was assigned the sole nursing care of a mentally ill father. While her mother worked, Dianne was left at home alone to care for him. She had to make sure he took his medication, and she had to keep him from committing suicide. There was no room for error. The child never wavered— she kept her father alive.

Dianne's parents lived a rigid, ritualistic lifestyle. They were obsessed with cleanliness, order, exactness. They were preoccupied with their weight and physical appearance, so much so that they disciplined themselves to the point of compulsion in their eating habits. When someone mentioned to an already over-whelmed Dianne that she was getting a little chubby, she set about immediately to control her body image by strenuous dieting. Never mind that it might have been normal for a child to be chubby at her age. She began systematically starving herself when she was only eight! Within a few months, she was hospitalized and tubed (force-fed) for the first of many times.

Twenty years later, looking like a survivor of the Holocaust, Dianne entered treatment for an eating disorder. Her physical-sexual development was stunted, her brain chemistry was imbalanced, and she looked more like a young boy than a mature woman (the Peter Pan syndrome). She was five feet five inches tall, and she weighed eighty-three pounds.

Behavior without choice

With her physical and emotional energy totally depleted, Dianne sat in group therapy one day weeping silently, help-lessly, almost lifelessly. "Why did I do this to myself?" she mourned. "I'll never be normal. I'll never get married. I'll never have children. My parents *tried* to make me eat. I knew better!"

Gently, pleadingly, Mel responded: "You couldn't help it, Dianne. It wasn't your fault. It was behavior without choice. You didn't *choose* to do what you did. You didn't *have* a choice. You did the only thing you knew how to do." And Mel, who had loathed herself for years and refused to forgive herself for her sexual acting out, sat back, stunned with the realization that she should apply her statement to *herself* as well. Her behavior, too, was behavior without choice. When a child has only one alternative in terms of survival, *there is no real choice*!

What does it mean to "know better"? Does intellectual knowl-edge or even religious conviction constitute knowing better? Or is there a motivation for behavior that bypasses the rational mind and responds to rules that are emotionally rather than intellectually mandated? Socially, morally, intellectually, each of these young women knew better: Dianne had a bachelor's degree in nutrition, but she was dying of malnutrition! As an Adventist Christian, Colleen knew that drinking intoxicating beverages was wrong, but she wanted to feel good. The physical torture and emotional agony that Mel endured as she prostituted herself was horrendous, but she needed lunch money.

Learning the rules

The casual observer might insist that if these girls had just obeyed their parents or conformed to society's standards, they would have stayed out of trouble. In reality, each of them was an obedient child. But obedient to what?

Earnie Larsen, a well-known lecturer in the field of addictions, tells of his boyish efforts to win the approval of his workaholic father. His dad was a plasterer, and Earnie worked with him, carrying mud in five-gallon buckets, conjuring up ways to carry more than one bucket at a time, calculating how to work faster and more efficiently, basking in his father's approval when he succeeded. The message he got from his dad was that only mortals rest, take lunch breaks, etc. "We're not weak like ordinary people," was the implication. Earnie lived a large portion of his life working harder and faster to prove his worth.

He describes his collapse at age thirty. He had his Ph.D. He was holding down several jobs. He had written numerous books. And as they were loading him into the ambulance, he found himself muttering, "I don't understand what went wrong. I was just obeying the rules."[1]

There are rules, and there are *rules*. I've often caught myself thinking, when my sons violate one of my rules, "They're not living up to what I taught them. They know better!" And then something reminds me, "They *are* living up to what I taught them." My dysfunctional attitudes and beliefs educated my children more surely than the principles and standards I was consciously trying to convey! I thought that if I taught them to be good, they would be saints. I didn't know I was also teaching them to be codependent.

Unspoken rules

What do we mean when we say that our children "know better"? What do they know? They know what the church requires. They know what their parents demand. And they know what society expects.

What else might they know?

If they were reared in a conservative Christian home, they might know *fear* of impending doom. A recovering Adventist alcoholic described his first memories of church: "When the pastor said Jesus was coming in our lifetime (or by 1964), I was terrified."

They might know *anxiety* about their eternal salvation because they are convinced they can never please God. A middle-aged man wept as he recalled his first-grade teacher telling him that one unconfessed sin would keep him out of heaven. He never forgot her remark. Whether or not her theology was correct is not the point. Her timing was incredibly poor!

Children might know the *pain* of loss—loss of nurturance from parents who are preoccupied with their own righteous pursuits. They might know *anger* as a result of suffering spiritual abuse at the hands of authority figures who batter them with Scripture and the Spirit of Prophecy in order to force conformity. Some of us are determined to get our children saved if it kills them (or us). And sometimes it does.

An overly zealous Christian father harassed his twenty-three-year-old son incessantly about his drinking and smoking, scolding and nagging the young man, to no avail. He didn't recognize the futility of his efforts or the compulsivity of his actions. When a concerned relative urged the father to seek professional help, he refused to do so because he believed that the Lord is sufficient.

In a fit of frustration during one of his father's verbal diatribes, the son picked up a heavy object and hurled it at his dad, who died from the blow. The son was sentenced to life imprisonment. If only his father could have let go and let the God in whom he trusted handle the problem instead of trying to force the issue himself! If only he could have *detached*! I am not suggesting that the father *caused* the tragedy. But had he been able to detach, the story might have ended differently. He could have learned detachment in a twelve-step support group or in therapy, but he was unable to accept that kind of help.

This man was not the first well-meaning Christian—nor will

he be the last—to die because he could not bring himself to reach out for professional help. The adamant refusal to accept help is not uncommon among conservative Christians. It is, in fact, a classic symptom of codependence.

Unintended lessons

When we think we're teaching our kids to obey Jesus, they may be learning to distrust Him. "You make Jesus sad when you do such and such," children are regularly reminded in Sabbath School. This does not inspire them to trust God *or* the church.

When we think we're teaching them to appreciate His death on the cross, they may be acquiring a distaste for everything it represents: "You deserved to die for your sins, boys and girls, but Jesus died for you. Isn't that wonderful?" Can an innocent three-year-old comprehend what he has done to deserve *death*?

When we think we're teaching our children to look forward to eternity, they may be learning to overlook the beauty of the moment. When we think we're teaching them high ideals, they may be learning low self-worth and fear of failure. When we think we're teaching them selflessness, they may be learning boundary-lessness.

When we think we're teaching them to focus on the needs of others, they may be learning not to practice healthy self-care. When we obsess about the behavior of others, we may be teaching them to ignore their own character defects in favor of judging other people. When we think we're showing them how to work hard, they may be learning that they are only valued for what they do. When we demand perfection of them, they may be learning to abuse themselves for our approval.

The child's dilemma

If children learn one set of rules on an intellectual level and another set of rules on an emotional level, which rules will they obey? There's no contest! People behave compulsively when they respond to an inner force or drive that bypasses the rational mind. They are not *consciously* or *deliberately* choosing to do so. They are driven to self-destructive or self-defeating behavior by unconscious beliefs and motives that reflect their childhood trauma—the fear, pain, hunger, guilt, shame, loneliness, or loss they suffered in their family of origin. Compulsivity is a mechanism for avoiding these undesirable feelings.

People who behave compulsively are not bad or rebellious. They are simply obeying the "commandments" they learned in childhood—rules dictated by the dysfunction in their immediate environment. In painful surroundings, children take on a survival role. That is the role they know best how to play. In fact, it is the *only* role they know how to play! Codependence and other compulsions develop when the damage sustained by children in dysfunctional, traumatized, or addictive social systems is carried into adulthood and acted out.

Addictive disorders are caused. People don't just fall out of the tree full-blown addicts. The predisposition comes from somewhere. I believe that the seed of addiction falls from the family tree. It flourishes in the soil of a painful social environment. And it develops into codependence, which may then evolve into addictive diseases such as alcoholism, workaholism, sexaholism, compulsive eating, etc.

I am not implying that addicts are not accountable for their actions or responsible for making changes in their lives. I *am* suggesting that addiction is as much about the addict's environment as it is about him and that he should not be held *solely* responsible for changing and recovering.

Unholy commandments

Did Mel choose the life of a prostitute and drug addict? Did Colleen make a rational choice to become a victim, or did she act on injunctions planted in her mind and heart by the abuse she suffered as a child? Did young Dianne decide to commit slow anorexic suicide, or did she respond to the demands of a family system in severe distress?

Did any of these women have a choice? In my opinion, their behavior was not based on informed consent and free, unencumbered choice. They were obedient to inner commandments that were not of their own choosing. Their decisions were determined by a disease of the spirit developing insidiously within them without their knowledge or consent. Sadly, that disease—which they did nothing to deserve—would progress in each of them until they were totally depleted and nearly dead.

Understanding compulsion

Compulsive behavior is behavior without choice—behavior dictated by an impaired will. Emotionally abusive environments damage the individual's will (his power and ability to choose).[2] When one's will is impaired or broken, he is robbed of his freedom of choice.

The apostle Paul clearly understood this phenomenon: "I do not understand my own actions," he says. "For I do not do what I want, but I do the very thing I hate." "I can will what is right, but I cannot do it. For I do not do the good I want, but the evil I do not want is what I do" (Romans 7:15, 18, 19, RSV).

Many Christians identify with Paul's dilemma. They promise themselves they won't stay up so late, overeat, overwork, watch TV too much, gossip, or bite their nails, and then they find themselves doing the very thing they resolved not to do. Often, the harder they try *not* to repeat the behavior, the more deeply it becomes entrenched, which is precisely the experience of the alcoholic. In a real sense, we are all addicts. But few of us realize it.

---

1. Earnie Larsen, "Life Beyond Addiction—Identifying Learned Self-Defeating Behaviors," videotape produced by Fuller Video, Minneapolis, Minn.
2. Ellen White, *Testimonies to the Church* (Mountain View, Calif.: Pacific Press, 1948), 6:513.

Chapter 3

Sin, the Ultimate Addiction

I believe sin is addictive in nature and we are all addicts. In his exquisitely written book *Addiction and Grace*, Gerald May suggests that the psychological, neurological, and spiritual dynamics of full-fledged addiction are at work within every human being: "The same processes that are responsible for addiction to alcohol and narcotics are also responsible for addictions to ideas, work, relationships, power, moods, fantasies, and an endless variety of other things. . . . All people are addicts," he says.[1] Alcohol and drug dependency are simply the more obvious and tragic addictions. "To be alive is to be addicted," he says, "and to be alive and addicted is to stand in need of grace."[2]

The underlying issue

If there is one underlying issue in both sin and addiction, that issue is codependence. Codependence is the self-absorption set up by emotional deprivation and loss in childhood. In this context, the term *self-absorption* does not equate with *selfishness* as most of us understand it. It equates, rather, with the preoccupation an individual experiences when he has a hangnail, a paper cut, or a missing tooth.

Codependence is that kind of preoccupation—an awareness of one's woundedness, an intense self-consciousness, an extreme sensitivity to pain. It is caused by deprivation, abuse, or lack of nurturance in childhood.

The codependent's behavior is characterized by compulsive attempts (1) to control people in order to get unmet needs satisfied and/or (2) to seek gratification in some substance or activity that supplies the missing sense of identity and self-esteem. This is what Keith Miller describes as *sin* or the *sin-disease*. He says that specific acts that are usually considered sin (murder, rape, theft) are actually symptoms of a basic, all-encompassing self-centeredness, a need to control in order to get what we want. Note the similarity between Miller's description of sin and the above description of *codependence*.

A child is wounded when anything interferes with his parents' ability to meet his needs. When he is denied vital nurturance, his ego development is stunted. In a painful, driven, addictive family system, he learns the ABCs of self-destructive behavior by watching the people closest to him act destructively and relate to one another in dysfunctional ways. He learns to cope the same way his models do—by avoiding reality, medicating feelings, running away, isolating, raging, blaming, controlling, and demanding. He does not develop mature social skills. In a real sense, he is an addict waiting to happen.

Sin and addiction synonymous

If, as Keith Miller suggests, sin is *more* than a simple deed—if it is a basic, all-encompassing self-centeredness, and if that is truly synonymous with codependence—then we're all in trouble, because codependence is the norm in this society. We have been socialized to be sick. Self-destructive behavior modeled by one generation becomes "normal" for the next!

Satan cleverly designed self-destructive behavior (sin) in such a way that it is self-perpetuating (addictive)! Perhaps our problem with sin is not merely that it is a *sin* problem. It is sin multiplied exponentially—in other words, *addiction*.

Because addiction has such a tremendous social impact, we Christians need to understand its true nature. In addition, we may need to reevaluate the approaches we have traditionally advocated for recovery from addiction *and* sin. While it is true that the principles of recovery are found in God's Word, our application of these principles may be of little practical value to the alcoholic, the drug addict—or the sin addict. Our pat answers about sin don't always work. Why? Because they fail to encompass the underlying issues of abuse and neglect in the sinner's life—the childhood roots of codependence. Emotional deprivation and abuse in childhood damage the will. The victim is thus robbed of the freedom and ability to make healthy choices.

Perfecting our dysfunction

Here's how Theresa described it: "The children in each generation understudy the roles played by their parents," she said. "My father learned his addictive behavior from his father, and I learned it from my father, and my daughter learned it from me." She went on to explain that in each succeeding generation, the children *refine* the roles played by their parents. Thus, the disease "perfects" itself. "My dad played his role better than my grandfather did. I play mine better than he did. And my daughter plays it better still."

Theresa was a petite, impeccably groomed ex-Adventist cocaine addict. For three generations her family had made material success their highest priority. Money was their drug of choice. Theresa would do anything to get it, legal or otherwise. She was willing to risk her life and jeopardize the safety of her children for financial gain. She was involved in extremely dangerous "enterprises" and, more than once, both she and her children were victims of violence. Her actions fit the simplest description of addiction: repeating harmful or negative behavior in the face of adverse consequences.

A diabolical scheme

Where did this deadly disease originate? According to Ellen White, after his fall from heaven, Satan called the evil angels together for a brainstorming session. The agenda: To figure out how to do the most possible harm to the human family. "One proposition after another was made," she says, "till finally Satan himself thought of a plan. He would take the fruit of the vine, also wheat and other things given by God as food, and would convert them into poisons, which would ruin man's physical, mental, and moral powers, and so overcome the senses that Satan should have full control."[4]

Addiction in Scripture

From the beginning, addiction has been Satan's most potent weapon. There are numerous accounts of compulsive behavior in Scripture, starting with Eve in the Garden of Eden.[5] Her troubles began with the compulsion to seek better feelings from a source outside herself, which is exactly where all potentially addictive behavior begins.

Eve was the most beautiful woman who ever lived—perfect mind, perfect body. Miss Universe personified! Yet she was dissatisfied. She wanted something she didn't have. Unfortunately, when anyone looks outside himself for whatever he feels is missing (meaning, identity, self-esteem), there is in the source to which he looks addictive potential. Eve wanted what God had forbidden her. She obsessed about it until she could no longer resist the urge to touch it. When she did, nothing happened. It seemed harmless, so she decided to eat.

The same psychology is often at work when religious parents try to scare their children into abstaining from drugs and alcohol. They imply that the child will die instantly or at least destroy all his brain cells if he ever touches a drink or drug. When his parents' prophecy doesn't come true, the child doubts their credibility.

Eve doubted *God's* credibility. Because she didn't die when she bit into the apple, she assumed that God must have been wrong and that she was right. Thus she manifested the character defect that epitomizes all addiction: arrogance. *She* knew what was best for her. Eve didn't have to listen to anybody. She would do as she pleased. God just didn't understand—she was different! She was different, all right. She had a serious case of terminal uniqueness.

Immediately upon eating the apple, she felt a strange sense of power: "It was grateful to the taste, and as she ate, she seemed to feel a vivifying power, and imagined herself entering upon a higher state of existence."[6] Eve got high. She didn't realize that what goes up must come down. So-called recreational drug users rarely realize that either, until they are on a roller coaster from which they can't get off.

Eve was heading for a crash. She thought she was in control—

a common illusion of alcoholics. She had no idea that a physical and moral disease was taking over her mind and body and that she would soon be doing things that were totally contrary to her nature. Gerald May says that addiction exists whenever people are internally compelled to give energy to things that are not their true desires.[7] This was Eve's experience.

Codependence in Scripture

As quickly as she succumbed, Eve became a pusher: "In a state of strange, unnatural excitement, with her hands filled with the forbidden fruit, she sought his [Adam's] presence and related all that had occurred."[8] And she urged him to partake.

Already Adam was thinking like a typical codependent: "I can't live without her. I *have* to please her. If I don't do what she wants, she'll leave me. I'd rather *die* than lose her." This is the first example of addiction and co-addiction in Scripture.

All the classic characteristics of addiction are present in this story: (1) a compulsive looking to some source outside of self for positive feelings; (2) preoccupation with the substance or behavior; (3) loss of control; (4) a compulsive urge to continue doing the behavior in the face of negative consequences; and (5) the ultimate loss of everything that matters.

Adam's and Eve's natures were so weakened by their transgression that they could not, in their own strength, resist the power of evil. They could not control their thoughts and actions. Their physical and emotional environment grew bitter and cold. They lost their freedom and their intimacy with one another and with God.[9]

Immediately they began to deny their guilt and blame others—another behavior typical of addiction. It's her fault. It's his fault, the serpent's fault, God's fault. Thus Adam and Eve set in motion a transgenerational cycle of addictive behavior that would threaten the very existence of humankind, which is precisely what Satan had in mind!

Other scriptural examples

Moses suffered severe childhood trauma, which set him up to be codependent. His codependence took the form of compulsive controlling. At a fairly young age he *lost* control of his controlling, which nearly cost him his life. Then he got an extremely stressful job rescuing the children of Israel. As long as Moses didn't try to be his own higher power, he got along fine. But when he took the burden on himself and tried to do things his way, his symptoms recurred. When he tried to control others, he lost control of himself.[10]

How many spouses or parents of drug abusers could testify to the same experience? The more we try to control other people, the less capable we are of controlling ourselves!

Moses' preoccupation with the children of Israel[11] was akin to an addiction. Codependents become as addicted to their troubled loved one as he is to his drug. It is as difficult for a codependent to abstain from care giving and controlling as it is for an addict/alcoholic to abstain from drinking and drugging.

Moses' sister Miriam was also a flaming codependent. She felt obligated to manage her brother's life long after she should have quit. As a child, she had shielded him from danger day in and day out. Taking care of Moses became a habit. But when it was time to let go, she couldn't. Her addiction to care giving and control created serious problems for Moses while he was guiding the recalcitrant Israelites through the wilderness. Miriam's interference in his business led to her being smitten with leprosy for seven days and shut out of the camp.[12]

Noah had difficulties with alcohol and sex.[13] Lot and his daughters committed incest while he was in an alcoholic blackout.[14] Samson was a relationship addict. He persistently pursued Delilah (his drug of choice) in the face of negative consequences,[15] which is, by definition, addictive behavior.

Saul was a rageaholic whose out-of-control behavior was homicidal in its intensity.[16] David lost control of his sexual impulses. His obsession led him to act inappropriately in the face of *extremely* negative consequences.[17] And Solomon refined his father's obsession to the point that he had 700 wives and concubines,[18] which would certainly indicate a degree of insatiability!

The prodigal son was hooked on excitement, women, and alcohol,[19] and Judas was addicted to status and success. [20] Before he became Paul, Saul was addicted to power and control,[21] and he acted in behalf of an addictive organization (the Sanhedrin), physically and spiritually abusing people in order to prove himself right,[22] which is a mark of religious addiction. Based upon Romans 7:23, 24, I believe Paul's "thorn in the flesh" could have been an addiction.[23]

The Pharisees were arrogant perfectionists who were hooked on their rigid belief system. The fact that they were willing to abuse others in order to force compliance[24] suggests that their behavior was indeed addictive. Repeatedly in Scripture, we see the ravages of sin and addiction.

The set-up for addiction

Painful, traumatized family systems set the stage for addiction. In an environment characterized by high stress and low nurturance, children develop feelings of worthlessness and abandonment that prepare them to medicate their emotions later on. Their pain and emptiness demand anesthesia.

And so from generation to generation, the beat goes on. According to Janet Woititz, author of *The Adult Children of Alcoholics*, addictions perpetuate themselves for three or more generations unless there is a therapeutic intervention.[25]

Is it any wonder that good kids from good Christian homes get into trouble with drugs and other druglike compulsions? To the extent that Adventist families replicate the dysfunctional patterns of alcoholic family systems, our children will develop addictive personalities. They didn't invent addiction. They caught it from us!

A prayer for liberation

"Father, we come before You today in the name of all Your confused children for whom alcohol and drugs have become false gods. We ask that through Your love they may gain release and find their way to wholesome living. We bow our heads in humility, *mindful that each of us knows the power of a destructive habit*, whether it be food or tobacco or gossip, gambling or grudge holding, ambition or greed. Lord, let us see ourselves, not separate from those we call 'addicts,' but comrades in a common struggle—bearing one another's burdens, sharing faith and courage on our imperfect journey toward Your perfect eternity."—Anonymous.

---

1. Gerald G. May, *Addiction and Grace: Love and Spirituality in the Healing of Addictions* (San Francisco: Harper & Row, 1991), 3, 4.

2. Ibid., 11.

3. J. Keith Miller, *Hope in the Fast Lane* (New York: HarperCollins, 1991), 26, 27.

4. Ellen White, *Temperance* (Mountain View, Calif.: Pacific Press, 1949), 12.

5. Concept drawn from Greg Goodchild, "Addiction in Scripture," presentation to the General Conference Study Commission on Chemical Dependence, Loma Linda, Calif., May 1988.

6. Ellen White, *Patriarchs and Prophets* (Mountain View, Calif.: Pacific Press, 1958), 56.

7. Gerald G. May, *Addiction and Grace*, 14.

8. White, *Patriarchs and Prophets*, 56.

9. See ibid., 57.

10. Exodus 2:1–4:13; Numbers 20:2. All Scripture references, unless otherwise marked, are from the King James Version.

11. Exodus 32:9-25; Deut. 31:24-29.

12. Numbers 12:1-15.

13. Genesis 9:20-24.

14. Genesis 19:31-36.

15. Judges 14-16.

16. 1 Samuel 14:44, 45; 18:8-11; 19:10-17; 20:30-33; 23:15-17.

17. 2 Samuel 5:3; 11:2-5, 14-27; 1 Chronicles 3:1-9.

18. 1 Kings 11:1-3.

19. Luke 15:11-32.

20. John 12:4-6; Matthew 26:14, 15

21. Philippians 3:4-6; Acts 8:1-3.

22. Acts 26:9-11.

23. 2 Corinthians 12:7-10.

24. Matthew 23:1-36.

25. Janet Woititz, lecture given at Rutgers Summer School of Alcohol Studies, July 1987.

Chapter 4

Anesthesia for Wounded Spirits

Medical science has developed some very effective ways of relieving intolerable pain: anesthetics. When I was introduced to the idea that alcohol and other drugs serve essentially the same purpose that analgesics do—only they numb psychic rather than physical pain—I felt an instant rush of self-righteous indignation.

"A handy excuse," I thought. "A neat way to evade responsibility. We *all* have problems, but we don't *drink*! We *cope*!" Such judgmentalism was my stock in trade. I had to develop an addictive disorder of my own before I could appreciate how wrong I was.

I was horrified by a statement often made to alcoholics: "It's not your fault you have this disease, but it *is* your responsibility to recover." I had no problem with the *responsibility for recovery* part, but I was bothered by the *it's not your fault*. I wanted to blame. I needed to keep sin and addiction sewn up in airtight packages that made me feel safe, secure, and sure of my salvation. Sin is sin, I thought. It's a black-and-white issue. I learned later that all-or-nothing thinking is characteristic of addiction!

I sincerely believed that the disease concept of addiction was a cop-out, an excuse. Today, after working in the field of addiction for almost twenty years, I can say that I have met very few real alcoholics who use the disease concept as an excuse to keep on drinking. They use it, rather, as a means of understanding what they need to do to recover.

Hope for the hopeless

Several years ago I met a clean-cut college student at a camp meeting where my husband and I were conducting a seminar on chemical dependency. "I came today because I have an alcohol problem," he confided. "My father is a well-known church leader. If I told you his name, you would recognize it. I got a DUI last summer [a traffic ticket for driving under the influence], and my dad was so embarrassed that he insisted I drop out of school and transfer to a college on the West coast where no one would know me.

"I went, determined to turn over a new leaf. But I couldn't quit drinking, even though I tried my best. I kept busy, which is supposed to solve everything, according to my parents. They believe that idle hands are the devil's workshop. I took a full load of classes and got into all kinds of extracurricular activities. I committed my life to Christ, prayed, read the Bible, witnessed, and started dating a good Christian girl. Surely that would keep me sober!

"I didn't know I was an alcoholic, and I didn't know that alcoholism is a disease. Once I had tried everything everyone had suggested for quitting and failed, I decided I must be a hopeless case. When you said tonight that alcoholism is a disease, I felt hope for the first time. I thought I was doomed, but if I have a disease that is treatable, then I'm not."

Becoming a savior

Initially, I had only a vague idea of what addiction was and how to help alcoholics. I had been exposed to "experts" who had strong opinions on the subject, but little understanding. They emphasized the moral component of addiction and largely ignored the medical aspect. They were utterly sincere, and I respected them. I still do.

One thing I was sure of: Christians are supposed to help sinners. If alcoholics were sinners, which was undebatable, then somebody had to help them. Maybe *I* should be the one. Working with alcoholics would require careful, prayerful, painstaking labor, according to Ellen White,[1] but I could do it. The difficulty of the task made it even more of a challenge.

So off I went to be a Good Samaritan, not realizing that en route I would act out my own compulsions and succumb to my own addictions. I had no idea that I was starting on a downhill slide into workaholism, perfectionism, care giving, and control that would not hit bottom for almost fifteen years. I didn't foresee that my addictions would eventually bring me to the brink of losing my family, my career, and my life.

Fledgling attempts to fix them (or me?)

My first victim was about to appear. Karen, an old classmate, had been through more than her share of trials. Her sister had been injured in an accident, her father was terminally ill, and her husband deserted her—all within just a few months. She was left alone with two children to support. I really wanted to help her. I was as naive as I was sincere, but that didn't deter me for a moment.

Karen's physician prescribed a tranquilizer to get her through the crisis. The Valium created more problems than it solved, because Karen was an addict waiting to happen. She had a family history of alcoholism, and her childhood had been very traumatic. At the time, I had no idea that a heredity of alcoholism multiplies the drug taker's risk of addiction by at least four times.

In short order, Karen was hooked. I watched it happen. Immediately I launched my first campaign to save a helpless addict. When she overdosed, I rushed her to the emergency room. When she overdosed again, I admitted her to the hospital. She became more and more helpless and depressed. I became more and more solicitous.

She couldn't work full time, do her housekeeping, and take care of her children, especially under the influence of Valium ("gin in a capsule," as some alcoholics call it). She was immobilized. She couldn't function at home, work, or anywhere else.

I tried everything I knew to save her—prayer, reading the Bible, claiming promises. Nothing worked. Her inability to respond (be healed) by my care giving made me feel like a failure. Eventually I gave up.

Since I had failed so miserably with Karen, I took on four more alcoholics. All at once. I thought I would succeed if I managed them better, so I invited them to move into our house. I did everything but handcuff them to myself. This was my first shot at doing the same thing over and over again and expecting different results (A.A.'s unofficial definition of insanity).

A deadly combination

Addictive diseases occur as the result of a combination of the same three factors that cause any other illness, including the common cold: (1) an agent, that is, the germ or, in this case, the drug; (2) a host, i.e., the individual with all his physiological and immunological advantages and disadvantages; and (3) the environment—the physical/social setting or climate in which exposure takes place. Where these elements interface unfavorably, disease occurs.

Karen's addiction was created by a combination of these elements. The host: she was the product of a painful, traumatized, addictive family. Not only was she genetically predisposed to addiction, but she was also psychosocially predisposed by her chaotic family background. As a child, she lived in fear of her father's alcoholic rages and her mother's violence and repeated threat of suicide. She had very low self-esteem and no boundaries. Karen was the ideal host.

The agent was readily available through her family physician. When her environment created sufficient stress and insufficient options, Karen began to medicate her pain compulsively. She may have known better in theory, but she probably didn't have a choice, given the limited repertoire of coping skills at her command.

The transgenerational cycle

Ten years before, Karen had met and married Brad, a handsome young up-and-comer with an extremely dysfunctional family history. Karen and Brad had no idea that they were ACOAs (adult children of addicts). They were wounded souls in need of comfort. They found solace in one another.

They expected marriage to supply them with companionship, intimacy, affection, affirmation, yes, even identity. Karen married Brad because she thought he could give her everything her childhood home had lacked—comfort, companionship, stability, security. He would meet her unmet needs.

But Brad could not carry such a burden. He could not fulfill Karen's unrealistic expectations, nor could she fulfill his. In order to escape her incessant demands, he turned to wine, women, and work. They provided the ego support and self-esteem he didn't get at home. Working hard was *easy*. Making Karen happy was *impossible*!

When a husband becomes involved in an addictive behavior, he is not present to his wife. The addiction becomes his mistress. As Brad withdrew, Karen reacted by tightening her grip on him. She became more and more demanding. He became her sole focus. She was determined to wrest from him that which he had promised to give. He was her "fix." She was as obsessed with Brad as he was with his addictions.

Into this happy family, two precious little children were born.

The legacy of the newborn child

Ideally, when a child is born, his father and mother are prepared to parent. They are emotionally mature adults who can give from their abundance. They can *celebrate*—rejoice in the existence and affirm the uniqueness of—the newborn child. The God-given assignment of parents is to nurture their children to reasonably high self-worth. This requires a steady flow of attention, affection, and affirmation from parent to child.

If, instead, the father is preoccupied with work, success, church, alcohol, drugs, or any other addictive substance or process, and the mother is preoccupied with *him*, who is available to concentrate on the children? Who has the time and energy to take care of *their* needs? The nurturance necessary for them to develop into self-valuing, self-confident adults is not forthcoming. The children's social and emotional growth is short-circuited by the parents' preoccupation with their pain and problems.

In addictive family systems, the ideal nurturance cycle (parent-to-child) is actually reversed. *Children* are forced to draw from their limited supply of emotional resources to meet the needs of, to pacify, or to make their *parents* comfortable. They may even have to defend themselves against their parents' out-of-control behavior.

They keep everything nice and quiet so Daddy won't get upset. They protect Mommy from Daddy's rage. They fix meals and clean house when Mommy is too tired, depressed, or drunk to do it. They are very compliant because they don't want their parents to hurt each other or them. They take care of themselves and their parents as well. They literally *parent* their parents.

Karen and Brad's children expended their God-given energy on caring for their mother. Because her children were her only source of comfort, Karen used them to meet her needs. Instead of being on the receiving end of nurturance, they were on the giving end. There is little doubt that she was unaware of what she was doing. She would never have chosen to drain her children, to rob them of their own vital energy. Nevertheless, their emotional growth was stunted and their development arrested.

Emotional impoverishment

In these conditions, how must Brad and Karen's children feel? Afraid? Neglected? Insecure? Hurt? Lonely? Unloved? Growing up in a home where one parent is preoccupied with his addiction and the other parent is preoccupied with her avoidant spouse is not a happy experience for children. They feel hurt, angry, scared. They develop what one expert calls an *emotional abscess*.

How long can children tolerate such pain without attempting to alleviate it? By the time they are eight or ten years old, they will have their first opportunity to find relief. I believe the form of relief they select is almost random. Whatever they happen to find first that feels the best and works the fastest will become their drug of choice.

Some get hooked on adult approval and use achievement to gain it. Others use food for comfort. Some children's normal, healthy sexual curiosity develops into compulsive masturbating and other forms of sexual acting out. Many young teenagers medicate with romantic relationships. And thousands of children of all ages turn to drugs and alcohol and anesthetize their emotions chemically. Thousands more develop death-dealing diseases like anorexia nervosa.

If the child has a biochemical predisposition to alcoholism, as Brad and Karen's children do, if he is programmed by his painful home environment to addictive behavior, and if he continues to use his drug of choice into his late teens and twenties, then what will inevitably happen? He will become the alcoholic/addict in the next generation, or he will marry one. People with alcoholic parents who do not themselves become addicted have a 50 percent greater-than-average chance of marrying an alcoholic.

Cheated children

At birth, children are immature, wanting, and needy. That's how God made them. They need constant nourishment in order to grow to physical, psychological, spiritual, and social maturity. If *one* parent is absent from the marriage because he is having an affair with alcohol or some other drug or druglike compulsion, and if, in turn, the other parent is obsessed with regaining the attention and affection of her mate, *neither* parent is focused on the children. The children are cheated of what they need to mature normally. And children who don't get nurtured don't grow up.[2]

A child thus deprived develops a core of pain and shame that won't quit. He remains insatiably hungry for that which he has been deprived of. Children need to be filled with warmth and joy and love; if, instead, they are filled with loneliness, hurt, sorrow, anger, fear, and confusion, is it any wonder that they seek relief?

---

1. See Ellen White, *Gospel Workers* (Washington, D.C.: Review & Herald Publishing Assn., 1948), 208.

2. Pia Mellody, "Overview of Codependency," audiotape from Mellody Enterprises, Wickenburg, Ariz., 1988.

Chapter 5

Addiction as a No-Fault Disease

One expert in the field of chemical dependence asserts that addictions are present in this society to medicate the pain of the undeveloped self.[1] Brad and Karen's children are a compelling example. Because they were, for all practical purposes, *born* codependent, it is inevitable that they will seek relief from their pain sooner or later. Randomly, almost accidentally, they will discover some substance or activity that anesthetizes their undesirable emotions.

Because they are biochemically and psychosocially set up to become addicts or to marry people who are physically or emotionally unavailable, are they solely to blame if they develop problems? Hardly. Not having been given a database for normal behavior, they are programmed to dysfunction. To the extent that their primary care givers modeled immature coping skills, they developed self-defeating attitudes, beliefs, and behaviors. They learned to be codependent. They can't be anything else! As codependents, they are walking the fine line of addiction to any substance, process, or activity that has the ability to alleviate their pain. They are addicts waiting to happen.

In adulthood, they will be called "adult children of alcoholics"—individuals who act grown up when they're children and immature when they're grown up. ACOAs are emotionally and socially impaired. They have been robbed of the opportunity to develop normally. How frustrating, how frightening, how embarrassing to be biologically twenty-five years old and functionally five!

Pia Mellody speaks of *addiction* as any process used to remove intolerable reality. "Addiction is present in this society," she says, "to take away the pain, the shame, and the fear of the undeveloped self."[2] It must be more than intolerable for an adolescent to face adulthood with the coping skills of a child!

The responsibility for recovery

If, in fact, the thought and behavior patterns of addiction are passed down from generation to generation, then how far back should we look to find who is responsible? Who is to blame?

I believe *everyone* is to blame, and *no one* is to blame. Or maybe *it doesn't matter* who is to blame! What matters most is that every member of an addictive system take responsibility for his or her own recovery. The more members of a family who are willing to share the responsibility for recovery, the better their chances for achieving sobriety and developing high-quality relationships.

The best approach, then, is to consider addiction a no-fault disease and focus our energy on taking responsibility for recovery. That is the sanest, most realistic, most *Christian* attitude anyone can take.

Addiction—sin or disease?

Years ago, I asked a minister how he managed to reconcile the medical and moral models of alcoholism. I was having a "problem" with the disease concept and needed answers. Although my attitude was a trifle sanctimonious, I was acting with all the honesty and earnestness I possessed at the time. To this day, I deeply understand the struggle of conscience many Christians have regarding the nature of addiction. I understand the difficulty they have recognizing it as a disease.

My advisor shared a perspective that satisfied my confused conscience temporarily. He suggested that drinking was initially a wrong moral choice that could become a medical disease. For a while, his explanation satisfied me—until I began to understand compulsion. Although his answer may be *theoretically* correct, I now question whether the alcoholic/addict always has a choice. Intellectual knowledge is not enough. Knowing better does not guarantee an individual the freedom to choose.

Alcoholism is a spiritual and physical disease that thoroughly undermines the sufferer's power of choice (his will): "Among the victims of intemperance are men of all classes and all professions. Men of high station, of eminent talents, of great attainments, have yielded to the indulgence of appetite until they are helpless to resist temptation. Some of them who were once in the possession of wealth are without home, without friends, in suffering, misery, disease, and degradation. They have lost their self-control. . . . With these, self-indulgence is not only a moral sin, but a physical disease."[3]

If the Christian community has made one mistake, it is that of emphasizing the moral component of addiction and ignoring the medical. I am grateful that we are finally recognizing our oversight.

The nature of addiction

Stanton Peele calls addiction "an unstable state of being which is marked by the compulsion to deny all that one is and has been in favor of, for some new and ecstatic experience."[4] Gerald May, author of *Addiction and Grace*, would agree: "Our desires are captured, and we give ourselves over to things that, in our deepest honesty, we really do not want."[5] In order to get our needs met on the one hand, we betray ourselves on the other.

Dr. May aptly describes addiction as any compulsive, habitual behavior that limits the freedom of human desire. "It is like a psychic malignancy, sucking our life energy into specific obsessions and compulsions, leaving less and less energy available for other people and other pursuits."[6] I appreciate his use of the term *psychic malignancy*. I have always considered codependence a sort of *emotional* cancer.

People don't choose to become dependent. No addict aspires to his role; the gutter is not his goal. He initially opts for a behavior that he may or may not consider risky, depending on his background and belief system. For his own reasons—reasons relating to his residual childhood pain—he decides that taking the first drink or drug is worth the risk. As one addict put it, he knows he's taking a chance. He just doesn't care.

If the predisposing factors are present (a traumatized family history and/or a heredity of alcoholism), he is an ideal candidate for addiction. Should he fall victim to the disease, he will be robbed of his power of choice and left without self-control. When Satan came up with addiction as a way to perpetuate sin, he knew what he was doing!

Addiction defined

According to Pia Mellody, addiction is anything a person does that becomes highest priority in his life, robbing other priorities of time and attention and creating negative consequences that he ignores in order to continue doing the behavior.[7] Obviously, this includes more than drugs and alcohol.

In order to accommodate the full range of addictions, I think of a *drug* as any substance, activity, or process that one uses to medicate, cope with, or avoid his reality. If work becomes his highest priority, if it diverts time and attention from other priorities to his detriment or the detriment of those he loves, and if he continues overworking in the face of his loved ones' distress or at the expense of his own physical, emotional, or spiritual well-being, then he is an addict. If a person shops excessively, if he consumes an inordinate amount of time, money, and energy in the pursuit of material satisfaction, and if his compulsive overspending becomes detrimental to his own welfare or the welfare of his family, but he disregards the consequences and continues to do it, he is an addict.

Common factors

As previously noted, all addictions have five factors in common:

- A compulsive looking to someone or something outside of self for safety, security, and self-esteem.
- Preoccupation with that substance or process to the extent that attention is diverted from other important priorities.
- Loss of control over the use of the addictive substance or process.
- A tendency to continue doing the behavior in the face of adverse consequences.

- Significant personal losses or major life consequences.

When one looks outside himself to find whatever he feels he is missing—self-esteem, identity, meaning, love, affirmation—there is in the substance or activity to which he looks addictive potential (see Figure 1). And the more something changes the way he feels, the more addictive it is.[8]

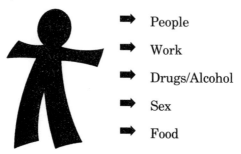

➡ People

➡ Work

➡ Drugs/Alcohol

➡ Sex

➡ Food

Figure 1 — The search for meaning.

There are many medicators that bring temporary relief from pain, anxiety, and low self-esteem. Almost inevitably, when an individual looks for something on the *outside* to compensate for a deficiency on the *inside*, he becomes preoccupied with whatever object or behavior he finds does the job best. It becomes his drug of choice. Eventually he may lose control of his behavior and suffer consequences. If he continues "medicating" in the face of these consequences, he is an addict.

Characteristics of addiction

Medical professionals consider addiction a primary, chronic, progressive, and fatal disease. Drug/alcohol dependence qualifies as a disease because (1) it has specific, recognizable signs and symptoms, (2) it has a predictable and progressive course, and (3) it is characterized by consistent anatomical and physiological changes.[9]

While the cause of addiction may not be fully understood, as is true with many other diseases, addiction is a *primary* disease—a disease in and of itself, and not merely a symptom of another problem (like craziness, weakness, or immorality). It is *chronic*—it can be kept in remission but never fully cured. The possibility of relapse is always present. It is *progressive*—it gets worse, not better. And it is *fatal*.

Stages of addiction

As a result of childhood trauma, many adolescents are predisposed to relief-seeking behavior. Media and peer pressure encourage them to anesthetize their feelings with alcohol and other drugs. The United States is actually the most culturally pervasive drug-abusing nation in history! Recreational and medicinal use of mind-altering substances is the norm. The progression into addiction moves through these four stages:[10]

Stage 1—Learning the mood swing. Whatever his reason for taking a drug, from curiosity to peer acceptance to a simple desire for better feelings, the individual learns by experimentation that if he ingests a particular amount of a certain chemical in a specific way, a predictable mood will follow. He discovers that drinking and drug taking are *a* way to feel good.

Stage 2—Seeking the mood swing. Having learned what to anticipate, he creates the desired mood change at will. Because he suffers few negative consequences at first, he concludes that drug taking is *the* way to feel good! Previously, he may have found meaning in relationships, achievement, and a variety of interests and activities. Once involved in drinking and drugging, however, his range narrows. Other sources of positive feelings lose their charm because they demand more of him than getting "high" does. He is about to get hooked. He took the bait in stage 1. The hook is set in stage 2. Now, although he may believe otherwise, he is no longer able to get off the hook (withdraw himself from chemicals) without professional help.

Stage 3—Preoccupation with the mood swing. In stage 3, the user concludes that drinking and drugging are the *only* way to feel good. Because what goes up must come down, his increasingly higher highs rebound into lower lows when the drug wears off. When he is high, he is really high. But when the euphoria wears off, the low is painful and depressing. Due to the tolerance factor, he now requires more of the drug to get intoxicated, and the highs aren't as good as they used to be. He spends much of his time pursuing the elusive quality of the highs he experienced at first. His pursuit will be in vain.

Stage 4—Using the drug to feel normal. At this point, the addict uses just to keep from feeling bad. He is depressed all the time. He can't function without his drug of choice. Beyond stage 4, there are only three alternatives: jails, institutions, and death. Or recovery. As the addict progresses through the four stages, the ante increases. The full progression is portrayed in Figure 2.

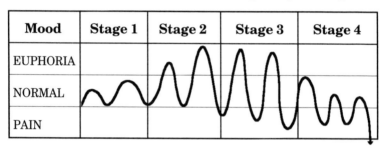

Figure 2 — The progression of chemical dependence.

Larry, a personable, intelligent cocaine addict in his late twenties, told this story: "I was reared in a strict Adventist home. I signed the 'temperance pledge' in church school. During my teens, I refused drugs a dozen times or more before I said Yes. But when I finally gave in and got high, my first thought was, 'Why did I wait so long? This is what I've been looking for all my life!' "

Over the course of ten years, Larry progressed through the four stages, descending rapidly to the bottom when he started using cocaine. "In the beginning, it was as if the devil came along and offered me everything I had ever wanted free of charge. It was nice for a while. I had a good time. But the devil came back to collect when I could least afford it." Larry lost his family, his business, his power of choice, and his self-respect.

The prodigal journey

Larry's prodigal journey was something like that of the young man in Scripture who went in search of excitement, fun, and freedom. The search for that elusive something is the point of departure for all addictions. The prodigal set out to learn the ways of the world—to *learn the mood swing*. With verbal economy, the Bible describes what happened next: "He squandered his wealth in wild living."[11] This is called *seeking the mood swing*.

"After he had spent everything, there was a severe famine in that whole country, and he began to be in need."[12] He was *preoccupied with the mood swing*. He invested everything he had in his addictive lifestyle. And, needless to say, he lost it all. He was left with nothing. The only job he could get was slopping hogs. He had hit bottom—a painful experience that seems to be a necessary prelude to recovery.

The prodigal son went from stages 1 to 4 in three verses of Scripture. Ultimately, "he came to his senses" and headed for home (recovery).[13] The response of his self-righteous older brother is classically codependent—an issue we will examine later.

Causes of addiction

It is virtually impossible to pinpoint the exact cause of addiction. There are biochemical factors. There are psychosocial factors. And there are unknown factors. In other words, addiction is a bio-psycho-social-spiritual phenomenon that is not fully understood. We *do* know, however, that it must be addressed with therapeutic care that is as comprehensive as the disease is complex.

Addictive disorders are *not* caused by weakness, lack of character, immorality, sinfulness, craziness, stupidity, disloyalty, or lack of love for family, church, or God.[14] Nor is addiction merely an issue of rebelliousness. We can't even say that addiction is caused by the addictive agent per se, although an addictive substance must be present for the disease to become active.

Alcoholism and addiction are not directly related to volume, frequency, dosage, duration, or drinking/drugging style. A diagnosis of chemical dependency cannot be made on the basis of how much, how often, or what kind of substance the user consumes.[15] We *do* know that there is a heredity factor. At least 80 percent of all addicts and alcoholics have chemical dependence in their parent or grandparent generation.

Because addiction is a function, not just of the individual, but of families, institutions, communities, and society as a whole; and because it involves complex social, psychological, physiological, and spiritual factors, we may never completely understand its cause. Perhaps giving the devil credit is as reasonable an explanation as any! If the end point of all addiction (by the testimony of addicts themselves) is jails, institutions, and death, then it is not difficult to see why he who has been a murderer from the beginning and the father of lies would choose addiction as his most effective weapon.

Treatment of addiction

In order to target their redemptive efforts effectively, Christians must understand the nature and stages of addiction. Lacking such awareness, they will unwittingly accommodate the disease or *enable* the addict (help him stay sick).

Based on their misconceptions of addiction, I've seen many Adventist parents go to great trouble and expense to treat a child's "drug problem" with tough love; family therapy; Bible studies; psychiatric care; or isolation on Uncle Bert's ranch, where he will be at least a hundred miles from the nearest sin. While these approaches are not all bad (and some are useful in primary prevention), they rarely work when the addict has passed beyond the middle of stage 2.

A few years ago, I set up a drug intervention program at an academy. During the in-service training, an administrator asked me to comment on a decision they had made the week before. A former student who had been expelled for violation of the school drug code had applied for readmission. His drug-taking history suggested that he was in stage 3 of chemical dependence. Not anxious to accept him back, the ad council had recommended that he enroll in another school, where he could "start over."

"We were wrong, weren't we?" asked the administrator. "We should have referred him for professional assessment."

He was correct. Geographical cures (new friends, a different environment, stricter rules, conversion, counseling that is not drug-specific) are not adequate once the addict or alcoholic has reached a given point. The only thing these methods accomplish is to create an illusion of progress, which feeds everyone's denial. Meanwhile, the disease gets an even tighter grip on its unsuspecting victim.

Primary prevention

There is no question prevention is the ideal course. If half the efforts directed toward the treatment of addiction were aimed at prevention instead, we might achieve a thousandfold better results.[16] To accomplish this, we will have to go far beyond what we are now doing. We will have to find a way to prevent *codependence*. I am convinced that the best thing Christian parents can do to keep their children from becoming drug addicts is to address their own codependence and take responsibility for arresting their own compulsive behavior.

---

1. Pia Mellody, "Overview of Codependency," audiotape from Mellody Enterprises, Wickenburg, Ariz., 1988.

2. Ibid.

3. Ellen White, *The Ministry of Healing* (Mountain View, Calif.: Pacific Press, 1942), 172.

4. Stanton Peele and Archie Brodsky, *Love and Addiction* (New York: New American Library, 1976), 265.

5. Gerald May, *Addiction and Grace* (San Francisco: Harper & Row, 1991), 1, 2.

6. Ibid., 13.

7. Mellody, "Overview of Codependency."

8. Terry Kellogg, "Compulsive, Addictive, and Self-Destructive Behaviors," videotape from Terry Kellogg/Lifeworks Communications, Minneapolis, Minn., 1988.

9. G. Douglas Talbott, "Alcoholism and Drug Addiction—the Disease," audiotape from The Fortune Companies, Atlanta, Ga.

10. Adapted from Vernon Johnson, *I'll Quit Tomorrow* (San Francisco: Harper & Row, 1980).

11. Luke 15:13, NIV.

12. Luke 15:14, NIV.

13. Luke 15:17, NIV.

14. Talbott, "Alcoholism and Drug Addiction."

15. Ibid.

16. See Ellen White, *Temperance* (Mountain View, Calif.: Pacific Press, 1949), 178.

Chapter 6

Why Conservative Christians Are at High Risk for Addiction

Back in 1975 when I set out to save the world, I was busy ignoring my own character defects and eagerly soliciting someone else's to work on. I had become acquainted with a number of college students who were using drugs and alcohol regularly. They presented the perfect opportunity for me to defocus from my own problems. I could avoid *mine* by concentrating on *theirs*. My codependence was about to blossom.

Reared in strict Adventist homes, these young people had been taught total abstinence as an eternal value. They knew beyond the shadow of a doubt that it was a sin to drink and drug—a sin that would threaten their standing with family, church, and God. But they didn't know the facts of life about drugs and alcohol—they were extremely naive in terms of viable facts and information. They didn't know the birds and the bees about booze! Because they had not been exposed to social drinking in their environment, they knew nothing of moderation. Later, when they jumped their cultural barriers and began to drink, they didn't drink socially or moderately. They drank to excess. They drank to get drunk. Isn't that why everybody drinks?

For some reason, these youth got into more difficulty with drugs and alcohol than the average "wordly" young person would. Lacking essential information, they drank in a high-risk fashion, thus increasing the likelihood that they would become addicted or suffer other negative consequences. The effect was dramatic. They did crazy things. They overdosed and hurt themselves. They got falling-down drunk and passed out on our doorstep. They took combinations of chemicals that resulted in bad "trips." When they got their cars stuck in the middle of the golf course at 2:00 a.m., we rescued them. When they were arrested for public drunkenness, we bailed them out. When they got in trouble at school, we covered up for them. In short, we enabled them.

I rather enjoyed the excitement they brought into our lives, and I found great satisfaction in being needed. I thought I could heal them with my love. When that didn't yield the desired results, I tried adding control. That didn't work either.

The mystery

At the time, I simply couldn't (didn't want to) believe that children reared with a strict abstinence code were at higher-than-average risk for addiction and other drug-related problems. I had always hoped and believed that a careful Christian environment would insulate them against such possibilities. In fact, I was counting on it, because I was a conservative Adventist, and I was the mother of two small sons.

I couldn't imagine how good kids from good Christian homes could get hooked on drugs. I knew they weren't *bad*. They *couldn't* be *bad*. Were they just rebellious? Or were they simply unconverted? Maybe they were just plain stupid! Why were they hurting themselves like this? Whatever the reason, one thing was abundantly clear: somebody had to save them. My husband and I decided to volunteer. We would dedicate ourselves to a cause nobody else seemed interested in. We would rescue the lost sheep of the house of Israel! We would care for troubled youth—a job Ellen White said she would have done herself had God not given her another work to do.[1]

Our decision was probably motivated as much by our co-dependence as it was by our dedication. We sold our home, loaded up our car, and departed for a "far country" to start a ministry to save all the Adventist young people in the North American Division.

Like Gerald May, it was my well-meaning but misguided efforts to help addicts and alcoholics and my subsequent failure that convinced me *I* was an addict. In May's words, "I am glad. Grace was there."[2]

Possible answers

Little by little I began to unravel the mystery of why so many Adventist young people get into trouble with drugs. One of the first clues came in the form of a line from *I'll Quit Tomorrow*, written in 1980 by Vernon Johnson. He suggested that all alcoholics have one thing in common: guilt.[3] Surely no drinker suffers greater guilt than one who has been taught that the use of alcohol and drugs is a sin sufficient to cost him his soul! Normal teenagers go out on Saturday night for beer and pizza. Adventist kids go out and get beer, pizza, and *guilt*!

Another factor that contributes to the susceptibility of Adventist adolescents is the hidden dysfunction and addiction in their social environment. There is a striking similarity between alcoholic family systems and rigid religious systems. Both can have a negative impact on the child. The mechanism is somewhat different, but the results are the same. The alcoholic system tends to be chaotic and *underprotective,* and the religious system tends to be rigid and *overprotective*, but the consequences are identical.

Social acceptability

Being the member of a group for whom alcohol use is socially unacceptable increases the likelihood of the drinker's having problems, because he is breaking the norm. People for whom drinking or drugging is unacceptable (women, adolescents, Adventists) score higher on rebelliousness and emotional-problem measures than do those for whom the use of alcohol and drugs is acceptable. In other words, the risk of problems goes up as the social acceptability of drinking goes down.[4]

On the scale below, please note that the individual at highest risk for addiction is the teenage child of conservative Christian parents who are church employees.

10 **Adult unchurched males:** drinking and drunkenness are culturally acceptable

9 **Adult unchurched females:** drinking is accepted, but not drunkenness

8 **Adolescent unchurched males:** drinking and drugging treated as normal rites of passage

7 **Adolescent unchurched females:** drinking and drugging not accepted

6 **Adult "liberal" churchgoing men:** social drinking approved

5 **Adult "liberal" churchgoing women:** social drinking accepted

4 **Adolescent "liberal" churchgoing males:** use of alcohol discouraged

3 **Adolescent "liberal" churchgoing females:** alcohol use strongly discouraged

2 **Adventist men:** church policy is abstinence

1 **Adventist women:** sames as men

-1 **Adventist adolescent males:** no drinking allowed

-2 **Adventist adolescent females:** no drinking allowed

-3 **Church employees:** use of drugs and alcohol prohibited; violation brings loss of employment

-4 **Church employees' children:** drinking and drugging totally unacceptable; stigma against parents if their children violate the standard

Figure 3 — Social Acceptability Scale

The less socially acceptable it is for a young person to drink or drug, the greater the possibility that he will experience significant social consequences—including alcoholism or addiction—if he violates his cultural norms.

Dumb drinkers

Given their lack of training in relatively safe drinking practices, children from anti-alcohol environments may not know the simple facts of life about alcohol. In homes where alcohol is used socially, learning of this kind occurs spontaneously, but not in Adventist homes. Many Adventist families adhere to the *don't talk / don't feel / don't trust* rule of alcoholic families.

Clearly, all use of alcohol and drugs involves some risk, but certain drinking styles are less risky than others. Because instruction on this subject is not part of the curriculum in most conservative homes, children lack essential knowledge about the medical, social, and legal implications of substance abuse.

If and when drinking and drug taking are discussed, parents speak in condemning tones because they want their children to know they disapprove of such behavior. They come across in a "preachy" manner. And yet research indicates that the moralistic approach to drug prevention is highly *un*successful!

Many parents are similarly skittish about sex education. They're afraid that their children will take any mention of safe sex and birth control as permission to be promiscuous. One father took me to task for suggesting that parents tell children the low-risk options from which they can choose when they reach legal drinking age. (Drinking styles that are relatively low-risk include total abstinence; drinking in small quantities; limiting intake to one drink per hour; refraining from the use of alcohol when pregnant, when on medication, when driving, or if there is a family history of addiction.) He said that people who give such information to their children might as well tell them to wear ski masks and gloves if they rob a bank!

I had a little trouble responding to his comment because it made so much sense. Nevertheless, I disagreed with him. I hope that young people *will* choose not to drink or to engage in sexual activity prematurely. But if they should choose to do these things, I want them to know how to reduce the risk of disease or death! It is possible to teach children the birds and the bees about booze in a non-condemning manner—including all the choices that are open to them—in such a way that they will make the wisest choices and establish their own firm boundaries.

I believe that failure to be honest with young people is riskier than the alternative. What children don't know *can* hurt them. If they are unaware that drinking on an empty stomach, combining alcohol with other drugs or with prescription medication, drinking large amounts hastily, or mixing drinks in certain ways are dangerous, they could be badly hurt.

For example, there are several forms in which alcohol can be delivered to the stomach: straight, mixed with juice, mixed with water, or mixed with a carbonated beverage. The manner in which it is mixed will affect the speed with which it is metabolized, which will determine how drunk the drinker gets, which may determine whether he wraps his daddy's nice car around a tree! Unfortunately, most Adventist teenagers who use alcohol drink in the most dangerous of these four ways.

Few fundamentalistic families include Alcohol 101 in their course of study. But ignorance is not an effective form of prevention! It would be wise for us to talk about these matters more openly with our children, emphasizing the medical and social implications of drug taking rather than the moral. We can no longer assume that drugs aren't an issue for young people reared in Adventist homes. Drugs and alcohol are a fact of life, and we must prepare them to face it.

High-quantity/low-frequency drinking

The likelihood of a drinker's developing alcoholism is directly related to his drinking pattern. High-quantity/low-frequency use of alcohol is more predictive of alcoholism than low-quantity/high-frequency consumption. The adolescent who drinks one or two beers a day is less likely to become an alcoholic than one who drinks six or more once a month. I hesitate to share this with teenagers, because I don't want them to think I'm sanctioning low-quantity use. Although they might come to that conclusion, I believe it's more dangerous *not* to tell them.

I'm careful to explain that I support total abstinence because all use of alcohol, even in small amounts, involves serious risk, for two reasons: First, relatively low blood alcohol levels can render an inexperienced teenage driver more accident-prone than an experienced adult driver with a higher blood alcohol content. In some cases, teenagers are impaired with half the blood alcohol content required to impair a more experienced driver. And second, the younger the drinker, the greater the risk of addiction. An adolescent's biological immaturity makes him more sensitive to alcohol and other drugs than adults are. Youth who begin drinking and drugging in their early teens can be addicted in just a few months' time, while the average adult would take several years to become fully addicted.

Young people from totally abstaining families adopt the high-quantity/low-frequency drinking style as a matter of necessity. In order to avoid getting caught, they have to plan their drinking carefully. Because they can't drink as easily or as often as they might like, when they *do* drink, they tend to *overdrink* and thus place themselves in the highest risk category for alcoholism (high quantity/low frequency). When an Adventist youth buys a six-pack, he can't take the unused portion home and put it in his mom's refrigerator. He drinks the whole thing (because Mom also taught him not to be wasteful)!

Reluctance to intervene

On the level of secondary prevention (preventing existing drug problems from getting worse), parents leave much to chance. For reasons of naive optimism or naive faith, we postpone getting help for young people who are known to have a drug problem. We would rather wish or pray it away. In reality, we are enabling it to get worse.

Eric's mother was concerned about her son. During his junior year in academy, she noticed changes in his behavior that led her to suspect he was using marijuana. He had developed a negative attitude, and his grades were slipping. Before the year was over, he was dropped from the gymnastics team. Although being part of the team was very important to him, he preferred to party. Within a few weeks, he was expelled from school.

The fact that he smoked pot in the face of such serious consequences is in itself a mark of how committed he was to getting high, which means he was already well on the road to addiction. Potential social consequences are a red light to the "social" drinker or drug taker. Not so to the addictive user. The social drinker's red light is the addictive drinker's green light!

When Eric's mother called a counselor for advice, he suggested that she have her son professionally assessed. The thought horrified her. They were a *Christian* family. Surely there was some other way to deal with it! Perhaps if the women in her Bible-study group agreed together in prayer as Jesus advised in Matthew 18:18-20, God would dispel the problem.

Several weeks later she called the counselor and announced triumphantly that Eric had been born again. Praise the Lord! The promise she had claimed had been fulfilled. Eric had given up drugs. He was eager to go back to the academy, and she was confident that he would remain drug free.

The first semester went well. Eric became a religious leader on campus. He was enthusiastic about his newfound faith and eager to share it. The faculty were thrilled with his positive influence—they wished there were more students like him. But just a few weeks before graduation, he was caught drinking and was dismissed from school again. Some time later, when he got in trouble with the law, his parents finally sought professional help, but not before he spent several weeks in jail.

Faith plus works

Most Adventists look askance at sects that refuse medical treatment for *physical* illness. While we believe fully in God's power to heal, we are more than willing to avail ourselves of modern medical technology. But we drag our feet when it comes to seeking professional help for *emotional* problems.

There is no doubt in my mind that God has provided both human and divine resources for healing physical *and* emotional illnesses and that each manner of healing is equally miraculous! A physician may put a plaster cast on a broken bone, but only God can heal the fracture. Psychotherapy may provide a healing environment for a broken heart or fractured spirit, but it is truly God's power that accomplishes the miracle!

If addiction were just *sin*, then prayer alone would be adequate. But if addiction is both a medical and a moral disease, it may require prayer *plus* professional help. There is no question that people should pray for healing in medical crises. But the most effective prayers for physical healing are those prayed on the way to the emergency room. And the most effective prayers for healing from addiction are prayed on the way to treatment centers where professional help is available!

Quality of parenting

It is widely recognized that there is a relationship between the psychological health of a child and drug abuse. A lack of closeness and intimacy in the family system affects the psychological well-being of a child and thus the likelihood of his having social problems of various kinds.[5] The quality of parenting is of great importance.[6] Children who experience either too much freedom or too much control are vulnerable. Both underprotection and overprotection have negative consequences.

Parents in chaotic family systems (alcoholic or abusive) are described as cold, hostile, unresponsive, and underprotective. They give their children little encouragement on the one hand but have high performance expectations on the other.[8] In rigid family systems (religious or perfectionistic), parents are characterized as distant and unresponsive. They give their children more support and encouragement, but they simultaneously pressure them and show excessive concern about their performance. They tend to be authoritarian and domineering, to squelch spontaneity and creativity, and to demand conformity.[9]

Why are Adventist young people at risk for addiction and other problems? I believe the most significant reason is parenting style. The incidence of drug abuse is lowest in families that provide freedom, acceptance, and loving control for children. If parents lack boundaries, give their children too much freedom, and control their behavior in a harsh or hostile manner, the likelihood of drug and alcohol abuse is increased.[10]

Problem parenting is a byproduct of parental addiction and/or codependence. Sick parents can only parent in a sickly way. Thus, the prevention of drug abuse in the Christian community depends on our facing and coming to grips with the deep-seated, almost institutionalized codependence and compulsion among us. It is to this issue that we will look in Part 2.

---

1. See Ellen G. White, *Testimonies for the Church* (Mountain View, Calif.: Pacific Press, 1948), 4:423.

2. Gerald May, *Addiction and Grace* (San Francisco: Harper & Row, 1991), 10.

3. Vernon Johnson, *I'll Quit Tomorrow*, rev. ed. (San Francisco: Harper & Row, 1980), 2.

4. Ray Daugherty, "Talking With Your Kids About Alcohol," TWYKA Workshop, July 1985.

5. Fred Streit, *Through My Child's Eyes* (Highland Park, N.J.: Peoplescience, Inc., n.d.), 4.

6. Jonathan Shedler and Jack Block, "Adolescent Drug Use and Psychological Health," *American Psychologist*, May 1990, 612.

7. Streit, 4.

8. Shedler and Block, 626.

9. Ibid.

10. Streit, 4.

Chapter 7

Officially Approved Addictions

Gayle was the daughter of a pastor friend of ours. I had not seen her since childhood, till the day we met in the administration building of the academy where she was employed. We talked briefly about our families and agreed to meet later for lunch. Over soup and salad, Gayle and I talked about codependence. She had read several articles about it and recognized some of the symptoms in herself. She was uncomfortable in social situations and had trouble getting close to people. She had very low self-esteem and no boundaries. Yet she couldn't imagine how she could be codependent, because her family was neither alcoholic nor dysfunctional. She grew up in a *wonderful* Christian home.

Her brother was having problems too. He was a junior-grade dictator. He dominated people's lives. If his friends didn't give him their exclusive attention, he accused them of being disloyal and uncaring. He assumed the right to tell his women friends how to act, what to wear, and how to style their hair. For obvious reasons, his romances didn't last long! And when they ended, he became depressed and suicidal.

"Something's wrong," Gayle said. "My brother and I aren't doing very well, but we came from a perfect Christian family. Why did we turn out this way? I don't understand!"

"What was it like growing up in your family?" I queried.

"My father was an excellent pastor, and my mother was an ideal minister's wife. They couldn't have been more devoted to the Lord or their ministry. As children, we knew beyond the shadow of a doubt that if the telephone rang and somebody needed him, Dad would drop everything and rush to their side immediately."

Gayle had no idea what she had just told me.

Because her parents seemed so perfect and her family looked so good, she could find no explanation for her codependence. She had no idea that her parents were behaving addictively and that she was an emotional orphan. She thought she was simply defective.

Hidden addictions and what they cost

There are numerous substances, activities, and processes with addictive potential. Some appear to be harmless, but if used or practiced in the extreme, they are addictive. Conservative Christians are subject to the full range of dependency disorders. Even if they manage to avoid the more flagrant ones, many succumb to covert addictions that are just as devastating as alcoholism but more difficult to diagnose and treat.

Children of *alcoholics* know why they feel bad: Daddy acts weird when he drinks. He gets mad and breaks things. He hurts Mommy. He goes away and leaves them alone. They can't bring friends home because he might embarrass them.

Children of *workaholics* can't justify their anguish. Their father works overtime so he can buy nice things for them. Or Mom works double shifts to make ends meet because they don't *have* a dad anymore. The children think it's their fault that their parent or parents are killing themselves with overwork.

Alcoholic and workaholic parents are equally unavailable to their families. It doesn't matter if Daddy is at the bar or at the office—he isn't home. It doesn't matter if Mommy has passed out on the couch from an overdose of Valium or from exhaustion—she isn't present to her children. And the absence of the parent leaves a hole in the child!

When one member of a family uses mind-altering substances harmfully or food, gambling, work, or sex destructively, he is unable to be fully present to the others. They in turn retreat behind defensive walls, living like strangers in the same house. Or they enmesh, becoming overly involved with one another and trying to manage each other's lives.

Passing it on

These dysfunctional patterns are then transmitted from one generation the next as normal behavior. If a father teaches his son carpentry skills, the son will use the same techniques his father modeled to him when he grows up. Many housewives arrange and organize their kitchen cupboards exactly like their mothers did.

Similarly, children pattern their social relationships after their parents' relationship. They relate to their spouses and children the way their parents related to each other and to them. They build their houses and arrange their cupboards *and their relationships* the way their parents did. As Earnie Larsen says, "Children learn what they live with."[1]

Addiction may appear in one generation as workaholism; in the next as alcoholism; in the next as an eating disorder, spouse or child abuse, sexaholism, love addiction, compulsive spending, etc. Or it may emerge as workaholism in each succeeding generation. Inevitably, the devastating effects are passed along from one generation to the next.[2]

A smorgasbord of painkillers

When a person uses any substance, activity, or process to avoid, cope with, or medicate his feelings, he is using it as a drug. And when he uses it to the extent that other priorities suffer and he continues nevertheless, he is practicing addictive behavior.

Dr. Archibald Hart, dean of the Graduate School of Psychology at Fuller Theological Seminary, postulates that 10 to 30 percent of all Americans suffer from hidden addictions or closet compulsions: sex, work, overeating, over exercising, shoplifting, religious overactivity, etc. These serve the purpose, he says, of helping people avoid the real anxieties of life by disengaging from reality. They distance us from our true feelings.[3]

Ingestive substances. The first and best recognized category of painkillers is ingestive substances. These include drugs, alcohol, nicotine, caffeine, and food.

Activities and processes. Any number of activities and processes have addictive potential: achievement, gambling, shoplifting, stealing, excitement, procrastination, talking, joking, sports, fantasizing, watching TV, playing video games, saving the world—any action for distraction, as Terry Kellogg puts it.[4]

Relationships. Emotional dependence on people is variously called "relationship dependency" and "love addiction." The person in an addictive relationship finds meaning and identity in his or her partner. The relationship junkie's "fix" is approval, acceptance, or adoration. Powerful, painful dependence can exist between spouses, between parents and children, and between friends, colleagues, or church members.

Thoughts and feelings. People become addicted to ideas, beliefs, attitudes, thoughts, and feelings. Misery, martyrdom, depression, worry, pessimism, negativism, obsessing, analyzing, intellectualizing, and raging can be addictive. If an individual feels more alive, more significant, or more in control when he is practicing any of these behaviors, if he is thus stimulated or tranquilized, he is using the behavior as a drug. Therefore, it is potentially addictive.

Worry, for example, is a state of arousal that makes some people feel alive: "I obsess, therefore I am." Worrying is stimulating. Compulsive confessing, overeating, and excessive TV watching calm people down or relieve tension when they are anxious. They act much as a sedative does.[5]

The family disease in action

Ken and Anita dropped out of college to get married. They planned to work a year and then finish their education. Lacking professional qualifications, they settled for minimum-wage jobs, which made it impossible for them to save enough money to go back to school. Nor could they afford the children who were soon born. Starting a business of their own seemed to be the only option. So they did. Ken bought a pickup, created an office at home, and advertised his services as a subcontractor.

Because his income depended on volume of work, he took on

more than he could handle. Every time the phone rang and a customer was on the line, the customer's demands took precedence over the family's needs. The telephone became their master. They never had time to relax and have fun together. All their plans and decisions were made in the context of the business. They couldn't do anything or go anywhere without first considering the cost in terms of lost contracts.

Ken was never home. And when he *was* there, he was too tired to do anything and too preoccupied with his worries to be present to his wife and children. As the saying goes, he was home, but the lights were out! He would sit down to watch the news and be asleep in five minutes. By the time their income stabilized, Ken was so accustomed to jumping every time the phone rang that he did it automatically. It was a habit. And saying *yes* when he wanted to say *no* was a habit too. Even though he was making plenty of money, he didn't want to lose his customer's goodwill, so he kept working at a fever pitch.

He couldn't have made a success of the business without Anita and the kids. They enabled him to keep up his pace. As Ken grew older, his children worried secretly that he would die of a heart attack because he was under so much stress.

The progression of Ken's workaholism is remarkably like the progression of alcoholism: first, the man takes a drink; then the drink takes a drink; then the drink takes the man. This is precisely what happened to Ken and his family—only the drug that consumed them was work rather than alcohol.

When their eldest daughter developed anorexia, Ken and Anita were devastated. Where had they failed? The young woman didn't blame her parents for her problems; she condemned *herself*! The question is, did she develop her eating disorder in a vacuum, or did it develop within the larger context of her family's addictive lifestyle? Was her behavior a statement of personal weakness, or was it a commentary on the beliefs and behaviors of the entire family system?

Ken and Anita's daughter had no idea that she had learned addictive behavior from her parents. She thought her problems were entirely of her own making. She saw herself as the only imperfect member of a perfect family. In reality, although her drug of choice was different from that of her parents, they were equally addicted.

Denial and delusion

Because addiction is a problem that thinks it's not a problem, a disease that says it's not a disease, many addicts are oblivious to their condition. Denial and delusion are characteristic of addiction. The last person qualified to make a diagnosis is the alcoholic or addict himself. In many cases, even the family is blinded by denial.

One thing family members are acutely aware of, however, is their own pain. I don't ask people if their loved one is an alcoholic or addict. I don't ask them how often he drinks, drugs, or overworks. I ask them how they *feel*. If they are hurting, lonely, angry, resentful, or afraid; if they feel discounted, controlled, deprived, or neglected; and if they themselves are desperate and depressed, I suspect that addiction is present.

With alcoholism and drug dependence, diagnosis is relatively easy. The wreckage is obvious, though only to those who are directly affected, seldom to the addict himself. I talked recently with a forty-year-old man who had been addicted to heroin for twenty years. He stoutly maintained that his wife and children had not been affected by his addiction in any way. I wondered what they would have said.

If an individual happens to have a "clean" addiction, denial and delusion are an even greater issue. The damage is not as obvious as it is with alcohol and drugs. Wrecked cars are easier to spot than wrecked marriages, broken bottles easier to see than broken hearts.

Nonchemical addictions

The "clean" addictions are hard to diagnose and harder still to treat. Nonchemical addictions include workaholism, perfectionism, churchaholism, sexaholism, love addiction, eating disorders, shopping and spending, excitement, gambling, care giving, and control. Many of these are not only socially acceptable; they are considered a badge of honor.

Work. Employers are eager to hire highly motivated workers.

Executives drive *themselves* ruthlessly and expect their employees to do the same. Pastors and church administrators feel pressured by the Lord or by their constituency to work nonstop. Few addictions exact a greater toll on the sufferer's health and the welfare of his family than workaholism. But the church rewards rather than rebukes the work addict.

Food. Considering the alternatives, food is one of the safest tranquilizers a Christian can ingest. People comfort themselves by cramming calories. Compulsive eating manifests itself as overeating, undereating (anorexia), and bingeing and purging (bulimia). The purging may be accomplished by vomiting, abusing laxatives, or exercising excessively. Whether the food addict obsesses about what he puts in his mouth or what he *doesn't* put in his mouth, if his thoughts are dominated by food, he is suffering from an eating disorder.

Relationships. The relationship junkie places his self-esteem in the hands of another and extracts his identity from that individual. In her book *Perfect Women*, Collette Dowling speaks of relationships in which "each partner uses the other as a thermostat for regulating self-esteem."[6] The love addict assigns too much importance to the beloved and expects him to neglect his own needs in order to meet hers or vice versa.[7]

A simple slight by the loved one, a cross word, a disapproving glance, shatters the self-esteem of the dependent partner. Because he thinks he's nobody unless somebody loves him, he fears nothing worse than abandonment. If his lover leaves him, he ceases to exist and may become suicidal. Losing a relationship is painful for anyone, but losing the will to live when rejected is an indication of addiction.

Some love addicts act out their compulsion through "innocent" flirting, which provides a little ego massage. Their affairs rarely progress beyond the realm of fantasy. I call this kind of relationship a *vegetarian affair* (an affair that lacks physical/sexual contact).

Destructive, abusive relationships are a form of love addiction. In such situations, the "victim" is bonded to the "abuser" and unable to break away. The Steinberg-Nussbaum case in New York City is a classic example. Tragically and typically, it was the little girl Lisa who suffered most.

Emotional dependency between parents and children is another important form of relationship addiction. It is character-ized by intense struggles over money, power, and control. The child remains dependent long after the ties should have been cut, or the parent relies on the child for meaning and identity. He makes him responsible for his emotional well-being. It is *never* OK for a parent to use his child to meet his own neurotic needs.

Sex. Sexual addiction is not uncommon among conservative Christians. It is impossible to describe the anguish of the be-liever who has an addiction that involves so much shame. Unfortunately, there is little help for the sex addict in the re-ligious community. Many churches treat inappropriate sexual behavior as the unpardonable sin. Yet sexaholism is an addic-tion for which effective treatment is readily available.

Almost without exception, sexaholics were victims of sexual abuse in childhood. As adults, they rarely realize that their intrusive sexual thoughts and inappropriate actions are con-nected to their childhood trauma, and therefore they do not address it therapeutically. They turn instead to the church for comfort and pardon, only to be disappointed. While they may receive comfort and pardon, they are not likely to receive help in recovering from their addiction.

The sexaholic considers himself hopelessly perverted. Un-aware that his addiction is as much a medical/psychological problem as a spiritual one, he treats it as a sin problem, which he assumes will be cured by conversion. When he joins the church to find relief from his obsessive/compulsive behavior, he is dismayed to discover that he is still inclined to act out inappropriately.

He expends enormous amounts of energy trying to hold his sexual addiction in check. When his obsession with sex persists, he is confused. He can't confess his weakness to anyone because he might get thrown out of the church. But until he acknowl-edges his secret and asks for help, he will continue to act out, at least sporadically. Disheartened by the never-ending struggle, he loses faith in himself, and often in God as well.

The price sex offenders pay for their crimes is severe, as has been demonstrated by several high-profile religious personalities recently. No matter how earnestly such people repent or how sincerely they seek victory, they will remain enslaved until they address their sexual issues as an addiction and get professional help.

Gambling and excitement. Excitement addicts live on the edge. They get a rush from dangerous occupations, hobbies, and sports; from high-tension movies, television, video games; from personal crises and conflict. They avoid order and organization by refusing to plan ahead. They are always stirred up about something. They literally *thrive* on chaos.[8] Procrastination is a form of excitement addiction because it pushes the individual into his adrenalin.[9]

Some crisis junkies get high on the feverish practice of religion. In the church setting, excitement addiction may be acted out as intense involvement in noble causes, religiously motivated political action (especially if civil disobedience is involved), ecstatic forms of worship, and preoccupation with persecution.

I've worked with a number of chemically dependent young people whose fathers were evangelists. Although soul winning is a worthy endeavor, it is characterized by "evangelistic fervor," which generates considerable hype and excitement and, as such, is a mood-altering experience. Such children develop an affinity for excitement and often act it out later in less acceptable ways such as alcohol or drug addiction.

Although most Adventists wouldn't be caught dead playing the lottery or buying raffle tickets, some get involved in risky investing or *entrepreneuring*, which can also be addictive. This combines three potentially addictive activities—gambling, excitement, and work. An entrepreneur in recovery described his behavior in these words: "I was preoccupied with my ventures all the time. I misrepresented the risks involved to potential investors, thinking I was helping them find 'financial freedom.' My entrepreneurship had become my medication. It robbed me of intimacy with my family."

Shopping and spending. Dr. Hart speaks of "shopping for stimulation."[10] The shopaholic uses spending to enhance his image and shore up his flagging self-esteem. His spending sprees are much like alcoholic binges. I personally am a bulimic shopaholic: I buy things, feel guilty, and then take them back. I am not suggesting that purchasing something occasionally to cheer oneself up is pathological. It is the continual practice of detrimental behavior in the face of negative consequences that defines it as addictive.

Religion. The addictive practice of religion involves preoccupation with God and church to the exclusion of other important priorities in life to the detriment of one's own self and family. Religion addicts use religion like a drug—to medicate or avoid the pain, fear, and the shame of the undeveloped self.[11] As with any other addiction, the "user" ends up harming himself and those closest to him.

Balancing one's concern for the eternal with a proper concern for the temporal is difficult, especially for people with addictive tendencies. Unfortunately, many Christian parents model extreme behavior in the way they relate to God and church. As a result, their children approach life in an extreme or addictive fashion. When religion is practiced in this manner, it can have a profoundly negative effect on children.

Care giving and control. Care giving (rescuing and fixing people) is extremely rewarding and is thus very addictive. I consider it the Christian's cocaine. Codependents find meaning and esteem in caring for and controlling others or in being cared for and controlled. There is an implicit expectation in care giving. The care giver secretly longs for someone to take care of him the way he takes care of them. Although the contract is unwritten, it is very real. And it removes caring from the realm of generosity to the realm of a business deal.

Sooner or later, when a care giver has made a major investment of time and energy in another individual, he accelerates to controlling. After all, he has earned the right! He gives unsolicited advice and expects it to be accepted. Resentment is sure to follow on the part of both the helper *and* the helpee. And there is some question as to who is really doing the controlling. Each actually exerts control over the other. Both derive satisfaction from what they're doing.

Diagnosing addiction

The addictions discussed thus far involve nonchemical "drugs" that are part of our everyday lives—things that can't be completely avoided. Most Adventists wouldn't touch alcohol with a ten-foot pole, but we can't avoid eating, working, shopping, spending, being sexual, being spiritual, and taking risks. We have no problem recognizing alcohol as addictive and promoting abstinence. But with these clean addictions, the issue is not so clear-cut. One cannot entirely abstain from achieving, working, eating, spending money, or taking risks. And few are *willing* to abstain entirely from sexual behavior or religious exercises. How does one determine whether or not his behavior in *these* areas is healthy or addictive?

Actual diagnosis must be made by a professional in the field, not by a pastor, doctor, counselor, or layperson playing these roles, unless they are specifically trained in the assessment of addictive disorders. But it is possible to examine one's behavior and get some idea of whether it is normal or addictive. The following questions are helpful: (1) Am I seeking self-esteem and good feelings from doing this? (2) Am I giving this substance or activity priority over other important priorities (family, school, etc.)? (3) Am I continuing the behavior in the face of adverse consequences such as job loss, marital loss, financial loss, loss of health, etc.?

The biochemical connection

Many hidden addictions involve dependence on substances generated within the human body. Research on the biochemical component of "clean" addictions has proliferated recently, and the findings suggest that they have an underlying chemical basis. Chemicals manufactured in the brain are responsible for pleasant feelings. "Both substance addictions and process addictions may be caused by the body's tendency to become 'hooked' on chemicals. In this sense, all addictions may come to be seen as substance addictions," says Dr. Hart.[12]

The excitement addict gets an adrenalin rush. Adrenalin is a stimulant. The successful entrepreneur experiences the same flood of brain chemicals when he makes a swift business deal that the cocaine user experiences when he shoots or snorts cocaine.[13] Endorphins and other brain chemicals play a definite role in the hidden addictions. In the broadest sense, then, all of us who practice "officially approved" addictions are actually drug addicts.

1. Earnie Larsen, "Understanding the Basics of Recovery, Part I," videotape from Fuller Video, Minneapolis, Minn.

2. Janet Woititz, lecture given at Rutgers Summer School of Alcohol Studies, July 1987.

3. Archibald Hart, *Healing Life's Hidden Addictions* (Ann Arbor: Servant Publications, 1990), xiv, 6.

4. Terry Kellogg, "Compulsive, Addictive, and Self-Destructive Behaviors," videotape from Terry Kellogg/Lifeworks Communications, Minneapolis, Minn., 1988.

5. Hart, 24, 31.

6. Collette Dowling, *Perfect Woman: Daughters Who Love Their Mothers, but Don't Love Themselves* (New York: Summit Books, 1988), 220.

7. Pia Mellody, "Love Addiction," audiotape from Mellody Enterprises, Wickenburg, Ariz.

8. Hart, 101.

9. Kellogg, "Compulsive, Addictive, and Self-Destructive Behaviors."

10. Hart, 99.

11. This definition is built on Pia Mellody's description of the role of addiction in society.

12. Hart, 8.

13. John Wallace, "From Allergy to Neuroscience," lecture given at the Anatomy of Recovery Conference, sponsored by Father Martin's Ashley, October 1990.

Chapter 8

The Abandonment of Self

Children reared in addictive family systems are biochemically and psychosocially predisposed to alcoholism, drug dependence, or one or more of the so-called "clean" addictions. The hereditary factor has been widely recognized for some time,[1] and the environmental factor is becoming more generally acknowledged.

A recent study on the factors that precede addiction was reported in the *American Psychologist*. It suggests that early psychological factors are a central issue.[2] "There is a large body of research literature that explores the relationship between *unendurable life circumstances* and the development of addiction,"[3] according to Archibald Hart. We cannot say that such stressors *cause* addiction, but we know they contribute to it.

Behaviors modeled to children by those closest to them become "normal" to them. If they grow up in the presence of compulsive, addicted adults, codependence is woven into the very fabric of their being.[4] If they see dishonesty, chronic low self-worth, frozen feelings, avoidance behaviors, or control and domination, they consider these behaviors appropriate. Such negative input programs error into the brain's basic "software."

Just as a malfunctioning nuclear reactor releases invisible radioactivity into the air, so the troubled codependent family system also produces "a kind of harmful fallout that seeps into and upsets the delicate emotional and psychological balance of its children," says Robert Subby in *Lost in the Shuffle*.[5]

The afflicted and the affected

When one member of a family is preoccupied with drugs or a druglike compulsion, the other members are affected. Each seeks relief from pain through potentially addictive behavior.

Thus the pathology of the parents is passed to the next generation. "Psychologists believe that codependency is a love hunger that can be transmitted from generation to generation. Emotionally dysfunctional families beget codependent adult children, who then create their own dysfunctional families and beget more dysfunctional children."[6]

Typically, when a husband is dependent on drugs, his wife becomes emotionally dependent on him, and their neglected child becomes dependent on such things as approval, achievement, care giving, control, manipulation, martyring, etc. As a teenager, the child acts out his approval hunger by trying to be perfect. He thinks that if he can only find the right hairstyle, the right diet, the right friends, nice clothes, enough money, or the ideal body image, he will be acceptable. He ends up looking for love (self-worth) in all the wrong places.

The *impending* addiction is visible in its *infant* form. The teenage romance seeker grows up to become a relationship junkie. The compulsive eater develops anorexia or bulimia. The overachiever graduates to workaholism. The care giver finds someone to take care of—preferably a helpless addict. As the authors of the Serenity Bible so aptly put it, the "early codependent vacuum becomes the root of our later adult addictions."[7] Codependence, then, is the disease within all addictive diseases.

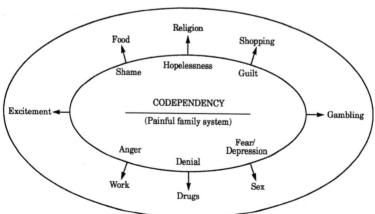

Figure 4 — The disease within the disease.

An addictive perspective

Within the framework of another person's addiction, the codependent child develops a skewed view of reality. He is dependent on someone who is dependent on something that is not dependable.[8] He learns to control internal feelings by manipulating external circumstances.[9] His coping mechanisms (survival skills) became habitual, but they also prove to be his undoing. As one addict put it, "The things I did to gain self-esteem separated me more and more from the people around me."

Much as reverse tolerance marks the drinker's final descent into alcoholism, the transformation of the codependent's survival skills into counterproductive social behaviors is an indication that he has hit bottom. When the things that worked for him in childhood push people away from him in adulthood, it's all over. The cost of continuing his compulsive behavior in terms of poor health, lost jobs, lowered self-esteem, compromised identity, and damaged relationships is no longer worth the benefits.

What is codependence?

Codependence is the pain in adulthood that comes from being wounded in childhood. It is a disease of the spirit that predisposes its victims to adult dependency disorders and dysfunctional relationships. Codependence is characterized by (1) lack of social competence, (2) low resistance to emotional stress, and (3) poor choices in expressing impulses.

In a study of adolescent drug use and psychological health, Shedler and Block determined that adolescents who use drugs frequently have personalities that are marked by these three characteristics. And they found that the offending personality characteristics were rooted in early childhood—that is, they developed before adolescence and the initiation of drug use.[10] For some reason, that doesn't surprise me.

Who develops codependence?

Codependence is the social, emotional, and spiritual illness that occurs when children grow up in a family system characterized by high stress and low nurturance. People subject to codependence are (1) those currently in close relationship with an alcoholic or addict; (2) anyone with an addictive parent or grandparent, including all addictive disorders ranging from chemical dependence to workaholism, compulsive overspending, sexaholism, and spouse or child abuse; (3) anyone suffering significant childhood loss due to causes other than addiction, such as death, divorce, physical or emotional deprivation; and (4) anyone from an emotionally out-of-touch or extremely repressive family background.

A portrait of pain

Elaine received enough mixed messages while growing up to confuse her for a lifetime. Her mother was antifeminine in her attitude and appearance and extremely unhappy in her marriage, yet she urged Elaine to look and act ladylike, or she would never get a husband. She seemed to hate men, but she was preoccupied with pleasing her husband and sons. She accepted the absolute tyranny of her spouse with apparent aplomb, but her outward calm masked enormous inward rage, which she transferred to Elaine.

Elaine's father was a demigod. He could do no evil. He was never wrong. He saw himself as spiritually and intellectually superior to everyone, particularly his wife and children. He was unmoved by any display of emotion on their part and considered the expression of feelings to be beneath him.

So there was no point in Elaine's expressing her opinions or feelings. She knew she didn't count. Because her father ignored her and her mother scapegoated her, Elaine developed a severe emotional abscess. She lost her sense of self-esteem. She spent her entire childhood calculating every deed and word so as not to displease anyone. She spent the better part of her adulthood trying to find identity and value.

In spite of their flaws, Elaine's family looked fine in the eyes of the community. The disease was so well hidden that Elaine thought she was crazy. She qualified for the diagnosis of codependence in all four categories. Her father was a religion addict, and her grandfather was a closet sex addict. Her parents were not physically divorced, but they were emotionally estranged. Her nurturance needs were not met, and she was deprived of warmth and affection. Her family system was the epitome of emotional repression.

Even after she became aware of her family's illness, Elaine found it difficult to excuse her codependence. She could easily recognize why the children of alcoholics were codependent, but she could not justify *her* symptoms.

Characteristics of codependence

Three characteristics of codependence are worth noting.[11] First is a *loss of self-identity*. This occurs both in the craziness of the chaotic alcoholic family and in the subtle insanity of a family like Elaine's. Elaine worked hard to regain her self-esteem. She became a respected professional. But in her heart, she still heard her mother saying she was worthless and her father telling her that her feelings and opinions didn't matter.

The second characteristic follows from the first: *overinvolvement with others as a means of gaining identity*. The codependent child panders to people in order to get his needs met. He plays the role of people pleaser, approval seeker, care giver, superachiever. His excessive care giving leads to a *lack of healthy self-care*, which is the third characteristic. A good codependent is more oriented to the feelings and needs of other people than he is to his own feelings and needs. He thinks he doesn't have the right to want or need.

Stages of codependence

Codependence progresses through the same four stages as chemical dependence. Like drinking and drugging, it is extremely rewarding and reinforcing in its early stages. The gratification that comes from care giving, the sense of power and control that accompanies rescuing and fixing people, the thrill of overachieving, the satisfaction of being needed—these things produce very pleasurable feelings. But, like drug highs, *codependent highs* are followed by *depressive lows*. The codependent may act out his compulsions for years with few obvious consequences, but eventually his tolerance reverses. His health breaks down, his relationships collapse, and he ends up alone and unhappy.

Stage 1—Learning to cope. While the alcoholic (workaholic, foodaholic, sexaholic) is *learning the mood swing* (stage 1), his codependents are *learning to cope.* They are vaguely aware that something is wrong. They walk on eggshells. They're afraid to be themselves. While there may be some cognitive dialogue among family members, there is little effective emotional exchange. Feelings are not factored into conversations. They are neither expressed nor discussed; they are unfelt and denied. An atmosphere of anxiety prevails. Emotional deprivation and neglect are the order of the day. There is little, if any, real warmth and intimacy. Everyone knows there is a problem, but no one can seem to do anything about it.

Stage 2—Seeking to control. As the addict/alcoholic *seeks the mood swing,* family members *seek to control* his behavior. They adjust their attitudes and actions to suit his varying moods. They absorb and act out his feelings. If he is tense, they feel stressed. If he is irresponsible, they take up the slack. If he is shameless, they carry the guilt.

Eventually, the primary codependent (usually spouse or mom) will become so enmeshed with the addict that the two of them are like Siamese twins. The rest of the family, whom I call *secondary codependents,* rotate around both the addict *and* his enabler. They feel abandoned by both the addict and the enabler, because all the enabler thinks about is the addict and his problems. It's as if the rest of the family doesn't exist anymore.

In his enabling role, the primary codependent unwittingly helps the addict stay sick. He moves the cushions around to prevent the addict from hitting bottom because he can't stand to see the addict suffer. The fact is that the addict *needs* to experience the consequences of his addiction if he is to muster up the energy to do anything about it. The enabler deprives him of the very pain that could motivate him to change!

Stage 3—Preoccupation with pain. Stage 3 for the chemically dependent is *preoccupation with the mood swing.* For the codependent, it is *preoccupation with pain.* Neglect, abandonment, and abuse by the addict create incredible pain in the codependent. The codependent's anguish may be so great that he feels compelled to seek relief in some dramatic way: running away, drinking, isolating. He eventually graduates from his coping role to the acting-out role. If he persists in practicing relief-seeking behavior, he is likely to roll into a full-fledged addiction himself (see Fig. 5).

Stage 4—Obsession with self. Finally, while the addict is *obsessed with the mood swing*, the codependent becomes *obsessed with pain*. The codependent no longer exists as an individual. His only significance is in relationship to the helpless addict. The only solution seems to be suicide or divorce. In a last burst of bravado, he rejects the addict: "If you're going to kill yourself, at least move out of the house so I don't have to watch you!"

Dependent Person (Addict)	Primary Codependent (Spouse, parent, friend)	Secondary Codependent (Parent, sibling, friend)
1—Learning the mood swing He/she discovers that a specific drug, process, or activity feels good; his/her attitudes begin to change.	**Learning to cope** He senses that he is losing the loved one and doesn't know why; he feels panicky.	**Learning to cope** He is aware something is wrong and thinks it is his fault.
2—Seeking the mood swing He decides that his new behavior is *the* way to feel good and makes subtle changes to accommodate it.	**Seeking control** He or she feels painfully anxious and begins adjusting his own behavior to restore the status quo.	**Seeking to compensate** He/she seeks attention by playing hero, bad guy, mascot, etc.
3—Preoccupation with the "drug" Addict is convinced that "using" is the *only* way to feel good and takes major risks to do it.	**Preoccupation with problem** He is obsessed with "fixing" the loved one and goes into orbit around him or her.	**Preoccupation with pain** He resigns himself to the situation and begins to grieve losses.
4—"Using" to avoid pain He lives to use; he is irresponsible to the point of being unable to care for himself; he is now "King Baby."	**Disintegration of personality** The individual is in such pain that he considers drinking, suicide, or divorce to escape.	**Obsession with self** He lives in constant pain and fear and seeks relief in addictive behavior.

Figure 5 — The development of codependence.

Note that the secondary codependent is ideally prepared to become a primary codependent (usually by marriage), and the primary codependent is likely to become an addict. Each is likely to graduate to the next "higher" role.

Fatal attraction

Lynda had exceptional professional qualifications, but she described herself as "a little pile of nothing." Her husband blamed her for his drinking, and she believed him! If dinner wasn't on the table when he came home, he slammed the door and headed for the nearest bar, declaring loudly that it was her fault. If the candles were lighted, the table was set, and the meal ready when he got home the next day, he trounced out again, declaring, "A man can't get a moment's peace in his own house." His agenda called for his wife to be in the wrong at all times so that he would have an alibi for his drinking.

Lynda dutifully accepted the blame. She didn't know that she hadn't caused him to drink, nor did she know that she could neither control nor cure him. She just knew she couldn't cope any longer. Her ego was shattered, and she wanted to die. Her codependence was killing her!

The contagion of codependence

Codependence, like chemical dependence, is a disease that is primary, chronic, progressive, and potentially fatal. Not everyone who drinks becomes an alcoholic. And not everyone who experiences childhood trauma develops a deadly case of codependence. But some do. Unfortunately, codependence is very contagious. And, according to Melody Beattie, if you want to get rid of it, you have to do something to make it go away.[12]

Jeff was a tall, lanky, twenty-year-old cocaine addict. His father was a workaholic, and his mother was a religion addict. Jeff's parents were so dedicated to God that they literally gave everything they had to support the church and its mission. They were what one of my colleagues calls *compulsive do-gooders*.

For almost ten years, they moved their children from pillar to post, donating their time and talent to one lay ministry after another, until they had exhausted their physical and financial resources. Jeff's only happy memories were of early childhood, before his family embarked on their misguided sojourn. The rest of the years were lost to him. Jeff and his siblings sacrificed their childhood to their parents' compulsions.

Generosity is a wonderful trait. But in this case, it was carried to an extreme. Jeff and his brother and sisters suffered negative consequences, which their parents chose to ignore in order to continue "doing their thing.". Ultimately they ran out of money and energy. The whole family was left disheartened, depressed, penniless, and exhausted.

All four children developed severe codependence, which eventually evolved into addictions to drugs, alcohol, relationships, and compulsive overwork. Thanks to his cocaine problem, Jeff was the first member of the family to hit bottom and seek help. Through professional treatment and the program of Narcotics Anonymous, he found freedom.

Within three years, eleven other members of his immediate and extended family sought treatment for addiction or codependence. Jeff introduced hope and healing to the rest of his family. Recovery is possible. And it is contagious!

---

1. Terence T. Gorski, *Do Family of Origin Problems Cause Chemical Addiction?* (Independence, Mo.: Herald House), 11, 12.

2. Jonathan Shedler and Jack Block, "Adolescent Drug Use and Psychological Health," *American Psychologist*, May 1990, 612.

3. Archibald Hart, *Healing Life's Hidden Addictions* (Ann Arbor: Servant Publications, 1990), 66.

4. Timmen Cermak, *Diagnosing and Treating Co-dependence* (Minneapolis: Johnson Institute Books, 1986), 54.

5. Robert Subby, *Lost in the Shuffle* (Deerfield Beach, Fla.: Health Communications, 1987), 93.

6. Robert Hemfelt and Richard Fowler, *Serenity, a Companion for Twelve-Step Recovery* (Nashville: Thomas Nelson Publishers, 1990), 15.

7. Ibid., 14.

8. Errol Strider and Lou Montgomery, "Family Baggage," videotape from Creative Recovery/Oak Creek Films, Boulder, Colo., 1988.

9. Hemfelt and Fowler, 14.

10. Shedler and Block, 612.

11. Subby, 21, 22.

12. Melody Beattie, *Codependent No More* (San Francisco: Hazelden, 1987), 16.

Chapter 9

Trying Too Hard to Do the Right Thing

The stunned voices on the other end of the line were the most heart-rending sound I had ever heard. And I've heard it many times: desperate parents, numb with shock, calling at three o'clock in the morning, agonizing over the news that their son has just overdosed on cocaine. "We never dreamed he was on drugs. Where did we go wrong?"

There is an abundance of information available to Christian parents on how to rear their children in the nurture and admonition of the Lord. What happens when parents follow all the expert advice, but things don't turn out the way they're supposed to?

Parents who leave no stone unturned, who read all the books and listen to all the sermons, who are as conscientious in their child-rearing practices and as dedicated to God and church as possible, are totally bewildered when their children end up in trouble. For some reason, their best efforts failed.

Why?

Job's comforters

In almost every church, there is an amateur analyst who knows precisely what went wrong. He could have told them years ago that they were being too lax—they should have been more strict. Or they were too strict—they should have been more patient. They should have sent their son to church school. They shouldn't have let him quit Pathfinders. They shouldn't have let their daughter start dating when she was so young.

They should have forced her to go to church whether she wanted to or not, etc.

Most of these "Job's comforters" are well-meaning people who wouldn't deliberately offend a soul. "We were *so* sorry to hear that your son is in jail. *Our* boy has never given us moment's worry," they console, oblivious to the subtle dose of shame they have just administered. One heartbroken mother was reminded by a Christian friend, "You can ask, believe, and claim promises to your heart's content, Lucy. Just remember, God doesn't force people against their will."

Ill-timed, inappropriate admonitions like this can crush a parent who is already in despair.

Obsessed with eternity

If anything, the average Adventist parent tries *too* hard to do the right thing! Parents who are obsessed with eternity may be so single-minded in their approach to life that their kids are robbed of the opportunity to achieve healthy balance and moderation. In spite of their efforts to create an ideal environment, their children develop addictive personalities.

Extreme behavior is extreme behavior, even if it is built around God and church. And addiction is a disease of the extreme. If temperance in all things is the biblical ideal, then we may need to learn to practice moderation in the way we exercise our faith and go about winning our children to it. Obsessive efforts to perfect a child's character can backfire. It is possible for parents to monitor a child's behavior so closely, trying to keep him from offending God, that they prohibit him from living![1] A fifteen-year-old academy student complained, "I'm tired of being perfect. I just want to be normal!"

Of *course* our children's salvation is important to us! That's as it should be. But young people can lose their individuality in the flurry of religious overactivity that characterizes many conservative Christian homes. And parents can lose their *own* identities in the addictive practice of religion, when the substance of faith gives way to a form of godliness.

I believe God wants our worship to be a joyful expression of devotion, not an exercise in drivenness! How much better to make our children's salvation high priority and still encourage them to explore a variety of options as they seek identity and meaning! How much better to refrain from playing God and let *Him* win our children to Himself without undue interference from us!

When we look at our sons and daughters, we need to see more than just souls in need of salvation, more than just characters in need of development. If we lose sight of them as people and make our beliefs and values more important to us than our children are as individuals, they may come to hate our values and beliefs.

Perhaps we would be better role models if we exhibited a spirit of serenity and eternal security rather than an aura of religious frenzy. Perhaps, as one expert suggests, it is best for us to do the works of religion as we go about living *without obsessive concern about whether or not we will be eternally saved*.[2] That may bode better for our children's salvation, and our own, in the end. If our hope of salvation lies in the righteousness of Christ and not our own merits, then we can't maneuver our way into God's grace anyway.

A well-ordered Christian family

Most Christian parents could afford to lighten up a little. I've often wished that somebody had told me that a long time ago! Unfortunately, I probably couldn't have done so anyway, because I was addicted to being perfect. I was obsessed with saving my children. Like the pious, proper character on "Saturday Night Live," I was a real "church lady."

To ensure my children's salvation, I dedicated myself to making sure that they saw no evil, heard no evil, and did no evil. An Adventist physician described his behavior similarly: "I was the father the kids couldn't do anything right for. I didn't know I was supposed to *enjoy* my children. I thought I was supposed to *exhort* them. I didn't know I was supposed to *celebrate their existence*. I thought I was supposed to *develop their characters*." And he wept openly, grieving the loss, both to himself and his grown sons.

The lengths to which one Adventist mother went to be an

ideal parent were unbelievable. She baked homemade bread and made gluten and granola. She sewed all her children's clothes, gave them piano lessons and taught them the music to every hymn in the church hymnal, helped them learn their memory verses every morning and read them bedtime stories every night, and home-schooled them until they were ready for academy. She (puff, puff) set a sterling example of Christian virtue in every aspect of her life. She literally drove herself crazy. She ended up physically, emotionally, and spiritually exhausted (clinically depressed).

Codependence, translated into the Christian setting, can be a cruel and heartless taskmaster!

Religious overactivity

Had I been aware that my religious overactivity was counterproductive, which I was not; and had I, in the light of that knowledge, been unable to change, I would have been considered a religion addict, which I was! And to the extent that I found it necessary to continue controlling my children long after I should have quit, I would also be considered a compulsive controller. I believe that the combination of these two addictions is deadly.

The reason my workaholic, churchaholic activities would be considered addictive is that when I realized my behavior wasn't healthy, I couldn't stop. When my husband and I attended professional meetings where workaholism was decried (but, ironically, high achievement was demanded), I made firm resolutions to cut back and take more time for myself and my family. But I couldn't keep my resolutions. I couldn't go a day without succumbing to the compulsion to overwork! Therein lies the difference between an addict and a "problem" drinker or a "social" overworker. The social drinker can quit. The alcoholic, addict, workaholic cannot.

According to Pia Mellody, perfectionists, working people, and religious people who can stop behaving compulsively probably are not addicts. Those who *cannot* quit probably *are* addicts. It is the inability to quit or control one's harmful behavior that identifies a person as an addict.[3]

Says Gerald May, "If you are successful [in stopping], there is no addiction. If you cannot stop, no amount of rationalization will change the fact that addiction exists."[4]

Loss of control

Geneva, a talented pastor's wife in her mid-fifties, was intensely involved in her husband's ministry. Her children were grown, so she worked around the clock giving Bible studies, visiting the sick, etc. She was her husband's unofficial, unpaid assistant, as well as the church choir director, Sabbath School superintendent, and social committee chairwoman.

Out of genuine concern for her mother's health, Geneva's eldest daughter chided her one day for giving so much time to the church that she had no time for herself. "Mother, you're doing too much. You need to slow down."

Clenching her fists, Geneva turned and screamed, "I *can't* slow down!" And then she collapsed to the floor, weeping. Both she and her daughter were shocked. Neither had realized how "spent" Geneva really was nor how compulsive and out of control her behavior had become.

As difficult as this may be to understand, the addict's inability to alter or control his addictive behavior is *not* a question of lack of desire, determination, or willingness. Nor is it lack of willpower. Most addicts have made strenuous efforts to change. They have exercised phenomenal willpower, but without success. It is impossible to arrest addiction with willpower.[5] In fact, the more a person struggles and strains to pull himself out of the quicksand of addiction with willpower alone, the more bogged down he or she becomes.[6]

Defending the disease

The tendency to defend or deny compulsive behavior is an earmark of addiction. A prosperous Christian businessman defended his workaholism on the basis of his financial generosity to the church: "If I weren't a workaholic, I wouldn't be able to give as much money to the Lord!" But his children were emo-tionally impoverished.

An "unselfish" Christian woman who was abandoning her

children and driving her husband crazy with her compulsive care giving justified her behavior with this pious question: "How can anyone say it's wrong for me to give of myself when Jesus gave His life for me?" Meanwhile, her family was being sacrificed on the altar of her ego!

A zealous Adventist whose controlling, critical spirit had driven his children and grandchildren completely out of his life defended his offensive behavior as "standing up for principle." He believed it was his Christian duty to rebuke and exhort everyone around him. Sadly, people's efforts to escape his badgering led many of them away from the Lord.

A young teacher shared her feelings of frustration: "Every time I call my mom, she wants to know if I've given my heart to the Lord yet. She doesn't think I've been 'converted,' because my lifestyle doesn't meet her standards. She pressures me constantly to conform to her beliefs. She's so burdened for my soul that she's miserable to be around." The mother thought she was just witnessing to her daughter. She was in total delusion about how hurtful her actions were, both in terms of her relationship to her daughter and in terms of her "cause."

The generous workaholic and the compulsive do-gooder found great satisfaction in giving. The zealous grandfather and burdened mother were confident that they were doing what was right. But the very behavior from which they were deriving such positive feelings brought negative returns. Yet they continued doing it. No matter how noble and righteous the deed, if the consequences are detrimental to self or others, it is inappropriate as well as addictive to persist in doing it.

A lethal overdose

"Because I was raised a Roman Catholic, I've had religion on my mind most of my life," says John Bradshaw. "At the parochial school I attended in Houston, the subject was bred into us. I've thought a lot about religious addiction—the mood alteration that comes with the feeling of righteousness, the feeling of being pure and blessed, specially selected, saved."[7]

I, too, have had religion on my mind most of my life. I don't think that's all bad. But it may not be all good either. Breeding religion into children from the moment they're born may have a downside. I've met many young adults who feel their parents overdosed them on religion. "Mom and Dad crammed God down our throats," they complain.

Overdosing children on religion may create an *antipathy* to religion on the one hand or *religious addiction* on the other. Neither outcome is desirable.

Salvation by behavior modification

It is an unchangeable fact that "firsthand spiritual experiences cannot be handed from one generation to the next."[8] Christian parents who genuinely love the Lord and have a personal relationship with Him are hard put to pass their experience on to the next generation. Our efforts to "convert" our children often turn into compulsive controlling of their outward behavior. To this end, we create lists of approved and disapproved activities—the *dos* and *don'ts* that children so resent.

According to Donald Sloat, author of *The Dangers of Growing Up in a Christian Home*, many parents define sin as a list of specific behaviors to be avoided. This master-list approach lays the groundwork for a dangerous kind of self-righteousness.[9] Behavior-oriented parents "try to teach their children to avoid certain actions, and as the children succeed in doing this, they fail to develop an appropriate awareness of their inner state of being."[10]

Dr. Sloat describes his own childhood: "There I was, being carefully monitored by my parents so I did not engage in any of the major sins (they even prohibited me from seeing a puppet show at school when I was in second grade), and at the same time I was told at church that I should be so very grateful that Jesus died to save me from all my terrible sins. What sins? What had I done?"[11]

I myself must have belonged to the same school of parenting. Once, years ago, my sons set out to design costumes for a Halloween party. Being creative, resourceful boys, they found an old sheet and, instead of doing the obvious (making a ghost costume), they tore it into strips and swathed themselves in "bandages." Then they added a little authenticity by soaking

TRYING TOO HARD TO DO THE RIGHT THING 89

the bandages in "blood" (food coloring). Instead of enjoying their creativity and exercising good humor, I judged their costumes gross and un-Christian and refused to let them wear them.

Compulsive as I was, I felt duty-bound to turn every situation into an opportunity to educate, moralize, or develop character. I was eternally vigilant, because I thought something might sneak up on one of my boys and tweak his sinful nature. He would be lost forever, and it would be my fault. Much of the joy and spontaneity that we could have shared as mother and children was lost to my perfectionism.

Pounding children to perfection

Children are not so evil by nature that they generate perverse behavior spontaneously. Our sons and daughters may be born into sin, but it is as much *our* sinfulness as theirs. They may have carnal natures, but they are not defective blobs that need to be mercilessly pounded to perfection in the holy name of character development. Unfortunately, our emphasis on the carnal nature of man, sometimes called original sin, leaves many young people feeling defeated before they start![12]

Once parents take on the divinely commissioned task of subduing a child's evil nature, it is possible to rationalize almost any means for accomplishing their purpose. Christian parents who consider it their sacred duty to break a child's will are very likely to slip into physically or emotionally abusive behaviors.

The need to vindicate *ourselves* is what drives most of us to overcontrol our children. We're afraid of what other people will think of us if they misbehave. Thus, we offer up our children as sacrifices to our lofty religious values.[13] We do such a thorough job turning our kids off on God that Satan doesn't have to bother! One old preacher called this "working for God like the devil!"

Chaotic Christianity

I once heard James Dobson speak of families that live in a state of routine panic. That's the way I functioned. I was obsessed with saving the world. I worked frantically during every daylight hour because I knew the night was coming! I never walked when I could run, and I never sat down. I operated in hyperdrive at all times. I sacrificed myself to the point of losing my own identity, if indeed I ever had one. My children suffered accordingly.

I don't think my obsessive practice of Christianity was good for me or my family, and probably not for the people I was trying to help. I consider my religious overactivity, my perfectionism, and my workaholism to have been spiritually abusive to myself and my family. Yet I doubt that I am the only Christian who has adopted this kind of insane lifestyle in order to do "the Lord's work."

Pushing children away

In an effort to cement the bond between their children and the church, many parents inadvertently push their children away from themselves and God. Anxious to establish his own identity, the normal adolescent gradually distances himself from his parents (and sometimes from their values). When he does so, the natural reaction on the part of the parents is to try to close the gap and restore the status quo. Thus, they unwittingly deprive the child of the distance he needs, which forces him to distance himself even more.[14]

As the young person continues to back away, his parents cross his boundaries in an effort to draw him back. They snoop, ask leading questions, and make subtle suggestions. This pushes the child farther away. Each time the parents try to close the gap, the child moves farther away. Parents who persist in their efforts to hang onto a child are working against their own purposes. Each step they take toward him pushes him farther in the direction of bizarre or antisocial behavior.

The more parents worry about their children's salvation, the more "driven" they become. And the more driven parents are, the more they drive their children away. It's that simple. We have to "let go and let God!"

When a parent has taken care of a child from the moment of his birth, it's hard to let go. Parenting can easily become an addiction. A tragic incident made me realize how habit forming parenting really is. Some dear friends of ours lost their three-year-old son in an accident several years ago. They were devoted to him, and the loss was crushing. Every Sabbath for the first three years of his life, they had held him in their arms during the worship service and entertained him with books and toys while the pastor (my husband) was preaching. I can still hear Chad lisping my husband's name: "Pathtor Cannon."

During church the week after Chad's death, I was painfully aware that his parents were sitting with empty arms. I could almost feel the awkwardness they must have felt. What do bereaved parents do with the arms that have held their child when he is gone?

The sense of loss we feel when we are bereft of the responsibility for leading and guiding our children is like that. Suddenly, our children are grown. They don't need us anymore. It's hard to break the habit of worrying about them, of trying to solve their problems, of telling them how to run their lives. But break it we must.

I am deeply grateful for counselors and support groups that have helped me work through the painful process of detaching from my children and learning to let go. I could not have made it without that kind of help.

---

1. Donald Sloat, *The Dangers of Growing Up in a Christian Home* (Nashville: Thomas Nelson, Inc., 1986), 153.

2. John Bradshaw, "Praying for a Dose of Mood-Change," *Lear's*, January 1991, 52.

3. Pia Mellody, "Overview of Codependency," audiotape from Mellody Enterprises, Wickenburg, Ariz., 1988.

4. Gerald G. May, *Addiction and Grace* (San Francisco: Harper & Row, 1991), 28.

5. Ibid., 30.

6. Ibid., 60.

7. Bradshaw, "Praying for Mood-Change," 52.

8. Sloat, 31.

9. Ibid., 31, 106.

10. Ibid., 107.

11. Ibid.

12. John Bradshaw, Healing the Shame That Binds You (Deerfield Beach, Fla.: Health Communications, 1988), 64.

13. Alice Miller, *For Your Own Good* (New York: Farrar, Straus & Giroux, 1990), 31, 66.

14. Sloat, 303, 304.

Chapter 10

Using Religion as a Mood Modulator

I referred earlier to religious practices that are an *exercise in drivenness* rather than an *expression of devotion*. It is possible to be so compulsive in our relationship to God and church that we hurt ourselves and our families, which is, by definition, addictive behavior. I don't think that's quite what God had in mind. The line between healthy spirituality and neurotic perfectionism is a fine one that bears examining.

I believe God enjoys His children best and appreciates their devotion most when they practice healthy spirituality. However, He doesn't condemn people who practice religion addictively any more than He condemns any other addict. Churchaholics can make *themselves* very unhappy, though, and not at all appealing to other people, which affects the viability of their witness. And sooner or later they hit bottom, much as the alcoholic does, and when that happens, they suffer major losses—sometimes even the loss of faith.

Almost everyone is acquainted with someone who was once on fire for God, whose initial practice of religion was so hot (enthusiastic, zealous) that he eventually burned out and went to the opposite extreme, leaving the Lord altogether. Religious addiction, like any other addiction, has fatal potential.

The very idea that the abuse of religious practices could be considered an addiction is an affront to many Christians, and understandably so. We consider religion the solution to our problems, not the problem itself. Christ is the Answer, the Alpha and the Omega, the Beginning and the End. Unfortunately, what we do with Him between the beginning and the end "is often a tragicomic roadshow of religious one-upmanship, distortion, and addiction,"[1] says William Lenters, a certified counselor and ordained minister.

Lenters suggests that religion has addictive qualities, or, more accurately, that "our addiction-prone selves are drawn to using religion in an addictive manner, because it makes us feel better."[2] A Christian with a painful family history is inclined to use religion as a medicator. He abuses it or uses it to abuse himself. Getting high on religion is like getting high on romance, Lenters says. "And, like romance, religion can become an object of obsession that causes serious life problems."[3]

By no means is every devout Christian a churchaholic! But people who take religion seriously and use it to medicate emotional pain are vulnerable to becoming harmfully involved or addicted.[4] Ideally, one's religious practices should be a meaningful expression of spirituality, a manifestation of mature devotion, rather than addiction. The issue at stake is how to distinguish between healthy religious practices and addictive religious behavior.

What is religious addiction?

"Healthy expression of belief is one thing. Using God as a giant aspirin is another," says John Bradshaw.[5] Addiction-prone people expect Jesus to do what booze does—make them feel better fast.[6] The individual who is operating out of a codependent emotional vacuum uses religion to relieve his feelings of loneliness and emptiness. Once his pain is thus numbed, he may overlook the underlying pathology (issues of immaturity carried over from childhood).

The unconscious goal of the codependent's religious striving is to modulate his mood, to fill the aching void. People who use God in this manner rarely realize what they are doing. But if an individual has always felt insecure, inadequate, and "different"; if he has felt that he doesn't belong anywhere, that he's not good enough, then he may use religion to compensate.

Unquestionably, one's hungering and thirsting for fulfillment is appropriate. Jesus *is* the "balm in Gilead." This makes

Christianity especially appealing to the wounded adult/child. I have personally found great comfort and hope in my beliefs. While my relationship with God and church is deeply meaningful to me, however, I consider it a perversion of the ideal to use religion as an emotional painkiller.

The codependent seeks relief in his beliefs. In Christ he finds acceptance he has never felt before. In the Holy Spirit, he finds companionship he has never found before. His quest for identity and meaning, however, may lead to a mindless dependence on religious leaders, rituals, and even doctrines.[7] In recovery, he may not have to change his religion, but he will have to change his motives.

Religious addiction can be defined as a psychological dependence on religious beliefs and practices to repair one's damaged ego and integrity. Lenters calls this "escaping to God." He reminds us that while here on earth, Jesus "gave no indication that his bosom was fair game for the terminally anxious looking for a way to ride out the storm."[8]

The function of religious addiction

Religion, when used addictively, (1) medicates intolerable emotional pain, (2) gives the needy codependent a sense of self-esteem and identity, and/or (3) acts to arrest other addictive behaviors such as alcoholism, sexaholism, love addiction, etc. Again, these things may appear to be healthy and appropiate, but carried to the extreme, they are not. The codependent tends to incorporate his religion into his emotional sickness. Thus his beliefs are perverted. This is a function of the addiction, not the religion.

Codependent Christians expect too much of religion. They expect a lifetime of lost social and emotional development to be restored instantly when they are converted. They hope (trust!) that they will be miraculously delivered of their defects of character so as to avoid the grinding responsibility of learning better ways of relating to self and others. They use religion as a shortcut to wellness. As one of my clients put it, "It was easier to control my outward behavior than it was to face my codependence. It was easier to act pious than it was to get well."

Who wouldn't prefer miraculous healing to major surgery? A young woman suffering from a late-stage eating addiction (bulimarexia) sought healing through her church and experienced a miraculous deliverance. Her condition improved temporarily. But when the symptoms of her eating disorder recurred, she was so ashamed that she kept her relapse a secret, which deprived her of help when she needed it most. The wonder is that she didn't die! By the grace of God, she got professional help before it was too late.

The real issue

It is relatively common for a new convert with a painful family history to remain in denial and delusion about his or her social and emotional deficits. Such Christians are often unaware that they are emotionally and socially handicapped. Though they may be faithful in their religious practices and utterly sincere, *they remain immature children in adult bodies.*

They are attempting to build a spiritual house on the sands of codependence instead of the solid foundation of recovery in Christ. Because they are unable to bring a well-defined, adult self into their relationship with God, the structure does not stand. The ultimate crumbling of their Christian experience is only a symptom of a much deeper problem. Neither they nor God is at fault.

Unfortunately, being woefully unaware of their social liabilities, they continue to act out their immaturity. They are oblivious to their arrogance, grandiosity, and "King Baby" behaviors. They violate other people's boundaries. They manipulate to get their needs met. They are irritable, offensive, blaming, and judgmental. And for good reason: They are "sanctified" dry drunks.

If they are using religion as a narcotic, the religious highs make them feel better, but these highs don't fix what ails them. They are still immature children in adult bodies! Dysfunctional attitudes, beliefs, and behaviors set these people up for ongoing emotional pain and problems, which they continue to anesthetize rather than address. They may seek and find solace in Scripture, but they continue to sabotage themselves because they lack adult coping skills.

As these problems persist and their mood swings grow more and more dramatic, these unfortunate Christians attempt to modulate their uncontrolled feelings with religious disciplines (fasting, prayer, Bible study). This may work for a while, but eventually these exercises will stop making them feel better, because the underlying problem is still untreated. Their tolerance will increase, as does the alcoholic's, so that they require more and more of the "drug" to bring about the desired mood change. Eventually, their tolerance will reverse, creating a crisis of faith.

Am I suggesting that God cannot heal such individuals? Not at all. I am suggesting, however, that God may choose to use available means, just as He does with physical illness. The therapeutic technology available today for healing from codependence and other obsessive/compulsive disorders is unsurpassed. For that, I praise Him.

The roots of religious addiction

How does religious addiction develop? Like other addictions, the roots of religious addiction are firmly planted in childhood. When a child has been abused rather than affirmed, neglected instead of nurtured, he is wounded. He bears the scars of his abuse and uses religion to cover them up, which is really unnecessary. He has nothing to be ashamed of! He is the child upon whom the sins of the fathers have been visited! He is bearing a load of shame that is not his own! He is paying the price for sins that are not of his own choosing. He may feel unworthy, but he is not *worthless*!

Filled with a sense of his own unworthiness, he begs for affirmation. Because of his history, he cannot believe that anyone—least of all *God*—could really care for *him*. So, feeling terribly inadequate, he approaches God in a groveling, apologetic manner. What a skewed approach to a generous, accepting, loving heavenly Father! And how unattractive and pathetic the result. He has yet to find the abundant life.

Shame-based codependents who are attempting to repair their damaged integrity slip readily into perfectionism.[9] They want so badly to be acceptable. Religion lends itself well to compensation of this kind. The mood alteration that accompanies the feeling of righteousness, of being pure and blessed, of being specially selected, of being saved, is enormously attractive to the shame-based person.[10]

Wounded children cry out for relief. While they deserve healing, and while the healing power comes from God, I believe that the healing *process* must be addressed on many levels, including religion, but not just religion.

Using religion to rebel

Researchers have learned that many families alternate between chemical dependence in one generation and religious addiction in the next.[11] When children from conservative homes rebel against parental values and forsake their religious upbringing, they often act out their defiance by violating the family's abstinence norms.

Children of alcoholics tend to act out their rebelliousness in the opposite manner—by getting involved with religion. Either way, they embrace one potentially addictive substance or activity in order to escape another.

Most teenagers who grow up in abusive alcoholic homes are determined not to be like their parents, so they avoid alcohol at all costs. This isn't a bad idea. Because children of alcoholics are predisposed to addiction, they probably *should* avoid alcohol. But if they use religion to assuage their pain instead, they are likely to abuse *it*. A codependent walks the fine line of addiction to any substance, process, or activity that he uses to avoid, cope with, or medicate his feelings, *including religion*.

Kinds of religious addiction

Two basic kinds of religious addiction have been identified: the ecstatic and the somber, the Pentecostal and the Puritan.[12] The fervent, ecstatic practice of religion involves hype, excitement, and exuberance. The convert expects to be hap-hap-happy all the time. He feels he must praise the Lord always, no matter what happens. This is a worthy ideal, to be sure. But when a person does not feel happy and joyful (and who does *all* the time?), and when his failure to exhibit adequate enthusiasm is seen by the church as a lack of dedication or an indication of spiritual inadequacy, the climate can quickly become judgmental, controlling, and cold.

When a member thinks he has to hide negative feelings from his fellows because he is afraid he will be accused of being un-Christian, something is wrong! In order to protect himself, he is forced to hide behind walls that make intimacy with God and fellow believers impossible. Unable to share his repressed feelings with anyone, the pain and pressure build to the point that the sufferer may feel compelled to return to his negative patterns of behavior. Thus the church enables addiction, much as a dysfunctional family does. Nuclear families and church families stay as sick as the secrets they keep.

The Puritan type of religious addiction is characterized by rigidity and rigorous rule keeping. If it feels good, it's wrong. (I call this *pleasure anorexia.*) Believers spend a great deal of time moralizing, analyzing, criticizing, and judging. They are preoccupied with sin and salvation. They tend to be coercive and controlling. They think being too happy and joyful shows a lack of commitment.

Some people combine these two religious addictions and flip-flop between them. I lean in the Puritan direction myself, being somewhat somber by nature. However, I no longer enjoy being negative and critical. Recently I met someone who was decrying the sinful condition of humanity, and I felt like running the other direction. For me, that's progress, because I used to get high on conversations like that. They made me feel so righteous.

Being right and being righteous are the churchaholic's source of self-esteem and security. That's why it's unnerving to look at the issue of religious addiction—it threatens our sense of security, which is precisely what *needs* to happen so we can get one thing straight: we are not in charge. God is. He is responsible for our salvation, and He is well able to accomplish it.

If we could get that concept clearly into focus, if we could present ourselves to our children as power*less* (unable to save ourselves) instead of power*ful* (capable of earning merit)—in short, if we could stop playing God and acknowledge that we are fallible human beings—we would be much less likely to abuse our children in the interest of saving them!

Symptoms of imbalance

Following are some signs of religious addiction:

- A tendency to focus on external behavior and acts of piety rather than true spirituality.
- Preoccupation with religion or church to the exclusion of other important priorities.
- A unidimensional lifestyle in which one finds one's total identity in church activities.
- Dependence on feelings of righteousness and holiness for meaning and self-esteem.
- Using God or God's Word as a "fix" while refusing to face the underlying symptoms of codependence.
- Projecting one's wants and wishes onto God and claiming that subsequent choices are "His will."
- Care giving to earn merit or feel worthwhile.
- Excessive reliance on rigid, ritualized forms of religion.
- Loss of spiritual spontaneity.
- Using asceticism (austere self-discipline) to prove one's dedication.
- Inability to allow oneself to be human and fallible.
- Acting in the religious extreme—fanaticism.
- Beating oneself up with guilt.
- The tendency to overcontrol or overprotect children in order to ensure their salvation.
- Doing the Lord's work to the detriment of one's health and well-being or the well-being of one's family.
- Obsessive "worry" praying.
- A judgmental spirit.
- Isolation from "the world"—the effort to live in a sin-free environment.
- Avoidance of anything or anyone whose beliefs are not harmonious with one's own.

Certain of these traits or behaviors appear, at first glance, to be positive. As a Christian, I *do* want my fondest thoughts and tenderest feelings to be of Christ. I want to be useful to the Lord and a blessing to people. But I have to recognize my human limitations. And I must maintain balance. While I don't want to be lukewarm, I do want to practice moderation in all things, including religion, so that I can be a healthy, viable witness to the faith I love.

I want to worship the Lord out of the abundance of psychological health, not out of an emotional abscess. I believe He deserves to be worshiped by a person with a well-defined identity who can make a mature choice to love Him freely, without expectation of temporal or eternal reward. I am a wounded soul, but I want God to be my Surgeon, not my anesthetic. I want to get rid of the headache, not mask the pain. I am entirely willing to undergo a radical intervention so that I can be healed of my unhealthy dependencies. And I'm confident that God is the ultimate Source of recovery.

----

1. William Lenters, *The Freedom We Crave* (Grand Rapids: Eerdmans, 1985), 81.

2. Ibid.

3. Ibid.

4. Ibid.

5. John Bradshaw, "Praying for a Dose of Mood-Change," *Lear's*, January 1991, 52.

6. Lenters, 83.

7. Ibid., 88.

8. Ibid.

9. Fred Downing, "The Family Disease Workshop," videotape from Paradox Productions, 1984.

10. Bradshaw, "Praying for Mood-Change," 52.

11. "When Religion Is Used Addictively," *AddInfo News* (Andrews University Institute of Alcoholism and Drug Dependence, 1988), 3.

12. Bradshaw, "Praying for Mood-Change," 52.

Chapter 11

Confessions of a Churchaholic

Nancy Lee was the firstborn child of a perfectionistic mother and an alcoholic father. Her mother didn't want children, and her father didn't want a *girl*. Needless to say, Nancy Lee felt unwelcome. "At age three," she says, "my mother got mad at me for complaining of an earache, and I remember feeling rejected and abandoned." When she was five, a life-changing incident occurred. It was Sabbath, and Nancy Lee was ill again. Her mother didn't want to miss church, so she left her daughter at home with her brother (the child's uncle), who had a history of sexually abusing little girls.

Since it was Sabbath, Nancy's mother insisted that she dress up, even though she wasn't going to church. So when her uncle molested her, Nancy came to associate the abuse with having worn a dress. From then on, she got hysterical whenever she was forced to wear dresses. And, as is always the case when children are molested, Nancy absorbed the abuser's shame. She was the victim, not the perpetrator, but she bore his guilt and shame just the same.

Because her father had rejected her gender, her mother refused to accept her imperfections, and her uncle violated her, Nancy saw herself as hopelessly flawed. Anxious for approval and desperate for her mother's acceptance, Nancy drove herself to be more perfect. Nevertheless, feelings of unworthiness haunted her continuously. She agonized over her sinfulness when, in fact, she barely qualified as a sinner! Her feelings of shame were related to the incest and little more.

Shortly after her marriage at twenty, Nancy's sense of defectiveness drove her to despair. For a victim of incest, entering a serious adult relationship may bring deep-seated feelings of anger and fear to the surface. Not recognizing the source of her distress, Nancy Lee spent night after sleepless night begging God for some sign of acceptance, but it didn't come. Why did peace elude her? Was it because she was bad? Was it because God is cold and unforgiving? No! It was because of the abuse she had suffered and the fact that she had never been able to express her anguish.

She became more and more miserable. She describes herself as being a "seething cauldron of rage" erupting frequently on her husband and children. She took her frustrations out on each of them in turn. She used her eldest child as her confidante. She scapegoated the second child, rejected the third, and loved the fourth obsessively. Her poor performance as a mother only served to increase her burden of shame.

By the time she was thirty years old, she was severely depressed. A concerned friend told her that busy-ness was the best-known remedy for depression. She suggested that Nancy Lee forget herself and concentrate on serving others, which she obediently did. She dove headlong into church activities and began laboring feverishly for the Lord.

It worked!

"Those years were a religious high for me," she says. "My experience parallels that of Bill Wilson. In the 'Big Book' of Alcoholics Anonymous, he talks about the 'inviting maelstrom of Wall Street' having him in its grip. My inviting maelstrom was religious overactivity. He says that business and financial leaders were his heroes. Religious leaders were mine. Out of this 'alloy of drink and speculation' (for me it was prayer, work, and penance), he 'commenced to forge the weapon that one day would turn in its flight like a boomerang and all but cut [him] to ribbons.'[1] That was my experience with religion."

Her next words are telling: "I became more and more legalistic and perfectionistic. I clung to a false piety and religiosity that bolstered my faith and gave me a euphoria that I thought was spirituality. All I succeeded in doing was to drive my children away from me and turn God, religion, and moralism into an addiction. That's when I hit bottom and wanted to commit suicide, but I was afraid to because I didn't want to hurt my loved ones or look bad in the eyes of the church.

"Then our son acted out my sickness. He stole thirteen thousand dollars of our money and spent it on cocaine in two months. We took him to a treatment center, little realizing that we were the ones who were sick. When we attended his Family Week, I got a glimpse of my problem and the way out. For the first time in my life, I saw light at the end of the tunnel.

"I've been in recovery now for over five years. It has been a long, hard battle with lots of pain and joy and help from many sources—family, friends, sponsors, twelve-step programs, therapists, pastors, and codependency treatment. At present, I know a new freedom, serenity, and comfort in God's love and acceptance that I never felt before."

Stages of religious addiction

Based on the experiences of several recovering churchaholics and religious addicts, I have attempted to superimpose the four-stage model developed by Vernon Johnson for alcoholism onto religious addiction:

Stage 1—Learning the mood swing. The codependent seeks relief from his pain and shame through religious practices. The people at church say they're happy. They have bumper stickers that read, "I've Found It!" and "Honk if you love Jesus." He hopes to find their secret. He is enamored with the promise that religion holds out to him.

Stage 2—Seeking the mood swing. He accepts Christ and is born again. He learns church doctrines and standards, which give him a sense of security. He is gratified to have found the "truth." Belonging to the right church makes him feel better, but the pain is still gnawing away at his insides. Whenever it surfaces, he pushes himself harder to make God happy. He begins to depend on being right and being righteous for feelings of self-esteem. He tries to be the best Christian he can be.

For the first time in his life, Someone is listening to him and responding to his needs. That feels wonderful. Gradually, unintentionally, he begins to use God as a vending machine.

Stage 3—Preoccupation with religion. He decides that more is better. He connects with religious leaders and gets attached to them. He multiplies his self-imposed requirements and places greater and greater demands on himself. He practices strict adherence to the letter of the law but has little awareness of the spirit of the law. He becomes obsessed with rules and regulations, with forms and rituals. He isolates himself from worldly people and pursuits in order to concentrate on religion. Thus he manages to control his sinful thoughts and actions. Sooner or later, he begins slipping occasionally into acting-out behavior (his old addictions or sins), and then promises himself that he will never do it again. And he believes he won't.

Ellen White describes stage 3 in *Steps to Christ*: "There are those who profess to serve God, while they rely upon their own efforts to obey His law, to form a right character, and secure salvation. Their hearts are not moved by any deep sense of the love of Christ, but they seek to perform the duties of the Christian life as that which God requires of them in order to gain heaven. Such religion is worth nothing. . . . A profession of Christ without this deep love is mere talk, dry formality, and heavy drudgery."[2] This is the classic Laodicean state.

Stage 4—Practicing religion obsessively. Now, like the drug addict, the religion addict is "using" just to keep from feeling bad. He is using religion to avoid doubt and self-condemnation and to escape eternal damnation. The guilt he experiences every time he fails (falls short of God's or the church's expectations) attaches itself to his existing shame core and, rather than leading him to a healthy repentance, sets him up to seek relief in his addictive behavior again.

The internal conflict intensifies. Feelings of sinfulness and unworthiness escalate. His efforts to be perfect alternate with major relapses into sinful behavior. Failure leads to suicidal thoughts. Spiritual bankruptcy is impending.

Elijah's addiction

I have often wondered if some of the trials and tribulations of the prophets of old might have been related to religious addiction. The rather dramatic life of Elijah is a case in point. Whether Elijah was indeed a religious addict is not for me to say. But his story does exemplify some of the characteristics of religious addiction that I want to point out.

Elijah was a man singularly chosen by God to check the spread of apostasy.[3] The importance of his ministry, the intensity of his burden, may have led him to work addictively. And although he may not have been addicted to religion as such, he was certainly a co-addict. Why? Because he lived with a whole nation of religious addicts!

From the time of Jeroboam until Elijah's appearance before Ahab, the Israelites gradually slipped away from a healthy relationship with God into an addictive relationship with a false god. The shift occurred little by little. They moved from what was a vital, personal experience into a stale observance of the forms of religion. They lost touch with the essence of their faith.[4] Finally, they regressed into heathenism.

I began to suspect that the Israelites of Elijah's time were religious addicts when I read a statement in *Prophets and Kings* suggesting that God called Elijah to free his people from their *delusion*.[5] In addictions treatment, we talk a lot about denial and delusion, so the word *delusion* caught my attention.

Then I noticed a second clue: "In the face of calamity, they [the children of Israel] continued to stand firm in their idolatry."[6] If one of the characteristics of addiction is continuing to do harmful behavior in the face of negative consequences, then that applies to the children of Israel.

I found yet a third characteristic. Their disease was transgenerational, as are all addictions. When Elijah confronted the king with God's message, Elijah boldly asserted that the apostasy of his people involved both Ahab and his father's house.[7] Ahab responded with a major symptom of addiction: blaming. He knew the consequences of Israel's relationship to Baal, but he blamed Elijah for their troubles rather than looking honestly at his own behavior and taking responsibility for it. This leads me to believe that Israel was an addictive society!

Elijah maintained his serenity throughout most of the ensuing drama, which I find encouraging. But at the very last, he experienced a severe mood swing—a catastrophic high, followed by a devastating letdown. The excitement of those dramatic hours on the mountain gave Elijah an adrenalin rush that was followed by a rebound into depression. He went from the mountaintop to the pit of despair: "A reaction such as frequently follows high faith and glorious success was pressing upon Elijah. . . . Depression seized him."[8]

Finally, Elijah ran away. This is the fourth stage of codependence—isolation. Forgetting God, he fled from Jezebel's threats until he found himself "in a dreary waste," alone. "A fugitive, far from the dwelling-places of men, his spirits crushed by bitter disappointment, he desired never again to look upon the face of man."[9]

Did God forsake Elijah when he hit bottom? No! "He loved His servant no less when Elijah felt himself forsaken of God and man than when, in answer to his prayer, fire flashed from heaven and illuminated the mountaintop."[10]

God forsakes no one, addict or otherwise.

The road to recovery

Can religion addicts find recovery and live normal Christian lives? I believe they can. I have no doubt that God understands all the circumstances that have led them into the condition they are in,[11] and that He will gently lead them to better health *if the rest of the saints will refrain from trying to do the job for Him!*

There are certain pitfalls in early recovery that make the process less than gracious, especially in the eyes of the onlooking church. There are at least two detours, normal but awkward, that may be unavoidable. One is a developmental issue, and the other involves the post-acute withdrawal syndrome.

Developmental arrest. People in early recovery are developmentally immature. It is unavoidable, and it is not their fault. When an addict begins the process of recovery, he is somewhere between the ages of zero and twelve developmentally. This is a fact that the church must accept. His emotional and social growth were arrested when he started drinking and drugging, or earlier still, when the trauma in his life became profound.

For example, if his parents divorced when he was four, if he was sexually molested at six, if he was neglected and abandoned by alcoholic or workaholic or churchaholic parents from infancy, then his development was arrested at that point. Never having had the opportunity to process his pain and anger therapeutically, he will begin his recovery at the point where the emotional energy for his growth was diverted into surviving the major crisis of his childhood.

What are the implications for the recovering religion addict? Like any other addict, he is emotionally and spiritually a pre-adolescent. He will probably struggle through the typical questioning of values, examining of ideals, and the search for identity that any normal adolescent would. He will not become a thirty-five-year-old Christian overnight, even if he is biologically thirty-five or even forty-five. Church members need to adjust their expectations, or they will run the risk of judging such an individual harshly and assuming that he is not committed to Christ when his growth doesn't fit *their* timetable or *their* definition of holiness.

Post-acute withdrawal. An issue even more threatening to the uninformed observer is what is known as the post-acute withdrawal syndrome. In normal recovery from drug dependence or any other addiction, there is a withdrawal phase that can last for a year and sometimes longer. This is nothing more than a reaction to the absence of the addictive substance and the reality of facing life without the emotional painkiller. The backswing can be as deep and dramatic as the original high. This reaction varies in intensity from uncomfortable to unbearable.

What happens to co-churchaholics—children who are co-dependent to religiously addicted parents? They often go through a similar withdrawal when they leave the addictive environment. It is a well-documented fact that "crack babies" go through withdrawal when they enter the world. Children of religion addicts have much the same experience. They go through a painful period of "wandering in the wilderness" when they leave home, and they may experience real difficulty in their struggle to find peace with God and church.

The worst thing a church can do is to overreact and condemn

such people or judge them as lost because they don't fit the church's profile of a born-again Christian. These people may be going through their spiritual and emotional adolescence and/or experiencing the rebound phenomenon. One such young person was told that the church was praying for him. "I'd rather have them accept me than pray for me," was his response.

Therein lies a valuable truth!

Can religion addicts or their children ever become normal Christians? I believe they can. But they must be patient, tolerant, and gentle with themselves. And they need a great deal of understanding. It takes time to grow up. That's actually the way God meant for it to be. Recovery is a *process*, not an *event*. As a matter of fact, sanctification is the work of a lifetime.

---

1. *Alcoholics Anonymous* (New York: Alcoholics Anonymous World Services, Inc., 1976), 2.

2. Ellen White, *Steps to Christ* (Mountain View, Calif.: Pacific Press), 44, 45.

3. Ellen White, *Prophets and Kings* (Mountain View, Calif.: Pacific Press, 1917), 119.

4. Ibid., 109.

5. Ibid., 127.

6. Ibid., 128.

7. 1 Kings 18:18.

8. *Prophets and Kings*, 161.

9. Ibid., 162.

10. Ibid., 166.

11. See Ellen White, *The Ministry of Healing* (Mountain View, Calif.: Pacific Press, 1942), 172.

Chapter 12

The Hurry Disease

If there is one officially approved addiction in Christian circles, it is workaholism. A person who overworks for a good cause is not only exempt from the judgment placed on other addicts, he is exempt from the judgment placed on other workaholics! Who can fault a person for working hard if he or she is working for the Lord?

The truth is that the workaholic is as chemically dependent as the alcoholic, according to Diane Fassel, author of *Working Ourselves to Death*.[1] Workaholics are hooked on their own adrenalin. Some experts believe that the damage to one's health from workaholism is as serious as the damage from alcoholism.[2] The organic damage caused by stress is as serious as the damage done by drug addiction.[3]

Workaholism is a deadly disease. "Held hostage by their illness, work addicts live in misery and despair amid accolades, slaps on the back, fat paychecks, and gold plaques. It is the only disease that draws cheers from onlookers," says Bryan Robinson, professor of child and family development at the University of North Carolina.[4]

For years, I assumed that God would exempt me from the consequences of battering myself with overwork because I was doing it for Him. Thinking that God would overlook my self-punishing behavior because I was doing Him a favor, I invoked the promise, "They that wait upon the Lord shall renew their strength. . . . They shall run, and not be weary; and they shall walk, and not faint."[5] I expected Him to be my divine Enabler—to defy His own natural laws to protect me from the consequences of my workaholism! The biblical term for this is *pre-*

sumption. I didn't care about the fat paycheck and gold plaque because I was going to get something better: a mansion in heaven and stars in my crown!

Characteristics of workaholics

Workaholics are hurried, harried people. Haste is a way of life. In the presence of a workaholic, no one can catch his breath. Work addicts operate in hyperdrive. They move quickly, walk swiftly, type rapidly, act abruptly, listen distractedly, and calculate constantly how to get things done better and faster.

They love the sound of motors running. I used to get high on the sight and sound of busyness. I loved it when I had the washer, the dryer, the dishwasher, and the vacuum cleaner all running at the same time. I felt exhilarated when the computer, the printer, the typewriter, and the copier were whirring simultaneously. Accomplishment was my drug of choice, productivity my *piece de résistance.*

They keep notepads at their bedsides. Some of my best problem solving took place at night. In order to remember any good ideas I might have while I was asleep, I kept a notepad at my bedside. (This is resting?) I woke up every morning with my computer printout in hand. After all, there was work to be done!

They are consistently overcommitted. The workaholic is always running behind. He has more on his agenda than he can possibly do. The very act of crossing a completed task off the list is gratifying. Once, when I finished a job that *wasn't* on my list, I added it quickly so I could cross if off! The workaholic's appetite for accomplishment is insatiable.

Work addicts operate in the superlative. Work addicts are compelled to be the very best—the most valuable player, the valedictorian, the top salesperson, etc. Failure to be number one brings shame, loss of self-confidence, disproportionate anger, and blaming.

Workaholics don't do just one thing at a time. Work addicts dry their hair and brush their teeth at the same time. Some even read while they're *driving a car.* Saner workaholics limit themselves to dictating letters or listening to tapes as they drive. The sickest of all *sleep* at the wheel! They're so exhausted from overwork that they doze off the minute they get on the highway. And we think driving under the influence is limited to drinkers!

They compete with the clock. Dr. Gilbreth, the efficiency engineer in *Cheaper by the Dozen*, is the workaholic's hero. I know a retired woman who sets a timer for simple tasks like dishwashing and doing laundry. She can't relax for a second because she believes she's accountable for every moment of her time. She is practicing a valid principle in a compulsive manner.

Workaholics value the product more than the person. It came as an embarrassing eye-opener to me when a client told me that he felt like an intruder every time he came to my office— he could tell I had more important things to do than talk with *him.* Somewhere along the line, my work became more important to me than the people I was working for. My goals had become my gods.

Workaholics are greedy for glory. A good workaholic can do *anything.* The more impossible it appears, the more determined he is to do it. I have moved railroad ties, pianos, and organs singlehandedly. Once I even tried to be a bulldozer. I thought I could lower the level of our huge backyard with a pick, shovel, and wheelbarrow. A close friend commented that I was the most driven person she had ever met. I thought I was normal.

Workaholics hide their "booze." Just as alcoholics hide their bottles and compulsive overeaters conceal the evidence of their bingeing, workaholics hide their overworking. They sneak paperwork into their luggage when they go on vacation and then stay in their rooms to "nap" so they can work without getting caught.

Workaholics have blackouts. Blackouts are another phenomenon of workaholism that parallels alcoholism. A workaholic can go from one side of town to the other and not remember how he got there. He can pull up to a red light in his own neighborhood and not know where he is. He can walk into a room and not remember why he's there. This is called an *emotional blackout.*

They are irritable when interrupted. Alcoholics are irritable when deterred from drinking, and workaholics are irritable when interrupted. Once a workaholic's mind is set on finishing a task, he can't quit until it's done. Because workaholics are restless when not busy, they find work to do everywhere they go.

Workaholics are insatiable. There is a truism in recovery circles that goes like this: for the addict, one drink or drug is too many, and a thousand are never enough. The same could be said for the workaholic: one accomplishment is too many, and a thousand successes are never enough.

They don't do *their work—they* are *their work.* Workaholics see themselves as human *doings* rather than human *beings*. They are only as good as their accomplishments. Their self-esteem is built on outworking everybody else.[6] Their identity is based on the role they play in the workplace. The line between their personal and professional lives is indistinct. People refer to them by their titles instead of their given names: "What do you think, Doc?" "Yo, Coach." "Hello, Pastor." Certain vocations lend themselves particularly well to this blurring of identities: politics, medicine, corporate administration, counseling, law, and the ministry, to name a few.

Workaholics are boring. Only a full-fledged, card-carrying workaholic such as myself would dare say this! Workaholics are uneasy in non-work-related conversations because they have nothing to say. Their interests and activities are so limited that they have trouble holding an intelligent conversation about anything but work. They're trapped in the middle of a barren, lonely existence, with projects piled all around, but few, if any, people in sight.

They abuse themselves and their families. Normal people stop working when they are tired or sore. Not the workaholic. He ignores the signals his body is sending him and plunges on, even though he is exhausted and in pain. Like the drug addict, he is willing to risk his health in order to get high.

The family of a workaholic feels as unloved and neglected as the family of an active alcoholic or drug addict. But it is nearly impossible to intervene on workaholic behavior, because the workaholic has such good reasons for everything he does!

Excuses for excesses

Workaholics tend to give one or more of several excuses when anyone complains about their compulsive behavior. Here are some of the most common ones.

I'm doing it for you. Franci was concerned about her husband, a physician in family practice. His office hours and hospital duties kept him away from home during every waking hour of the day. Their children were suffering. They never saw their father except at church and Sabbath dinner, if they were lucky. Sometimes he didn't even make it to Sabbath School because he worked nights in the emergency room and had to catch up on his sleep. Their four-year-old was misbehaving in Sabbath School, and the nine-year-old was balking at going to church. "They might as well not have a father," their mother mourned. "And when I try to talk to him about it, he tells me I shouldn't complain, because he's doing it for us."

Doing it for the Lord. This is an airtight excuse if there ever was one. To challenge this would be to challenge the Almighty!

Tina and Lynn, teenage twins of workaholic missionary parents, were caught in this bind. They were isolated on a remote island, terribly lonely, and desperately unhappy. Their parents' work was their *life.* They had dedicated their lives to mission service as newlyweds and felt they couldn't go back on their promise now. After all, they had put their hand to the plow!

The only way the girls could escape was to return home alone and go to boarding school, knowing that they would only see their parents once or twice a year. They were forced to choose between two undesirable alternatives. Nothing mattered to their mother and father except their work. Not only were they workaholics, but it was God's fault! Tina and Lynn dared not question their parents' commitment, or they would be questioning God. Not surprisingly, they developed a serious dislike for God.

Doing penance. The shame-based Christian works hard to pay for his crimes. He forgets that Jesus has already paid the price! Guilt-ridden Christians who are struggling with some hidden addiction (besetting sin) frequently use overworking for the Lord as a way to relieve shame and guilt or as a means of controlling addictive behavior. They "delve into work as consecration for their unforgivable sins."[7]

Doing it for the boss. Blaming the boss is probably not as bad as blaming God, but it's still a cop-out. When a work addict allows his employer to make unreasonable demands on him and doesn't set limits, his children learn by example not to maintain healthy boundaries in the presence of authority figures. Watching a parent's boundaries crumble at the whim of an employer teaches children that personal and family priorities are expendable when the stakes are high enough.

Doing it for the bill collector. Financial responsibilities are a fact of life. Everybody's got them, and almost everybody worries—perhaps even obsesses a little—about them. But obsessing out loud in the presence of children is inappropriate. I've known many adult/children who have developed a neurotic relationship to money as a result of their parents' financial worries and woes being dumped on them when they were young. *Children shouldn't be burdened with their parents' financial problems.* Ideally, parents should confine their complaining to the therapist's couch or to their adult peers, outside of their children's hearing. If every time he asks for something a child is told, "We can't afford it," he feels ashamed for having needs and wants. He feels he must apologize for his existence.

Sacrificial parents who love to give to the Lord can easily give the message that they are unable to meet their children's needs because they've pledged so much money to the church building fund or some other worthy cause. The children naturally become angry at God, because in this case *He* is the bill collector.

Doing it for "them." Arthur was driven in his career as a conference administrator. He was sorry that he had to spend so much time away from home, but it was part of his job. Advancing in the church political structure was important to him. He had an obsessive need to excel. He was a third-generation preacher, and family tradition demanded that he rise in the ranks to an administrative level. He was willing to compromise his children's well-being and be physically and emotionally absent from them during the most critical years of their lives.

Who was he trying to please? God knows! The real taskmaster was probably the internalized parental demands that drove him to make career choices that were not in his or his family's best interest. He was driven to perform in order to prove himself to "them."

Somebody has to do it. This rationalization is very real to the workaholic. He thinks that if he doesn't do it, it won't get done, or it won't get done right. The misconception that fuels the workaholic church employee's overdrive is the notion that God's reputation depends on his accomplishments. It's fine for a Christian to be a worker worthy of his hire, but God's reputation does not hinge on any one person's Christian service! No human being is capable of carrying that kind of burden. Yet I've seen many try, including myself, and I've seen how broken they become before they discover that God has not placed that burden on them. Note these lines from a missionary's letter: "The needs in this country are so great! We can never do enough. After fifteen years of mission service, my husband is suffering from burnout, and I have been through months of depression. Being conscientious Adventists, we're finding it a bitter experience to be in trouble and not know where to turn. We thought we were doing the right thing."

The bottom line

It's not normal to grow up in a home where chairs are thrown down the stairs and windows are broken by an inebriated mother. It's not normal to live in a house where a drunken father comes home at midnight and terrorizes his wife and children. Nor is it normal to grow up in a home where children are locked outside all day to be sexually abused by neighbors while their parents "sleep it off."

And it's not normal for children to be banished to play noiselessly in their rooms with nothing to eat but a box of crackers while their father studies for his sermon and their mother works! Nor is it normal for children to be left unattended and undernourished while their parents take care of every needy soul they can find in order to earn stars for their heavenly crowns! The consequences to children from officially approved addictions such as workaholism are every bit as devastating as the consequences of the more socially unacceptable addictions. And the effect on the next generation is identical, if not worse.

Denial and delusion

I've heard many children of workaholics express feelings of resentment and loss directly related to their parents' overworking. I've watched them try to tell their parents how lonely they feel but fail to penetrate the parents' wall of denial and delusion. And I thought alcoholics had incredible denial and delusion! I've *never* seen denial and delusion as impossible to deal with as that of Christians who see their work addiction as a virtue.

One mother said, "I'm not workaholic. I *love* my work!" I empathized with her—that rationalization was one of *my* favorites. Now, when workaholics tell me they love their work, I tell them alcoholics love their booze too, and coke addicts love their cocaine! There's no difference. Enjoying an addiction doesn't make it OK.

A "retired" workaholic was attending a family therapy group with his wife and three grown children. Since retirement, he had become deeply involved in church volunteer work. One of his children was a cocaine addict, and the other two were medical professionals. As the three of them explained to their dad how they felt about his lifelong preoccupation with work, he stared at them incredulously. "I never worked more than eight hours a day when you were young. How can you say I'm a workaholic?"

Alcoholics say, "I don't have a problem. I never drink hard liquor. I only drink beer." Or, "I don't drink every day. How can you say I'm an alcoholic?" Or, "I only get high on weekends; I'm not an addict."

It's not how much you drink or when you drink or how often you drink that classifies you as an alcoholic. It's *why* you drink. And it's not how long you work, how often you work, or how much you accomplish that makes you a workaholic. It's *why* you work so hard.

We don't overwork for our families, God, the boss, or the bill collector. If we're doing it for any reason, it's to measure up to our own unrealistic expectations. We're trying to prove something. We're trying to repair our damaged integrity.

Signs and symptoms of workaholism

Workaholics live to work rather than work to live. They work for the sake of working. "Work addicts find it hard to slow down, relax, have fun, and enjoy themselves," says Brian Robinson. "Even in social situations, their thoughts are preoccupied with work, and they remain uneasy, uptight, and have trouble letting go."[8] As children they learned that it was not OK to play or be playful, so as adults they are only able to play if they work at it!

Many workaholics develop a pattern of binge working followed by hangovers, just like the alcoholic drinker. Denial is obvious in the binge worker's rationalization that he will do it just this once. No one will know. After almost two years of abstinence, I had a relapse based on this kind of thinking. I waited until my husband and colleagues were out of town for the weekend and then binged for thirty-six hours, taking only short naps. I didn't realize until afterward that I was rationalizing exactly the way alcoholics do.

The workaholic lives in a constant state of physical emergency. As Dr. Hart puts it, he is jammed at full throttle. Hyperarousal of the adrenalin system disrupts normal bodily functions and destroys the body's normal immune defense mechanisms. The anti-pain and anti-anxiety systems become depleted, resulting in chronic pain and panic attacks.[9] The individual experiences what are known as stress-related illnesses: headaches, fatigue, joint and muscle pain, indigestion, ulcers, back pain, hypertension, sexual dysfunction, sleep disorders, nervous tics, dizziness, etc. Like alcoholism and drug addiction, workaholism accelerates aging.[10] Other symptoms include irritability, impatience, forgetfulness, restlessness, difficulty concentrating, mood swings, depression, anxiety, and isolation.[11]

The following questions will help you identify workaholism:

- Would I rather work than sleep?
- Do I have a tendency to overextend myself?
- Do I feel depressed when I'm not working?
- Do I base my self-esteem on my productivity?
- Do I think about my work when I'm away from it?
- Do I use work to avoid people and problems?
- Do I feel guilty when I'm relaxing or having fun?
- Do I believe that the harder I work the more God will be pleased?

- Do I believe that souls will be lost if I don't work hard enough and long enough?

Progression of workaholism

In a previous chapter, I described the progress of religious addiction according to the four stages that have been identified for chemical addiction. Now I will do the same for workaholism.

Stage 1—Learning the mood swing. The child's appetite for approval is whetted by positive strokes based on his performance that are given by key persons in his life. Their response to his achievement is ego reinforcing. He gains a feeling of worth when his efforts are recognized as valuable. He concludes that good feelings come from doing a good job.

Stage 2—Seeking the mood swing. He begins chasing the carrot. He has tasted approval, and he will do anything to get it again. His achievement is calculated to win attention. His mood is determined by people's reaction to his accomplishments. If he is extremely undernurtured, he will contort himself in bizarre ways just to get a crumb from the master's table.

Stage 3—Preoccupation with achievement. The child becomes a superachiever. He is obsessed with winning the prize. If he fails to be number one, he is disheartened. He abuses himself to accomplish his goals.

Stage 4—Working just to feel normal. He relentlessly pursues, but never achieves, the emotional highs he once enjoyed. Like the drug addict who switches chemicals and alters his drug-taking style in order to recapture the first high, the achievement addict changes jobs, pursues new goals, takes on more responsibilities, starts another project, etc. Yet the returns are invariably diminishing. He will reach the point where nothing works anymore.

I am uncertain how long it takes to move through these stages. Certainly the "clean" addictions progress more slowly than chemical dependency does. Many workaholics trace the onset of their disease to early childhood. Few hit bottom before age forty. But they are forty going on a hundred. And they have usually picked up a few other addictions along the way. Perhaps drug addicts and alcoholics are the lucky ones. They generally hit bottom years sooner than the workaholic does.

The workaholic woman

The authors of *The Addictive Organization* speak of the cultural rewards that society holds out to the workaholic woman. They describe how magazines for career women tout the example of workaholic women who make their first million before they're thirty; superbeings who start up new companies, jog and swim daily, put in sixty hours a week at the office; who have husbands and children; and who bring work home in the evenings and work weekends, all the while being impeccably groomed and emotionally unflappable. Collette Dowling says, "A belief in the possibility of perfecting ourselves is the chief illusion seducing women today. . . . The drive to become better is a compulsion, a never-ending quest for admiration because there's nothing warming us from within."[12] And she adds, "*Accomplishment* is what separates the women from the girls. Accomplishment, 'excellence,' and deadly fatigue."[13]

For some reason, I feel like weeping when I read that line.

How Christians unwittingly encourage workaholism

I've often asked myself where I got the messages that programmed me to compulsive overwork. Some came from my religious heritage. I still appreciate and honor that heritage, but I am very aware of how distorted some of my beliefs were.

I was greatly influenced by my grandparents, who were pioneer missionaries, and who were and are my heroes to this day. Grandma used to say, "We must hasten to do the Lord's work. Jesus is coming soon." She and Grandpa spent most of their lives in South America preaching the gospel. They sailed from New York City when they were in their early twenties with one young child (my father) and didn't return home, even for a furlough, for nineteen years! The United States—their homeland—was foreign to my father and his brother and sister when they finally returned to it.

Grandpa used to sing "Work for the Night Is Coming" and "We'll Work Till Jesus Comes." He actually taught his pet parrot to sing, "To the work, to the work, we are servants." And the parrot always squawked on the word *servants*.

These are the messages that I picked up: "We should never waste a moment." "We must account to the Lord for every second of our time." "Whatever our hands find to do, we must do with all our might." "Laziness is a cardinal sin." "We must never become weary of well-doing." "Time is short." "The more we sacrifice, the greater our reward." If these messages aren't fodder for workaholism, I don't know what is!

I realize that the church leaders who convey these attitudes mean well. They don't realize the damage they are doing. They certainly don't *intend* to destroy their workers or their families. For that reason I don't blame the church for these diseased messages, and I certainly don't blame God! But I want to be more cautious about the example I set for my children and grandchildren. I want to give them a balanced impression of the value of self and the value of work. I want to show them that I esteem them for who they are, not for what they do or how well they do it. And I want to model taking very good care of the most precious gift God has given me next to Jesus—myself—so they will have permission to do the same.

Perhaps it's because I'm a workaholic that I consider workaholism to be one of the most difficult addictions to recover from. For addictions that involve behavior from which a person cannot entirely abstain, recovery is an ongoing struggle. The workaholic has to discover what triggers his symptoms, then define and redefine abstinence. For the workaholic, abstinence is defined by moderation. And finding moderation is a trial-and-error process that includes a fair amount of learning from one's mistakes.

The workaholic needs people to whom he is accountable, people who will monitor his behavior without condemning or controlling. He needs a safe place where he can go to find nurturance and encouragement as he progresses toward recovery. Perhaps hardest of all, he has to accept the reality that his goal is progress, not perfection.

Finding support for recovery from workaholism is not easy. There are not many Workaholics Anonymous groups in the United States. After all, workaholics don't have time to attend twelve-step meetings!

I hope that twelve-step groups for workaholics will become more widespread. It means a lot for an addict to be able to go to a place where he or she is fully understood and receive guidance and support from others who have suffered similarly and who have found sobriety and serenity.

————————

1. Diane Fassel, *Working Ourselves to Death* (San Francisco: Harper Collins Publishers, 1990), 3.

2. Anne Schaef and Diane Fassel, *The Addictive Organization* (San Francisco: Harper & Row, 1990), 130.

3. Archibald Hart, *Adrenalin and Stress* (Dallas: Word Publishing, 1991), 70.

4. Bryan Robinson, *Work Addiction* (Deerfield Beach, Fla.: Health Communications, 1989), viii.

5. Isaiah 40:31.

6. Earnie Larsen, "Life Beyond Addiction—Identifying Learned Self-Defeating Behaviors," videotape produced by Fuller Video, Minneapolis, Minn.

7. Robinson, 29.

8. Ibid., 41, 42.

9. Hart, 22, 61-63.

10. Ibid., 7, 54, 55.

11. Ibid., 71.

12. Collette Dowling, *Perfect Women* (New York: Summit Books, 1988), 43, 62.

13. Ibid.

Chapter 13

The Making of a Martyr

So you love someone who has a problem. Look around you. As many as half the other people at church do too. Maybe more. For them and for you, every waking moment is filled with worry about your loved one. Even your prayers are tinged with worry. It's hard to trust God when someone you care about is gradually disappearing from your sight, and there seems to be nothing you can do to save him. Maybe he used to sit next to you in church, but he doesn't attend church anymore.

Sooner or later, the sorrow and pain begin to show on your face. People notice your distress. Some of the saints chide you for lack of faith because you're visibly upset. Others admire you for your tenacity. Still others question why you trouble yourself over someone who is rebelling against God and rejecting everything you stand for. "Remember him in your prayers. Otherwise forget him," they imply.

All you know is that it hurts.

For every person who has an addiction of any kind, several others will be deeply affected—burdened with anxiety, loaded with guilt, overwhelmed with responsibility, consumed by sorrow, haunted by a profound sense of failure. Because they don't know how to reach out for solace and support, they remain locked in their anguish, begging God for relief, pleading for healing for their loved one, and growing more and more disillusioned and discouraged.

Convinced that they caused the problem or at least failed to prevent it, they consider themselves responsible for curing it. And they exhaust themselves trying. They obsess endlessly about possible solutions. Their loved one's negative behavior is controlling them as surely as it controls him. If this goes on long enough, it will reach the point that they are addicted to misery. If they have children, their children will learn to worry compulsively and be chronically miserable too. They are martyrs in the making. Misery is the chief characteristic of the martyr.

Addicted to misery

For many, the process of addiction to misery begins long before they marry an alcoholic or give birth to an addict-to-be. If they are children of *abuse*, they grew up with lies, uncertainty, disappointment, broken promises, and shattered hopes. If they are children of *perfectionism*, they grew up with criticism, confusion, double standards, shame, and shattered spirits. Both the children of alcoholism *and* the children of perfectionism live in the land of fear and trembling. Their belief system is based on a single common premise: life is painful. This sets them up for addiction to misery.

A family system is like a puzzle in which each member is uniquely shaped to fit his or her designated place. When such people grow up and leave the family, they look for another puzzle with an opening the size and shape of their own so they will fit in. They conform to what they learned in their family of origin and continue to act it out.

Andrew's parents were the personification of marital disharmony. Although both were dedicated Christians, they were carriers of codependence. They lacked the ability to esteem themselves and to communicate their needs in healthy ways. Their marriage became an ongoing power struggle as each tried to force the other to be what he/she wanted him or her to be. Both were miserably unhappy, and Andrew was caught in the middle. His parents coped with their frustration by withdrawing from each other into a state of mild, chronic depression. Andrew developed a similar outlook. By the time he was twenty, he was seriously depressed. His parents' inability to resolve their problems set him up for addiction to unhappiness.

Joanie's mother suffered from severe migraine headaches. She spent days at a time in her darkened bedroom, unable to cope with the pressures of life. She was a lonely, miserable woman who was unable to take care of herself physically or emotionally. And she had no one to comfort her but her daughter. The child became her mother's counselor when she was just a tot. She absorbed her mother's misery and integrated it into her own personality. In family systems theory, this is called *martyring*. Martyrs carry the unwanted reality of others; they sacrifice themselves for someone else.[1]

A legacy of negativism

For children of trauma, unhappiness is a way of life. Feeling good, experiencing pleasure, expecting the best, looking at the bright side—these things are totally unfamiliar to them. They grow up waiting for the other shoe to fall. As heirs to a legacy of negativism, they are programmed to expect the worst.

Often their very expectation acts as a self-fulfilling prophecy. A martyr's pessimistic filters give negative meaning to events that are neutral or even positive. The negative meaning he assigns to situations sets off an emotional chain reaction that activates whatever disaster he may have anticipated. Some martyrs are so addicted to feeling terrible that they will sabotage anything good that happens and turn it into a catastrophe.

The martyr tells herself she's miserable because her parents fought all the time, she didn't have nice clothes, or she was ashamed of her house. She's miserable because nobody cares about her, she hates her job, or her husband forgot their anniversary. Such people really believe their misery is caused by other people. Someone in their life isn't living up to their expectations, isn't meeting their needs, etc. The martyr gives others the power to determine how he or she feels.

The game

His secret hope is that if he acts pitiful enough, people will feel sorry for him, realize that they have wronged him, and yield to his wishes. Whining and complaining become his *modus operandi*. He projects an aura of unhappiness. Unfortunately, there are just enough people around who are willing to rescue such pathetic creatures that they don't have to face their problems and learn how to solve them. That is, until their care givers get fed up. Then they either have to grow up and get responsible or find another hero. Of course, there is no shortage of rescuers—there are enough around to keep any good martyr in business for a long time!

When the martyr gets "fixed" or rescued, he experiences a temporary high. He feels loved and cared for. But the feeling doesn't last. Next time he needs something, he's got to find someone who will sense how miserable he is. Then he's got to manipulate that person into asking what's wrong and generate enough "sympathy" that this person will take care of him. His self-esteem always remains at a low level because he never has a chance to gain the self-respect that comes from taking charge of his own life. And he's never sure that the attention he extracts from others is freely given.

Hard-core martyrs

I've never seen rage like the rage of a child who has spent years watching his mother sit in the impotence of self-pity and whimper about the way her alcoholic spouse neglects his family. He drinks up his paycheck. The bills aren't paid. She has to slave twenty-four hours a day to provide for the children. She complains constantly, but she continues to tolerate intolerable behavior. She's like a doormat with a welcome sign emblazoned on it. Her position is painful, to be sure, but because it is all she knows, she accepts it as her due and does nothing to change it.

Some martyr-mothers seem to enjoy their pain so much that they practically invite abuse. They don't feel right unless they're being wronged. They nag the alcoholic when he's drunk and then cringe when he gets violent. The daughter of an Adventist alcoholic said, "I knew why my *dad* acted crazy. He was drunk. But what was *her* excuse? She egged him on. And then she wore her bruises to church like a badge of honor and soaked up all the sympathy she could get. I hated her."

Martyring and other addictions

Earnie Larsen says that martyrs measure their worth by their ability to suffer. They take pride in being able to endure more than anyone else.[2] They seek out opportunities to sacrifice themselves. They welcome suffering as a means of elevating themselves to a plane of piety above that of ordinary human beings.

Two other addictions easily link up with martyrdom: care giving and churchaholism. Codependent Christians are ideal candidates for these dual roles. They kill themselves trying to serve the Lord, and then they want everyone to hear about it. That's martyring. Their martyring has connected with their religious addiction, and they have no idea that their self-sacrificing and complaining are compulsive and unhealthy.

People who are addicted to care giving also make excellent martyrs. When, in order to feel good, an individual has to give to those who should be learning to help themselves, he is robbing himself and the people he is trying to help of social and spiritual growth. When he gives to feel self-righteous and at the same time he feels miserable and complains, he is martyring.

For their own sake and the sake of those they serve, such individuals must address their codependency issues if they are to avoid compulsive martyring.

Commitment to misery

I've already described martyrs in some detail, but listing a few characteristics of the disease may be helpful. Martyrs are committed to their negative heritage. They will defend it to the death. They ruminate incessantly about the past, massaging their painful memories until they drive themselves to depression or despair. They'd rather be unhappy than change. They pick the scabs off their wounds again and again in order to remain in anguish.

As a fifteen-year-old, Estelle married a widower with several children, the oldest of whom was not much younger than she. When her husband introduced his new bride to his family, he said, "I've found someone to clean house and wash dishes for you children." Instantly Estelle was reduced to the status of a maid. She never forgot the insult; she savored it for thirty years. She bequeathed her rage, low self-esteem, and misery to her youngest daughter, who acted it out in the form of an obsessive/compulsive disorder that nearly cost her her life.

Chronic complaining. Most martyrs leak their feelings on anyone who will listen. There is an air of painful resignation about them. They obsess out loud. They may not sound like they're whining, but they are. One's voice doesn't have to *sound* nasal to be whining. Whining is about being helpless and expecting someone else to make you OK, not about the tone of voice. Obsessing out loud in the presence of other people (who usually have the capacity to "fix it") is manipulative. When the martyr stands helplessly in the middle of the universe acting pathetic, expecting someone to come along and rescue him, he's manipulating.

Misery addicts look and act confused, but because they don't want to reveal their ignorance, they rarely ask for help. (They wouldn't want to be a bother.) When someone doesn't know what to do, his ignorance is fairly obvious. Why pretend? But the martyr is so full of shame that he cannot ask. Instead, he whines, giving detailed accounts of his problem to anyone who will listen. Eventually everyone close to him scatters, because his neediness drains them dry.

Feigned helplessness. There is a soundless kind of whining that is just as dishonest and disgusting as the verbal variety. When a martyr looks helpless and pitiful but doesn't say a word, he is unconsciously manipulating to get his needs met. This is very irritating to the people closest to him. They learn to run the other way when they see him coming. Some misery addicts see themselves as so undeserving and so unworthy that they dare not even hint at what they need. They just stand there and ooze their neediness.

Dedicated doormatting. Being in the one-down position is a source of self-esteem to the martyr. Actually, it's a very powerful position, because it keeps the people around him hopping or at least feeling guilty. The doormat gets his power by giving it to everyone else. If, in an unguarded moment, he happens to stand up for himself and take back his power, he tosses it away again like a hot potato. He *can't* feel good, because he gets his self-esteem from being persecuted. And it's all their, your, or God's fault.

The doormat's favorite expression is "Yes, but." I *know* I

should set a boundary, but I don't want to hurt anybody's feelings. I *know* I should take care of myself, but I can't afford it financially. The "yes, but" always leaves him on the short end of the stick, which is exactly where he feels most at home.

Recovery from addiction to misery

Misery addicts have to abstain from those situations that support the misery. "Worry is to the misery addict what alcohol is to the alcoholic," says Robert Becker, the author of *Addicted to Misery*.[3] If this is the case, then how can the martyr ever hope for freedom from his obsession? There are no easy answers. Becker makes several valid suggestions that are comparable to having a total brain transplant. His final answer seems to be, *Just do it!* Would that it were that simple.

I believe the process of recovery from addiction to misery is identical to the process of recovery from any other addiction. To begin with, the individual has to be sick and tired of being sick and tired. Then he has to face the fact that he is powerless and that addiction to misery and martyrdom has made his life unmanageable. He needs to appeal to a source of strength and wisdom outside himself if he is ever to find freedom. Through resources both human and divine, it is possible to recover. With appropriate help, even the most negatively programmed individual can find freedom from addiction to misery.

1. Fred Downing, "The Family Disease Workshop," videotape from Paradox Productions, 1984.

2. Earnie Larsen, "Life Beyond Addiction—Identifying Learned, Self-Defeating Behaviors," videotape from Fuller Video, Minneapolis, Minn.

3. Robert Becker, *Addicted to Misery* (Deerfield Beach, Fla.: Health Communications, 1989), 59.

Chapter 14

Shattered Dreams, Wounded Hearts, Broken Toys

There's a line in a song by Bill and Gloria Gaither that says, "Give them all, give them all, give them all to Jesus—shattered dreams, wounded hearts, broken toys. Give them all to Jesus, and He will turn your sorrows into joys."[1] Another Gaither song speaks of painful memories: "Hurt by hurt, the painful memories waited in line. Hurt by hurt, He healed them all, one hurt at a time."[2]

How do you heal wounds like the ones this adult/child sustained: "I'm suffering from the effects of childhood sexual abuse. Abused children are afraid to say anything, and they hide their feelings of self-loathing and shame deep down inside themselves. Abuse can destroy the best of anyone's life. I thought I could handle it on my own, but I couldn't. It nearly killed me."[3]

I'm amazed by the attitude of believers who act dumbfounded when the subject of child abuse within the Adventist community is raised. Hearing of a battered child, they demur, "*Surely* his parents weren't Adventists!" If we are all sinners, then we are probably all abusers. Consider the meaning of the word *trespass*. To trespass—sin—is to invade another's person's territory, to step on his or her boundaries, to violate his or her rights. To trespass is to abuse. It is important that we face the reality of abuse among us rather than denying it.

If I hurt or offend anyone, whether knowingly or unwittingly, subtly or flagrantly, I am an abuser. My motive makes no difference. Lack of intention to abuse does not remove the consequences of abuse. A person—yes, even a Christian—can accidentally run over a child with a car. The child will be injured whether the driver intended to hurt him or not.

An abusive society

In recent years, the media have focused a great deal of attention on child abuse and neglect. Society is beginning to acknowledge the most obvious forms—physical and sexual—but there is still considerable denial about other kinds.[4] If our society as a whole has been in denial about child abuse, then the church has been in even greater denial! Individually and institutionally, we get quite defensive when the subject of abuse is mentioned. We're willing to invoke the principle that children should honor their parents, but we overlook the biblical injunction that parents should not provoke their children to anger.

Christians *are* capable of abusing their children, their spouses, and their brethren. And the abuse we perpetrate against each other is often so subtle as to be even more evil than overt physical abuse. I have seen "godly" people inflict incredible physical and emotional injuries on their loved ones. I've seen grievous wounds inflicted on the bodies and spirits of children by Christian parents who were simply insensitive. I've watched rigid, religious mothers hiss hatefully at their children because they weren't behaving properly in church. I saw a church employee drag his daughter across a room by the hair of her head!

A *Christianity Today* article reported a survey of female students in a Christian liberal arts college. Of the ninety-six students who responded to the questionnaire, more than half said they had been abused as children. And almost all of them had been reared in Christian homes.[5]

Abuse: The cause of codependence

I concur with Pia Mellody, who says that the cause of codependence is child abuse. And she defines child abuse as "anything less than nurturing."[6] It's high time we Adventists became as zealous about the issue of child abuse as we are about our health message! It's time we adopted an ethic about our treatment of children that is as lofty as some of our other beliefs and standards!

On the next few pages I will describe the various forms of abuse, beginning with the obvious, overt forms and working toward the more subtle forms. As suggested above, covert (camouflaged) abuse is as devastating in its effects as overt abuse, if not more so. The more difficult abuse is to identify, the more deadly its effect will be on the one who is abused.

Physical abuse. This involves treating a child's body disrespectfully: spanking with instruments such as belts, rubber hoses, hairbrushes, flyswatters, wooden spoons, and switches; slapping a child's face, pushing, pinching, kicking, or shaking him; pulling, jerking, or picking up a child by the extremities; scaring, teasing, tossing a child in the air or tickling him into hysteria; overpowering or entrapping him. All of these are physically abusive behaviors.[7]

Threatening to do any of these things is also abusive, even if the threat is never carried out. A rageaholic father took his son fishing. When the boy handed him the wrong lure from the tackle box, the father lost his temper, grabbed his son, held a fishing knife to his throat, and threatened to cut his head off. Threatening to harm a child is verbal-physical abuse: "If you touch that again, I'm going to break your arm," or "If you do that again, the bogeyman is going to get you."

If a child is placed in a position where he has to witness the abuse of another person, he is considered a victim of "witness abuse." The terror he feels is almost worse than if he were being directly abused,[8] but he has no way to relieve his feelings.

Another form of physical abuse is neglect. Children need food, water, clothing, shelter, warmth, protection, and affection in order to thrive.[9] It is abusive to deprive them of the right to perform normal bodily functions like eating, drinking, and eliminating. It is abusive to force them to sit still for long periods of time, to force them to do tasks they are physically incapable of, or to leave them unsupervised where they are exposed to physical danger.

I recall sitting near a family with five small children in church one Sabbath. The children sat silent and erect, looking absolutely miserable. Their parents wore stern, forbidding looks on their faces. Toward the end of the sermon, one of the little ones dared to ask his father if he could go to the bathroom. The father noisily informed him that if he left just then, he would disrupt the service. He must wait until church was over. The father's admonitions were more disruptive than the child's leaving would have been!

At ten, Robert was small for his age. His father needed help on the farm but couldn't afford a hired hand, so he insisted that Robert drive the tractor and other farm machinery. If the boy failed to plow a perfect furrow, his father berated him mercilessly. The father's behavior was both physically and emotionally abusive.

Sexual abuse. Pia Mellody identifies four kinds of sexual abuse. Physical-sexual abuse includes intercourse with a child, oral or anal sex, masturbation (child to offender or offender to child), sexual touching (fondling), kissing, or hugging. Overt-explicit abuse is exposing a child to visual or verbal images that are inappropriate. This includes voyeurism (allowing a child to observe the sexual behavior of others), exhibitionism (exposing one's own sexual organs to a child), and allowing a child to see or listen to adult sexual materials such as pornographic magazines and videos or motion pictures. It also includes adult sexual talk in the presence of children, such as "dirty jokes" and "dirty stories."

It is highly inappropriate for a parent to discuss his or her sexual prowess in the presence of children. I have known a number of young people who were deeply shamed by such conversations. The sexual activity of the parent is none of a child's business. Children don't want to hear about it. Keeping pornography in the home is also sexually abusive. If material of this kind is *anywhere in the house*, children will find it.

Covert sexual abuse includes teasing or shaming a child about his body, violating his boundaries (his right to modesty and privacy), and giving him inadequate or skewed information about sex (too much too early or too little too late).[10] Failure on the part of the parents to model healthy sexuality to a child is also a form of covert sexual abuse.[11]

The fourth form of sexual abuse is especially subtle, yet just as destructive as the more obvious forms of abuse. I refer to *emotional incest*. This occurs when a child is placed in the middle of his parents' relationship, when he is made more important to one parent than the spouse is to that parent.[12] Emotional incest often develops when one parent is absent because of divorce, death, addiction, etc. The parent who stays with the child feels disillusioned, frustrated, and lonely, and may turn to his or her children for comfort. *This is highly inappropriate.* The needs of the parent should be taken to a therapist or a support group, *never* to the children. Children need to *receive* nurturance. They should never be required to give it.

Certain behaviors are abusive to children because they are sexually stimulating: a mother asking her adolescent son to rub suntan lotion on her body; parents who expose their children to parental nudity or partial nudity (Dad in his underwear, Mom in her sexy nightie); parents masturbating or making love at times and in places where the child can witness the activity. It is also abusive for parents to overreact to being "caught in the act."

Anything that is sexually shaming to a child is sexually abusive: showing nude baby pictures of him to his friends, teasing him about his sexual development, forcing him to take public showers, demanding that he drop his pants for spankings, making him change his clothes in public places, etc.

Failure on the part of parents to protect a child from sexual abuse is collusive abuse. When parents learn that a child has been abused but they do nothing to protest or protect him, they are committing an added offense against him. A teenage girl was raped and brutalized by a drunken friend of her brother's. The rapist pushed her out of his car miles from home. When she stumbled into her house hours later, her father called her a *slut*, slapped her, and threw her against the wall. He told her that if she ever wanted to stay out late and have a good time again, she shouldn't come home at all. Ravaged already, she needed her father's comfort and protection—not more abuse.

Two women informed their parents that they had been molested as children. In both cases, the abuse was perpetrated by a close friend of the family. The parents reacted to their daughters' revelations very differently. One mother contacted the offender and told him never to come near her daughter again, even though it was almost twenty years after the fact. The daughter was gratified by her mother's reaction. Her need to feel protected and cared for was satisfied.

The other woman's mother felt sorry for *herself*. "It's not my fault," she moaned. "I didn't know about it—you should have told me. Why didn't you tell me?" Instead of taking responsibility for neglecting her daughter, she shamed her for not reporting the abuse. The reason most children *don't* report abuse is that they are intimidated by the offender or afraid their parents will blame them. The parents of the abused woman continued to socialize with the offender and invite him into their home, even after they learned what he had done to their daughter. They didn't want to offend *him*. It appeared that they were more concerned about *his* feelings than *hers*, and she felt deeply hurt.

Emotional abuse. A few paragraphs back I discussed *sexual* emotional abuse. Here I want to talk about *nonsexual* forms of emotional abuse. Emotional abuse can be verbal (sarcasm, name calling, criticizing, etc.) or nonverbal (acts of silent violence such as glaring, eyeing contemptuously, etc.). Being overcontrolling, overprotective, or overly demanding is emotionally abusive, as is failure to give appropriate moral support, encouragement, and attention.

Other forms of emotional abuse include shaming children for making mistakes or scolding, nagging, or making fun of them for such things as bed-wetting, thumb sucking, and masturbating. Failure to model healthy life skills and provide structure, direction, and guidance to a child also constitutes emotional abuse.

Discounting a teenager by withholding information that involves him or by giving him misinformation is emotionally abusive. This includes failing to tell him he was born out of wedlock or that he is adopted, pretending that his stepparent is his real parent, or not telling him that he has half brothers or sisters. I've met many adult/children who are legitimately hurt and angry because such facts were withheld from them. Failure on the part of a noncustodial parent in a divorce to keep in contact with his children and pay child support is a major issue of abandonment and, as such, is emotionally abusive.

It is also emotionally abusive for the custodial parent to refuse to let the children see their noncustodial parent. And it is abusive for either parent to criticize the other parent to the children or to inform the children of conflicts in the marriage that they would not have known from their own observation. And, of course, allowing a child to observe profound parental conflict is also abusive.

Neglecting a child's need for attention and affirmation or scolding him for demanding time and attention is emotionally abusive. Providing for his needs but doing it grudgingly is abusive, as is reminding him frequently of the cost of feeding and caring for him, of the high cost of church-school tuition, etc.

Creating an emotionally repressive home environment is abusive. The home should be a place where children feel safe expressing their feelings. Many young people refuse to ask for what they want and need because they know their parents will lecture, scold, rationalize, or explain their needs away. Or, worse yet, they will betray their confidence. Children hide their feelings and keep secrets because they are afraid their parents will overreact or disbelieve them. Some hesitate to report sexual abuse for that reason.

Children are now being taught in school health classes how to defend themselves against sexual violations. If anyone attempts to invade their sexual boundaries, they are told to find an adult who is safe and tell him or her. What if the child goes to his mother or father to ask for help and is told that he's imagining things? Failure to provide a child with adequate support in such situations is emotionally abusive.

Failure to model appropriate expression of feelings to a child is emotionally abusive, and shaming him for expressing feelings is abusive: "Now don't be angry, or Jesus will be sad," or "Big boys don't cry." Children need to know that their feelings are normal and that they will be respected when they express them in healthy ways. People who suppress their feelings in order to gain approval are actually hurting themselves emotionally. Letting feelings simmer, especially anger, can be as bad for one's health as being overweight.

To model depression, addiction, or any other unhealthy behavior to a child is emotionally abusive. If a parent suffers from a mental illness and refuses to seek professional help for his condition, his children are abused. If the other parent refuses to do anything to solve the problem, he or she is equally responsible. Parents must take responsibility for their own mental health care.

Children are affected dramatically when a parent is depressed and/or suicidal. One mother put her children in the car and told them she was going to drive them all off a cliff. A teenage girl came home from school and found her father unconscious in the garage, with the car running and a suicide note on the seat beside him. She had to break the automobile window to rescue him. A deeply depressed woman forced her young son to spend hours on his knees at her bedside praying that Jesus would come quickly to deliver her from the depression. Jesus didn't come, and his mother didn't get better. The child ended up depressed himself, which is completely understandable.

An Adventist mother, who was straining to hold her family together in spite of her husband's infidelity, confessed to her thirteen-year-old son that she was having suicidal thoughts. "I feel I don't have anything to live for," she told him.

"What about *us*, Mom?" was his poignant reply.

Children who live with his kind of threat are permanently affected. According to Pia Mellody, parental suicide is an issue of abuse that children will never forget. Children must be protected from this kind of trauma.

Social abuse. When a child is attacked or made fun of for anything about his person—his race, size, intelligence, gender, religion, socioeconomic status; his kinky hair or big ears; his physical disabilities or handicaps—he is being socially abused. And when he is isolated, ostracized, or denied his human rights for any of these reasons, he is being abused.

Children often inflict abuse of this kind on one another. Emotionally deprived children can be exceedingly cruel to each other. There is little parents can do to prevent such cruelty, but they certainly can and must help their children identify, describe, and debrief their feelings when they have been hurt. Wounded children do not need to be lectured, scolded, or shamed. Failure to be supportive of a child who is suffering social abuse is abusive. Many a "macho" father has intensified the pain of a son who has been abused at the hands of a bully by shaming him and even battering him for not defending himself to the father's satisfaction. I've seen many grown men *agonize* over the memory of such incidents.

When a child is suffering abuse at the hands of his classmates or teachers, he needs understanding and affirmation. He needs someone to set boundaries in his behalf, to demonstrate that unacceptable behavior is not to be tolerated. Parents should intervene and even remove their children from abusive situations if necessary, regardless of the cost, inconvenience, or consequences in terms of what other people will think!

Intellectual abuse. Intellectual abuse occurs when anyone uses his "superior" intelligence, education, wisdom, or experience to coerce another person into compliance. The intellectual abuser batters his victim with facts and information until he acquiesces. He argues, reasons, gives proof texts or filibusters until the other person capitulates. The intellectual abuser demands that others think and believe what he thinks and believes.

Prying and mind reading are intellectually abusive, as are analyzing, criticizing, or judging another person's thoughts and beliefs. Interpreting his motives, discounting his ideas or opinions, and correcting, amending, or editing his views are forms of intellectual abuse.[13]

Grandiosity is intellectually abusive. Terry Kellogg defines grandiosity as "knowing everything about everything."[14] When a parent, grandparent, or authority figure is grandiose, everyone around him feels stupid. Giving unsolicited advice is a form of grandiosity.

Moralizing and preaching to unwilling listeners is intellectually abusive. Some Christians never miss a chance to turn an incident into an opportunity to moralize. This kind of witnessing is at least abrasive if not abusive. It is manipulative and, to the person on the receiving end, it is insulting. The line between inappropriate sermonizing and legitimate witnessing is indistinct. People who tend to be controlling, however, should exercise restraint. When I find myself feeling compelled to pop a homily into every conversation, I am running the risk of being intellectually abusive. Any good my witnessing might have accomplished is negated by my offensiveness.

Spiritual abuse. A great deal of abuse occurs within the sacred confines of the church. The devastating effect on the eternal welfare of its victims cannot be told. Spiritual abuse robs the victim of a healthy concept of God and a healthy relationship with self. Various forms of spiritual abuse and their impact will be discussed at length in the next chapter.

Silencing the victim with shame

Little Melissa had a frightening dream one night and ran to her parents' bedroom. Without hesitation, she crawled into bed with her daddy, where she would be safe. He proceeded to molest her sexually and then shamed her into silence by saying, "That's what happens to little girls who crawl into men's beds." Because Melissa thought it was her fault, she couldn't do the one thing that might have relieved her pain: tell someone and get help. Many suicides among young people are traceable to this kind of distress.

When the perpetrator of a sexual offense behaves in a shameless manner, his childish victim thinks that he or she is to blame. Many such victims carry their "guilty secret" with them to the grave, never realizing that they have done nothing to be ashamed of, that they were the *victim* of a crime, not the *perpetrator*. Sexual offenders often lead the victim to believe that she did something to cause her own abuse. Thus the victim takes on the abuser's shame and feels tainted, sinful. I have met several elderly women who lived their whole lives feeling ashamed for something someone else did to them when they were children.

A precious five-year-old was molested by her baby sitter's husband. He told her not to tell anyone because if she did, no one would ever love her. Abusers often tell their victims that they imagined the abusive event, that it never happened, or that it was just a bad dream. Many abusers threaten the lives of their victims or their families in order to coerce them into keeping the event a secret. Children are left to suffer alone and sometimes to die. Many victims are discouraged from reporting incest, because Daddy or Grandpa might have to go to jail, as if his being jailed would be *the child's* fault.

Blameless children

There is a phrase in the Big Book of Alcoholics Anonymous that speaks of the *warped lives* of *blameless children*. When a young person develops social problems later in life because of early abuse, the offending adult often accuses the child of being weak or bad—as if he (the offender) had nothing to do with the victim's problems. If the troubled adolescent mentions that her actions are related to the abuse she suffered as a child, the offender insists that she is just making excuses. Thus the child is re-abused.

A recovering codependent who was physically abused by her alcoholic father wrote the following lines when she was fifteen, which I quote with her permission:

MY TREE
by Beth B.

Once
my ego was a tiny tree
needing the light
  you, my sun,
were supposed to shed.
But you
  didn't
    care.
You ripped it,
roots and all,
from the safe, solid earth.

You shook it,

you stripped it
with your wooden fists
and heart of stone.

and with the blade of your
words
you cut it,
you whittled it,
to the size you desired.

Thank you for the toothpick, Daddy.

When the life of a blameless child is warped, he is not responsible. When he "acts out" his distress, he is not at fault! It's time that we stopped blaming victims and started taking responsibility for our own offensiveness!

An abuser can make himself accountable for his past actions by admitting his wrong, owning his guilt, making amends, and thus removing the shame from his victim. Many avoid this by rationalizing, "It happened so long ago and, after all, I was drunk." Or, "I didn't know better. I did the best I could. What's past is past. It's water under the bridge. Can't we just forgive and forget?"

That's great when you're the one who benefits from the forgiveness!

I'm watching five Adventist families right now who are struggling through painful issues of past sexual abuse. In each case, the abuse occurred years ago but is only now being made known. In one family, the perpetrator voluntarily made confession to the victim and is taking full responsibility.

In the second case, the perpetrator seems to be concerned only with damage control. He has not apologized sincerely or accepted responsibility for his behavior. Now that the truth is out, he is only concerned that no one else be told. He is more interested in containing the damage than he is in the well-being of the children he molested.

In the third case, the perpetrator will not admit his guilt at all and has enlisted a number of family members to aid and abet him in his denial. In the fourth case, the perpetrator and his spouse have retreated from their offspring, who were the victims of the father's abuse, leaving them to hold the devastating emotional baggage and refusing to take any responsibility for the therapeutic cleanup.

And in the fifth case the perpetrator was caught, and rather than being prosecuted, was given an opportunity to obtain professional help. Although the Christians who gave him this option were demonstrating a forgiving spirit, they may have enabled his disease. Time will tell.

No gain without pain

I cannot bring myself to write a comforting conclusion to this chapter. Better that we sustain our pain. Better that we take the issue of child abuse seriously. Better that we recognize the enormity of this problem. Change is called for. And there is no gain without pain.

1. Benson, "Give Them All to Jesus," Nashville: Justin Time Music, 1975.
2. Gloria Gaither, "Hurt by Hurt," Alexandria, Ind.: Gaither Music, 1987.
3. Paul and Carol Cannon, "Ask the Cannons," *Listen*, September 1991, 23.
4. Pia Mellody, "Codependence: An Overview," videotape from Mellody Enterprises, Wickenburg, Ariz., 1989.
5. Randy Frame, "Child Abuse: The Church's Best Kept Secret?" *Christianity Today*, 15 February 1985, 33.
6. Mellody, "Codependence: An Overview."
7. Ibid.
8. Ibid.
9. Ibid.
10. Ibid.
11. Terry Kellogg, *Broken Toys, Broken Dreams* (Amherst, Mass.: BRAT Publishing, 1990), 236.
12. Ibid.
13. Terry Kellogg, "Broken Toys, Broken Dreams," videotape from Terry Kellogg/Lifeworks Communications, Minneapolis, Minn., 1988.
14. Ibid.

Chapter 15

Shot Down by Friendly Fire

In the aftermath of the Gulf War came a number of disturbing reports that certain casualties were caused by "friendly fire." Americans were killed, not by the enemy, but by their comrades in arms. What could be worse than to die so needlessly? What could be more heartbreaking for the bereaved? Yet the same thing happens every day in Christian communities. The saints level their guns at each other, innocent souls are caught in the crossfire, and fatal injuries are inflicted.

Abuse at the hands of a fellow believer is especially painful because the victim is caught off guard. He's not anticipating an attack. After all, church is a safe place. Unfortunately, spiritual abuse by church members is responsible for more casualties from the ranks of the faithful than we will ever know. *Yet these losses are preventable.*

Loss of self/misunderstanding of God

In addictive family systems, children are abused and neglected. And abuse causes codependence. As Terry Kellogg puts it, "Abuse a child and create a codependent."[1] In the experience of abuse, children are robbed of the ability to love God *or* self. Unable to understand why God allowed them to be hurt, why He failed to protect them, they find it difficult to trust Him. An anorexic coed who was sexually abused by her churchgoing father said, "God was my *dad's* buddy. He was on my dad's side. God didn't take care of *me*."

Abused children see God as cold, distant, and uncaring. They see themselves as unlovable and unworthy of protection. This is a double strike against them. As a result of their abuse, they are literally robbed of the ability to know and love self and the freedom to know and love God. According to Matthew 22:35-40, we Christians are to love God with all our hearts and our neighbors as ourselves. "On these two commandments depend all the law and the prophets."[2] What happens to the individual who is unable to love God *or* self because he has been spiritually abused? He cannot fulfill the great commandment. To love God and self in a healthy, appropriate manner is virtually impossible for him. On this basis, I find spiritual abuse the most devastating of all the forms of abuse.

What is spiritual abuse?

Spiritual abuse is the abuse of a person's spirit—abuse that robs him of his sense of worth, value, and identity. It is anything that denies him the right to be the unique person God meant him to be. Spiritual abuse occurs any time one person steps between another person and God and makes himself that person's god. When a human being presents himself to another as all-powerful, all-knowing, and all-wise, he is standing in God's stead, and he will inevitably misrepresent Him. It can take considerable effort to undo the damage.

Specific forms of spiritual abuse include the following:
- Battering a child into conformity with Scripture or spiritual principles.
- Acting as the child's conscience, insisting that he fit the adult's preconceived mold, become what the adult wants him to be.
- Abuse of any kind perpetrated by an authority figure who represents God to the child—pastor, priest, church youth leader, or a parent who makes a big issue of being a Christian.
- Abuse of any kind that occurs in the church setting.

Unfortunately, much abuse occurs at the hands of parents, teachers, and church members. In the words of Ellen White,

"Prodigals have been kept out of the kingdom of God by the un-Christlikeness of those who claimed to be Christians."[3]

Major spiritual abuse occurs when anyone uses Scripture or church standards and traditions to coerce another person into conformity. If a Christian parent batters his child with the Bible, if he shames him with Scripture or Spirit of Prophecy, he is abusing the child. Donald Sloat comments on this in *The Dangers of Growing Up in a Christian Home*: "In my opinion, one of the most harmful practices in evangelical homes is parents' use of God and Scripture to control children, avoid personal responsibility, and justify negative child-rearing practices."[4]

In an article published by the Evangelical Women's Caucus, Elizabeth Bowman notes that some Christians use the fifth commandment to justify wielding undue power over their children. The kind of thinking that encourages abuse, she says, has this ring to it: "I know what is good for you and I have the right to do what I please with you. My superior status gives me responsibility for your life and the right to use whatever means are necessary to make sure you follow my advice. . . . Truth, authority, and personal autonomy lie with me and you receive them only through me."[5]

One researcher compared the child-rearing attitudes of fundamentalistic Christian parents, Jewish parents, mainstream Protestants, and known child abusers. She found no difference in the attitudes of the fundamentalists and the abusers where children were concerned. But there were significant differences in the attitudes of the abusers and the other, less rigid religious groups.[6] The fundamentalists and the abusers shared a common view of humanity: children are bad, selfish, etc. If an adult holds this view and sees himself as the mediator of God's wisdom—one whose divine mission is to remove evil from the child—the potential for abuse is great.[7]

Playing god

Many adult/children of dysfunctional families report having had a least one parent who was always right. He/she could do no wrong. The child was never allowed to question him. This, in itself, is spiritually abusive.

Acting as another person's conscience is abuse of the highest order. When anyone assumes the burden of governing another person's life and makes himself responsible for that person's salvation, when he attempts to interpret God's will to another human being, he is abusing him *and* presuming on God's mercy. This is not an appropriate role for a Christian, no matter how sanctified and holy he may claim to be.

When we try to play god and run our children's lives, especially beyond a certain age, we are abusing them spiritually. We are depriving them of reasonable autonomy. I'm not suggesting that the parents of young children should abandon their responsibility to give appropriate guidance and set healthy boundaries. To *fail* to do so is to abuse them. But there is a limit to the amount of controlling a parent can do, particularly beyond a given point.

Parents play god when they control their children's behavior excessively. Telling a child what he should think and feel, what he should believe, what he should wear, what he should be in life (vocation), whom he should marry or not marry, is spiritually abusive. Although some guidance is necessary and appropriate in early and middle childhood, there is a big difference between appropriate guidance and excessive control. There must be a progressive letting go on the part of the parents. The parent, pastor, priest, or friend who maintains too much control over another person is abusing him.

Hurtful healers

Some victims who turn to clergy or lay counselors for advice report being abused by those whose help they have sought. Occasionally, pastoral counselors treat victims of abuse with suspicion and disbelief. Some question the credibility of women who report marital abuse. Children who report sexual abuse are often accused of lying or fantasizing.[8] One minister's wife who went to a Christian counselor and reported that she was being emotionally and sexually abused by her husband was faced with this skeptical reply: "Surely a man of God wouldn't do those things!"

Virginia Mollenkott reports further atrocities within religious circles. She describes victims of abuse being counseled to submit to abuse as God's will.[9] A Christian counselor told a female client to submit to her husband's abuse, and if she died as a result, she could be at peace, knowing that she had laid down her life for the Lord! A prominent Christian lecturer made a similar comment in the presence of an audience of several thousand.

When sexual or physical abuse is going on in a Christian home, family members often ignore it rather than confront the guilty party. A successful, self-confident businessman wept as he described listening to his sisters when he was a small child. He could still hear them in the next room, pleading with their father to leave them alone. The father was a pillar of the church, and he was incesting his daughters on a regular basis.

Women have been counseled not to interfere with the ongoing incest of their children, but rather to pray for the offending partner and try to be sexier themselves.[10] That is classic co-addictive behavior. Whenever one person takes responsibility for another person's misbehavior, he/she is acting codependently. Abusers must take responsibility for their own inappropriate behavior. The wife is not responsible for her husband's offenses.

Unhealed wounders

When an authority figure who represents God (pastor, priest, youth leader, etc.) abuses a child in any way—physically, sexually, emotionally—he is abusing him spiritually.[11] If a youth leader is sexually inappropriate, if a priest or nun is harsh, disrespectful, or physically abusive to a child, he is abusing him spiritually.

Recently, a child molester wrote the following in a national magazine: "For more than forty years, I was a loving friend to hundreds of little boys. I took them fishing, helped them with their homework, and listened to their problems. Their parents never suspected I was also having sex with them."[12] When he took control of the children he mentored and abused them sexually, he was abusing them spiritually.

If a child is physically deprived, emotionally neglected, or otherwise mistreated by a representative of God or by parents who make an issue of being Christians, he will experience these behaviors as spiritually abusive.[13] Church nominating committees who hold the responsibility of assigning leadership duties within the church must be aware of this. No leaders should be more carefully chosen than those who have to do with the guidance and care of children and youth!

Perhaps this is a radical idea, but I believe that people who are untried and inexperienced in children's ministry should be supervised closely to see how they actually relate to children. Do they shame them? Bully them? Overlook their needs? Are they kind, tender, and loving? Are they sensitive and understanding? Even those youth leaders who are experienced and trusted should be made accountable to someone who is aware of the signs and symptoms of child abuse until they have proven themselves safe and effective. It would be irresponsible to do any less.

Suffer the little children

If the physical needs of a child are ignored while he is involved in a church activity—if he is required to sit still too long, if he is not permitted to go to the bathroom, if someone holds his nose and covers his mouth to hush his crying so he doesn't disturb the preacher, if he is jerked roughly in order to hurry him into the pew or pushed to make him kneel—these things may be experienced as spiritual abuse because they happen in church.

All-day religious rallies are a case in point. I watched a group of youngsters during one of these marathons. After the morning services and before the potluck, several children began to run and jump noisily in the church lobby. They were acting their age—a common malady of children. A stalwart deacon who was obsessed with reverence in the sanctuary stopped the children in midleap and marched them off to the fellowship hall to await the noon meal. The kids had been sitting still all morning, so reposing quietly at the lunch table was not what they had in mind.

If the deacon and the chairwoman of the social committee

had conspired together to plan the next scene, they couldn't have done a better job. When she saw the children sitting in the fellowship hall, she shooed them out: "Go play. We don't want you in here right now." The children felt they weren't wanted *anywhere*. I was smitten with the realization that if we tell our young people to get lost often enough, *they may*!

One isolated incident of this kind does not cause a child to be eternally lost. But if this is the standard way a church relates to its young people, there may be consequences. As Wes Haystead states in his book *Teaching Your Child About God*, the quality of a child's relationship with people at church does impact his view of God and church.[14]

On the inside looking out

All children deserve to be loved and blessed (celebrated). None deserve to be abused and neglected. One group, however, that probably suffers more than their share of spiritual abuse is denominational workers' children.

Twelve-year-old Katie's father was a teacher in the church school she attended. When the students complained about him and called him names, she stood by helplessly, not sure how to react. By the time she was in the eighth grade, he had been made principal of the junior academy. He reminded her frequently that she had to be a good example because of his position. Katie actually felt responsible for her father's career! Her strenuous efforts to uphold the perfect family image led her into bulimarexia and alcoholism.

Randy, a handsome college senior, wept as he recalled a childhood experience. His pastor-father halted midsermon more than once to scold him in front of the whole congregation. He took Randy out of the sanctuary, spanked him, brought him back in, and resumed preaching. How humiliating! As Randy relived this painful memory, I remembered doing similar things to our sons because we thought it was expected of us.

Pleasing people mattered more to us than the well-being of our children. And yet, we were just "obeying the rules." Today, I consider our excessive concern for the opinion of others very wrong. Our children had to carry the burden of our insecurities.

In this sense, pastors' children are caught between the devil and the deep blue sea. Their parents expect them to behave well so the church members will think well of them (the parents). The children's behavior reflects on their parent's vocation. That is just not fair.

Occasionally, church members scapegoat the pastor's or teacher's children when they are unhappy with something the parent is doing. The parent dares not defend his child lest a constituent be offended. There were times when I should have acted to protect my children from abuse but did not, because I didn't want to hurt our ministry. I wasn't fulfilling my parental duty. God could have taken care of our ministry. I should have taken care of my children.

Workers' children are often "hawked" by church members. Someone reported to us once that our son had been seen at a potluck dinner helping himself to a second dessert! On another occasion, a deacon rushed into the fellowship hall to report loudly that the pastor's son and some other children were throwing pebbles on the church roof. Fearful that we would be thought badly of, I abused my son emotionally in order to satisfy the complainer. My heart aches for the children of pastors and other denominational workers who have been the innocent victims of such institutionalized dysfunction.

How to offend your friends

Telling people of any age—even children—how they should feel is emotionally abusive. And if it is done in the name of the Lord or on the basis of Christian principle, it is spiritually abusive as well.

Other people's feelings are a personal matter and, as such, are none of anyone else's business. During the postlude one week, a cheery soul stopped and scolded the man behind me, "Don't look so unhappy, Bill." Bill was unhappy because his wife was ill and he was terribly worried about her. His unhappiness was appropriate.

A casual acquaintance of mine chided me similarly. "I haven't seen you smile all week," she said. "You should really try to look happier, like so-and-so," she added. "Christians are supposed to be happy." Her observations were accurate. My mother was dying of cancer, and my son was scheduled for painful surgery. I looked on the outside the way I felt on the inside—overwhelmed with fear and pain.

A young mother lost a child in a tragic accident. Coming to terms with her loss and grieving her little one's death was not easy. For weeks, she struggled with her sorrow and doubt. How it must have crushed her when a church member took her to task for grieving so long. She should just accept her loss, praise the Lord, and get on with life, she was told. "All things work together for good to them that love the Lord." And then came the ultimate insult: God must have known the deceased child was going to have problems later in life and laid her to rest to spare the parents, so she (the mother) should be grateful!

Abuse by withholding approval

I was touched by the words of a young cocaine addict who was raised in the church. Tears slipped from his eyes as he said he never felt good enough when he was growing up, no matter where he was—home, school, church, Pathfinders, or anywhere. He grew up in a world that expected perfection, and he could not achieve it. I wonder how many children in Christian families feel that way? And I wonder how it affects their relationship with God?

Once, when my husband was teaching college, he invited several students home after church. One of the girls offered to help me in the kitchen, so I asked her to make the punch. It was a simple task, but she was nervous and anxious to please. When she finished stirring the juice, she asked me to taste it. I took a sip and said, almost without thinking, "It's great, Debbie." When I turned and looked at her, she had tears in her eyes. "No one has ever told me I did anything right before," she said.

Informal excommunication

Janice and Roy were well-educated, well-to-do members of a large church. Their children were given every advantage. Their middle son, who was small for his age, suffered a great deal of social abuse in church school. In academy, he found acceptance with a partying crowd. His parents had no idea that he was drinking and drugging, so they were caught by surprise when he was arrested for possession of marijuana and his arrest was reported in the weekend edition of the local newspaper. "Do you think I felt like playing the organ in church that week?" his mother cried. "I wanted to crawl *under* it!"

Heartbroken parents feel the pangs of the church's rejection when their children develop drug problems. While it is true that shame isolates people, it is easy to increase parents' burden of shame by judging them and withholding encouragement and support in times of crisis. Hurting families frequently feel abandoned by the church. "It's as if we suddenly caught leprosy," they report. "People seem to understand when a child *dies*, but when he gets into *drugs*, they don't know what to do." Such neglect is more an issue of social ineptitude than deliberate condemnation, but it still hurts.

It's amazing how quickly a dysfunctional system can move to exclude a person who violates its norms. There seems to be a fear that somehow the misbehaving person will spoil the church's reputation, like the proverbial rotten apple. Perhaps he will have a negative influence on the other young people or make the church look bad in the eyes of the community (as if the community is paying any attention—pardon my cynicism). We Christians get a little grandiose at times, thinking that everyone's eyes are upon us. We're probably not that important to most people!

Few churches make enough of an impact for a single troubled member to attract that much public attention. And if someone *were* watching, I wonder what kind of influence it would have on him if he observed a struggling sinner being judged, condemned, and informally excommunicated by his own church in his weakest moment? Would that punitive measures could be postponed until young people were well out of their adolescence or that they could be used minimally as a method of church discipline for people of any age! Doesn't the Golden Rule apply in matters of church discipline? As a point of interest, the authors of *Toxic Faith* identify punitive discipline as one of ten characteristics of "toxic" religious systems.[15]

If the rod we read about in the text, "Spare the rod and spoil the child," is indeed the Shepherd's rod, then the concept of discipline is really built on guidance, not punitive punishment. The idea is to lovingly lead a child or a "lost sheep" out of harm's way.

I realize that the issue of church discipline is a complex one, especially when a member's misbehavior is considered a public embarrassment. But if the church is a family, I like to think that the "mature" members are in a better position to be flexible and forgiving of the sins of the younger, less-mature members than the younger are to tolerate the inflexibility and self-righteousness of the older members. In other words, if somebody has to be adult about the whole thing, shouldn't it be the mature Christians?

Spiritual shaming

I hide my head in shame as I write of this, because I am guilty of spiritual abuse. In training for the pastoral ministry, my husband and I were taught how to "work with" backsliders. The standard approach was to visit them in their homes and tell them we missed them. If they responded by telling us that they had been offended by a church member, we were to remind them that they should look to the Lord and not to people. Instead of apologizing for the fact that they were abused once, we abused them again. We pushed the church's shame back on them. I know that pastors and evangelists are trained to be much more empathetic now, but I still hear echoes of this attitude in some places.

Owning our own shame

There is no question that many have been hurt and offended in the church setting. We would profit very much by admitting our fault, owning our guilt, and taking responsibility for our actions. We cannot continue abusing people with impunity.

I am convicted by the words of Ezekiel 34: "Thus says the Lord God: Ho, shepherds of Israel who have been feeding yourselves! Should not shepherds feed the sheep? You eat the fat, you clothe yourselves with the wool, you slaughter the fatlings, but you do not feed the sheep.

"The weak you have not strengthened, the sick you have not healed, the crippled you have not bound up, the strayed you have not brought back, the lost you have not sought, and with force and harshness you have ruled them. So they were scattered, because there was no shepherd; and they become food for all the wild beasts.

"My sheep were scattered, they wandered over all the mountains and on every high hill; my sheep were scattered over all the face of the earth, with none to search or seek for them. . . . Thus says the Lord God, Behold, I am against the shepherds; and I will require my sheep at their hand."[16]

1. Terry Kellogg, *Broken Toys, Broken Dreams* (Amherst, Mass.: BRAT Publishing, 1990), 38.

2. Matthew 22:40, RSV.

3. Ellen White, *Counsels to Parents, Teachers, and Students* (Mountain View, Calif.: Pacific Press, 1943), 266.

4. Donald Sloat, *The Dangers of Growing Up in a Christian Home* (Nashville: Thomas Nelson Inc., 1986), 85.

5. Elizabeth Bowman, "When Theology Leads to Abuse," *Update*, Winter 1988-89, 3.

6. Ibid., 2, 3.

7. Ibid., 3.

8. Randy Frame, "Child Abuse: The Church's Best Kept Secret?" *Christianity Today*, 15 February 1985, 32, 33.

9. Virginia Ramey Mollenkott, "Evangelicalism, Patriarchy, and the Abuse of Children," *Radix*, January-February 1982, 15-18.

10. Ibid.

11. Pia Mellody, "Overview of Codependency," audiotape from Mellody Enterprises, Wickenburg, Ariz., 1988.

12. Ross Nelson, "Why I'm Every Mother's Worst Fear," *Redbook*, April 1992, 85.

13. Mellody, "Overview of Codependency."

14. Wes Haystead, *Teaching Your Child About God* (Ventura, Calif.: Gospel Light Publications, 1974), 84.

15. Stephen Arterburn and Jack Felton, *Toxic Faith* (Nashville: Thomas Nelson, Inc., 1991), 176.

16. Ezekiel 34:2-7, RSV.

Chapter 16

Robes of Righteousness, Coats of Shame

Although shame has been around for a long time, it has not been examined in depth until the last decade. The first scriptural reference to it is in Genesis 2:25. Adam and Eve, it says, were *not* ashamed. Created by God, they were pure and noble, happy and holy. They were healthy, glowing, physically perfect people. We picture them clothed in robes of light, visible to one another and to God—transparent, authentic, unashamed. They had nothing to hide, no inadequacy to defend, no secrets to protect, no need to be artificial.

The light and glory that surrounded them were what I would call an aura of openness (self-disclosure) and confidence (self-love). Nothing flatters—casts a person in a better light— than a humble but secure sense of self-esteem, of knowing how precious he is, of honoring his own existence as a child of God. I like to think that this is what constituted the light and glory that covered Adam and Eve.

God made the man and woman and gave them a glorious home in Eden. He was candid with them about their vulnerability, and He advised them to avoid the tree of knowledge of good and evil for their own safety. He let them know there was something about that particular tree they would be wise not to expose themselves to. They were meant to be human, not divine. The knowledge of evil was best left to God.

Healthy vs. toxic shame
Experts define *healthy* shame as an awareness of our human

condition, a recognition of our limitations. "It is necessary to have the feeling of shame if one is to be truly human," says John Bradshaw. "Shame tells us of our limits. Shame keeps us in our human boundaries, letting us know we can and will make mistakes, and that we need help. Our shame tells us we are not God."[1]

Shame as a *healthy* human emotion gives us permission to be fallible. It informs us that we aren't omnipotent. Healthy shame is the psychological foundation of humility and, in fact, the source of true spirituality.[2] Had Adam and Eve accepted their humanness and experienced their shame in a healthy fashion (as humility, teachability), how different their lives might have been.

"In the day ye eat thereof, . . . ye shall be as gods," Satan told them.[3] He didn't acknowledge the fact that his transgression had made him an outcast from heaven, nor did *they* realize that their transgression would separate them from God. According to a noted author on shame, the breaking of the interpersonal bond between two individuals is how shame is induced.[4] Adam's and Eve's sin separated them from God. It broke the interpersonal bridge between themselves and heaven.

The air in the garden had been mild and temperate until the fall of the first couple. With their sin came a chilling of the atmosphere. The self-esteem and serenity that had been theirs was gone, and in its place they felt shame—a nakedness of soul. They were exposed.[5] From that point on, they experienced shame as a toxic emotion.

To aspire to godlikeness—to plunge oneself into a knowledge of both good and evil—is to plunge oneself into toxic shame. I believe that one aspect of the knowledge of evil God was trying to steer His children away from was the experience of toxic shame.

No longer would Adam and Eve experience shame as a transient feeling. They would experience it as a state of being. "As a state of being," says Bradshaw, "shame takes over one's whole identity. To have shame as an identity is to believe that one's being is flawed. . . . Once shame is transformed into an identity, it becomes toxic and dehumanizing."[6] The following chart highlights the difference between healthy and toxic shame.

Healthy Shame	Toxic Shame
A transient emotion	A state of being
How I feel	Who I am
Realization that I am human, limited	Belief that I am flawed, defective
Awareness that I am not omnipotent	Feeling that I am subhuman
Acceptance of fallibility	Creation of a false self
Recognition that I need help	Conviction that I don't deserve help
Belief that I'm not alone	Feeling that I'm on my own
Humility, teachability	Grandiosity or groveling

Figure 6 — Healthy vs. Toxic Shame.

Hiding our shame

Bradshaw suggests that "toxic shame is unbearable and always necessitates a cover-up, a false self."[7] Once they had sinned, Adam and Eve's eyes were opened, and they knew they were naked. They sewed fig leaves together to cover themselves. It is in covering up for ourselves, refusing to admit our humanness, attempting to be what we are not, that we negate our authentic person. Internalized shame is the essence of co-dependence.[8]

The whole human race seems to be suffused with toxic, debilitating shame—a sickness of the soul that renders its victims emotionally and thus spiritually dead. In his landmark study *Shame: The Power of Caring*, Gershen Kaufman reports that shame is the source of such complex and disturbing inner states as depression; alienation; self-doubt; isolating loneliness; paranoid and schizoid phenomena; compulsive disorders; splitting of the self; perfectionism; a deep sense of inferiority, inadequacy, or failure; the so-called borderline conditions; and disorders of narcissism.[9]

Sources of shame

Children are born without shame. It is within our power to

affirm them or to shame them, to celebrate them or to devastate them. Where does toxic shame come from? From people. Toxic shame is induced by a child's primary care givers and companions: parents, grandparents, siblings, uncles, aunts, cousins, teachers, classmates, preachers, church members. Institutions, belief systems, and society in general can also instill shame.

Shame is induced in three ways: (1) by direct abuse or abandonment; (2) as an inheritance from parents and other ancestors, passed down from generation to generation; and, once it has been programmed into the individual, it is (3) internally generated and maintained. Once a child becomes shame-based, he produces shame spontaneously. His shame becomes self-perpetuating.

Externally induced shame. Shame originates primarily in significant relationships, including relationships with authority figures, care givers, and anyone else to whom the child is vulnerable. Even the smallest child who is brushed off by a parent who is "too busy" to meet his needs feels hurt and disappointed—ashamed. When he rushes home to show Dad something he made at school and is rebuffed because his father is preoccupied, he withers just a little. The parent has demonstrated to him the unimportance of his needs, and he feels discounted and ashamed. A little piece of his self-esteem is torn away.

The extent to which a child is shamed in a given situation is determined by who does the shaming and how important that person is to him. If his grandfather is important to him, the child will be very wounded if Grandfather shames him. The extent of the damage is also determined by what aspect of the self is shamed and whether the shaming occurs publicly or privately.[10] It's worse when done in front of other people.

Inherited intergenerational shame. Family shame is passed along from one generation to the next. A parent may be ashamed of his appearance, achievements, or actions. Dad may wish he were taller, or he may compare his meager accomplishments with others who are more educated or more prosperous than he. Mom may be ashamed because she didn't finish college. Both hope everyone has forgotten that their eldest son was born "prematurely." The shame is passed on to the next generation even though the reason for it may be forgotten.

Ellen grew up in the dust bowl during the depression. Her father deserted the family when she was small. Her mother and brothers managed to keep house and home together, but they lived in abject poverty. Ellen struggled to compensate for the shame she felt about her tattered clothes and worn-out shoes. She went to college, married an enterprising young man, joined a conservative church, and so distanced herself from her humble beginnings that no one would have guessed her history. She became a gracious lady, a scrupulous Christian, and a perfect mother.

Her friends and family saw only the image she created: a sweetly smiling, highly disciplined, very guarded woman who never made a mistake and was never wrong. Her children saw their mother as a package of rigid principles—a bundle of beliefs—rather than a person. She gave them religious books for their birthdays. When they were in boarding school, she wrote letters filled with Bible texts and thinly veiled homilies, which served to infuriate them rather than endear her to them.

Ellen's children had no idea who their mother really was. But in a moment of honesty, they told her how lonely and disconnected they felt. They told her how untouchable she was. When they encouraged her to get therapeutic help, she agreed. In counseling, she realized that because of her shame, she had hidden behind a false self. Gradually she found her identity and came to value herself. It was with great joy that she began to share herself authentically with her loved ones for the first time in their lives.

Internally generated shame. Experts agree that shame begets shame. The shame-based person learns to generate his own shame with little or no outside encouragement—like spontaneous combustion. With or without provocation, shame ignites and burns out of control. In the words of John Bradshaw, "Once internalized, toxic shame is functionally autonomous, which means that it can be triggered internally without any attending stimulus."[11]

Once it reaches this point, shame is more than just a feeling or emotion. It becomes a person's identity. He doesn't just act angry from time to time; he's an angry person. She doesn't just feel hurt and rejected; she's a martyr. He doesn't just have an occasional siege of self-doubt; he's an insecure person. She doesn't tell lies; she *is* a liar. He doesn't do bad things; he *is* bad.

Colossal shame binds

Five components of the self are so intrinsic a part of the person that undue shaming in these areas threatens one's very existence. These components are a person's gender, nature, emotions, dependency needs, and drives. When he is shamed about such basic aspects of the self, he is being shamed for who he is, and the offending characteristic is bound (locked) in shame. He copes by disowning the shamed characteristic, thus losing an integral part of himself.

Gender shame binds. If a child is shamed for being male or female, his identity is undermined in a very fundamental way. For example, in many families, daughters are deprived of the privileges accorded their brothers: "You can't do that because you're a girl."

If these kinds of family rules are based on a perversion of Ephesians 5:22, 23, if the domination and control of a female is justified on the basis of Scripture, the resulting shame is especially toxic because it affects the woman's relationship with God. The message is, "I am going to abuse you, and the Bible says it's OK." If her abuser is acting in the name of the Lord, the woman will feel betrayed by God. This is spiritually abusive.

Gender shame binds also occur when either parent rejects his or her own gender for reasons of low self-esteem. If Mom dislikes herself or dislikes being a woman, her daughter will identify with her and take on the shame. If either parent is abusive to the other, then one or more of the children will take on the victim's shame. Children react to their parents' feelings and act out their issues, whether or not they are expressed openly. Sexual abuse of any kind to a child of either gender places him in a sexual shame bind.

Binding one's nature in shame. A child's *nature* includes his disposition, his personality, and his temperament. If he is shamed for being an introvert or an extrovert, for being passive rather than aggressive, for being phlegmatic instead of sanguine, he is being shamed for who he is. That is his nature. The parent who is *himself* painfully introverted may reject his child's inward orientation and try to change him—"for his own good," of course.

Robert considered his preschool daughter a little too bossy for her own good. Instead of guiding her into more functional behavior, he shamed her by telling her she was obnoxious. Lewis thought his adolescent son was too passive. He insisted that the boy take martial arts courses even though the boy had no interest in them whatsoever. Both parents meant well, but the children were deeply shamed.

Binding feelings in shame. During the first years of life, a child needs parents who will reflect—describe or give words to—his feelings. Thus he learns to identify, label, accept, and express them. Children have to be taught to recognize and respect their feelings. They also have to be taught how to describe and discharge them. Lacking this skill, they will be unable to set functional boundaries in adulthood.

Some families demand that children be happy all the time. Cheerfulness is the only attitude that is acceptable; it's not OK to express sadness, disappointment, fear, or anger. When children are denied the right to express specific feelings, those feelings are shame-bound. From then on, whenever the child experiences the unacceptable emotion, he feels defective or bad.

Certain families allow children to be serious, but they don't permit them to be too happy, noisy, boisterous, etc. Often children are denied the right to express sadness or hurt. Lucy and her brother were routinely warned before they were punished that if they cried, they would be spanked again. "Quit crying, or I'll give you something to cry about," is a familiar threat to many children of dysfunctional families.

There are biases about feelings that are unique to each gender. It is acceptable for males in this culture to be angry, but they are considered weak if they express pain or fear. It's OK for females to be sad or scared, but not angry. A woman who expresses anger or behaves assertively is considered aggressive and masculine, and thus she feels shamed.

When a person is robbed of the right to feel, he is denied the opportunity to heal, for it is in expressing our trauma that we find relief. Alice Miller makes the point that "it is not the traumas we suffer in childhood which makes us emotionally ill but the inability to express the trauma."[12] To refuse a child the right to express his feelings is to bind his emotions in shame and cripple him in a deadly way.

Binding one's needs in shame. When a child has needs that are not given appropriate attention, he feels shame. Parents are not obligated to gratify a child's every wish, but children need to be accepted rather than accused or accursed for having needs and wants. Children need closeness, warmth, touching, holding, nurturance, affirmation, guidance, and direction. If a parent tells a child verbally or nonverbally to leave him alone, get out of the way, not be such a bother, not ask so many questions, etc., the child develops shame around his very neediness.

When children are shamed for being needy, it's usually because their needs clash with their parents' needs. Dad doesn't want to help his kids with their homework because he needs to relax and watch "Monday Night Football." Mom and Dad can't come to the school play because they'd rather be drinking, drugging, working, or whatever.

Binding healthy drives in shame. Normal drives are those appetites and needs that are physiologically or biologically based. It has been suggested that the drive most often associated with shame is sexuality. Behaviors that parents are likely to be uncomfortable with are genital exploration, masturbation, childhood sex play, teenage sexual activity, and issues surrounding sexual identity and sexual preference.[13] Parents, teachers, deans, and others who play a significant role in a child's life are capable of responding to any of these behaviors in shame-inducing ways. Associating masturbation with sinfulness, for example, can set up an addictive cycle of guilt, compulsion, attempts to control, loss of control, overwhelming shame, more compulsion, etc. We call this *sexaholism*.

When people shame children for their fledgling sexual behavior, the result may be a sexual shame bind. Lindy's mother was determined to control her daughter's sexual behavior. She made it a practice to hide behind the little girl's bedroom door at night to catch her masturbating. She violated Lindy's boundaries and created a sexual shame bind. "To the degree that sexuality becomes associated with and hence bound and controlled by shame," Dr. Kaufman writes, "the individual concerned is faced with an intolerable dilemma: how to come to terms with a vital part of the self that is seen as inherently bad."[14]

Mini–shame binds

Similar kinds of shaming occur around less critical issues, but the impact on a child can be profound. Children are shamed for their physical characteristics: being too tall, too short, too fat, too scrawny; having large feet, kinky hair, small breasts, broad hips, etc. Renee was a little lefty whose grandfather decided to convert her to right-handedness before she started school. He bribed her with everything from candy to flattery: "Eat [or write] with your pretty hand," he cajoled frequently. Kevin's parents were less positive in their approach; they tied his left hand to a chair.

John's peers resented him for being too smart, while his teachers shamed him for not doing his best. Lindsay's parents pressured her to develop her musical talent, while her peers considered her an attention grabber. Children are shamed for being ugly, pretty, poor, or rich. Thus they develop a double shame bind—not a comfortable place to be.

Deanna grew up in a small church school where there were few children her age. From the first through the eighth grade, her classmates treated her with disdain. Why? Because she was too pretty and her parents were too rich. She was unaware of her beauty and unassuming in every way, but the other children were jealous. She was confused, lonely, hurt by their rejection. But there was nothing she could do. She could not change who she was. Social abuse by Deanna's peers created debilitating shame.

When a child is smeared with shame, he takes it into the self and develops a shame core out of which he continues to generate his own shame with or without further outside help. He rejects the undesirable qualities and separates them from himself—

disowns his gender, emotions, needs, sexuality, etc. It is as if he were to bind one of his limbs in shame and chop it off. In so doing, he dismantles his person and puts in its place a false self that he hopes will be more acceptable.

Shaming words and actions

It is not difficult to induce shame in a child. The most efficient way is for an adult to transfer his own load of personal shame to the child by osmosis. When a parent's head is bowed with shame, his child's will be as well.

Another way to shame a child is to give him direct shaming messages, either verbally or nonverbally. Such messages appear as looks of disgust, disdain, or contempt. Refusing to acknowledge or be present to a child shames him. Glaring, sighing impatiently, and ridiculing children are shaming behaviors, as are disparaging and belittling. Comparing a child with his friends or siblings is shaming by implication. Showing contempt for a child's appearance or actions and being overly critical are shaming.

Verbal shaming messages sound like this: "You should have known better! Shame on you." "I'm surprised at you. Why did you do it that way?" "Didn't anyone teach you any manners?" "Why can't you be like Charlie? You idiot!" "That was a dumb thing to do." "When I was a kid . . ." "Can't you do anything right?" "Are you crazy? What's the matter with you?" "You embarrassed your mother. You should be ashamed of yourself!"

Placing high demands for performance on a child can set him up for disabling shame. Whenever such expectations are put on a person, says Kaufman, "binding self-consciousness can be induced." He becomes immediately aware of the real possibility of failure.[15]

Denying a child his privacy and otherwise refusing to respect his rights is shaming, as are discounting him (ignoring his feelings and needs), name calling, scolding him publicly when he makes mistakes, redoing his work, correcting his grammar, etc. Giving unsolicited advice and making suggestions can be shaming because the advice giver is implying that the advice receiver is inept or ignorant.

How to guide without shaming
Is it possible to guide children without inducing shame? I believe it is, relatively speaking, at least. In order to do so, parents need (1) to accept their own imperfections and allow their children to be imperfect and (2) give their children reassuring, affirming messages when they make mistakes. (3) They should correct and instruct in a nonscolding fashion. (4) Once guidance has been given, it should not be repeated more than once or twice. After that, as long as the child's life is not being threatened by what he is doing, he should be allowed to learn from his mistakes. (5) When he is embarrassed by his behavior, he doesn't need to hear, "I told you so." He needs to be comforted instead.

Is it guilt, or is it shame?
What is the difference between guilt and toxic shame? Guilt is associated with a specific behavior, a violation of one's own value system or another person's boundaries. Guilt is connected with inappropriate action. When I feel guilty, I regret my behavior, but I still respect myself. I know that I did something wrong or bad, but I do not identify with the deed and consider *myself* wrong or bad. To make amends for my mistake is to repair the breech and reaffirm my values. Throughout the process, I continue to esteem myself.

Living in shame
The shame-based individual who has been impelled to disown crucial parts of himself is not a happy camper. There appear to be only two ways he can survive: either outrun his shame or block it out. Outrunning the shame takes the form of addictions involving *loss of control*: alcoholism, workaholism, sexaholism, rageaholism, drug dependency. Blocking the shame out involves addictions that require *maintaining control*: anorexia, perfectionism, cleanaholism, rigidity, religious addiction, judgmentalism, image management, compulsive care giving, and controlling people.

In the one extreme, the individual is wildly running to get away from his pain and shame; in the other extreme, he's standing rigid and still, fending off the shame with asceticism. The bizarre thing about these two defensive styles is that each dips into the other's bag of tricks from time to time. A person whose behavior is out of control makes sporadic efforts to "rein himself in" or gain control. He practices a kind of white-knuckling abstinence. But he always ends up falling off the wagon and losing control again.

On the other hand, the rigid, controlled individual occasionally lapses into out-of-control behavior after periods of extreme self-deprivation. He may binge on food or alcohol or sexual acting out. But he convinces himself he is OK because he is able to resume management of his life, usually following a cycle of self-punishment (the Christian's purgatory). Then he musters up his self-discipline and goes for another stretch without doing anything shameful or sinful. Just when he begins to feel relieved of guilt, he blows it again.

Perhaps the only people who are able to practice moderation are those who have *healthy* shame and *functional* guilt (as described above). Christians struggling with addiction need to face the real issue—their codependence or toxic shame.

Shaming in religious systems

Shaming a fellow human being is generally an act of self-righteousness or an attempt to control him. Unfortunately, much shaming goes on in religious settings. There are some people for whom shaming others is a way of life—a way of acting out the feelings of rage, pain, and worthlessness that make up their own shame core.

Because I spend a lot of time in churches and at church-sponsored gatherings, I tend to notice a lot of shaming in these places, especially toward children and young people. I could write an entire book about that alone. One of the most poignant examples I've seen took place at prayer meeting.

A fatherless fourth-grade boy was invited by his pastor to conduct the song service one Wednesday night. The pastor was hoping to build the child's self-confidence by giving him this assignment. On the appointed evening, the child came early, dressed in his suit and tie, ready for his debut. He went to the platform and arranged two boxes of surplus Ingathering leaflets to stand on so he could reach the pulpit. Then he climbed up on the boxes and stood there quietly selecting hymns for the service.

Enter Brother X. He assumed the child was playing around and told him in a loud voice to get off the platform. The youngster complied. Mortified, he slipped down the aisle and out the back door of the church, never to return, *literally*.

The child was intensely ashamed. The only way to remove the undeserved shame would have been for the "good brother" to admit his error and apologize to the boy, which he did not.

An Adventist woman approached two recovering alcoholic church members who were lingering in the lobby after Sabbath School. "I need some advice," she said. "I have a niece who has a drug problem, and I don't know how to help her. *I've never had a habit I couldn't walk away from*, so I just don't understand what to do for her." There is little doubt that this patronizing woman meant well and that she was oblivious to the offensiveness of her remark. But it was subtly self-righteous and very shaming.

Two men in the church

Christ spoke a parable about a Pharisee and a publican. Both men went to the temple to worship. One had healthy shame and functional guilt; the other had toxic shame. Which was which? The Pharisee was performing an act of merit that would recommend him to God. He was trying to manage his image. He wanted to create the impression of piety. He presented a *false self* to others. He judged himself by other people, and he judged them by himself.[16] In his shame, he manifested the spirit of Satan, the accuser of the brethren. This is how toxic shame acts itself out in the church setting.

The publican was aware of his sinfulness. Self, to him, appeared to be nothing but shame.[17] His shame was, however, healthy shame. He recognized his limitations; he knew he could not do it alone. He didn't compare himself with others. He was overwhelmed with guilt, but he knew what to do about it. He desired pardon and peace, and he simply asked for God's mercy.[18] He didn't try to earn it.

The Pharisee did not recognize his sinfulness; he was in a toxic shame bind. "His soul was encased in a self-righteous armor which the arrows of God . . . failed to penetrate."[19] If that's not a shame bind, I don't know what is! He could not feel his wounds because he had disowned his feelings. We have to feel our wounds in order to desire healing.

The Pharisee went to his house destitute of the divine blessing. But the publican got what he needed. "I tell you," Christ said, "this man went down to his house justified rather than the other."[20]

1. John Bradshaw, *Healing the Shame That Binds You* (Deerfield Beach, Fla.: Health Communications, 1988), vii.

2. Ibid., 7-9.

3. Genesis 3:5.

4. Gershen Kaufman, *Shame: The Power of Caring* (Cambridge, Mass.: Schenkman Books, 1980), 15.

5. See Ellen White, *Patriarchs and Prophets* (Mountain View, Calif.: Pacific Press, 1958), 57.

6. Bradshaw, vii.

7. Ibid.

8. Ibid., 14.

9. Kaufman, 103-136.

10. Ibid., 10, 11.

11. Bradshaw, 23.

12. Alice Miller, *Thou Shalt Not Be Aware* (New York: Farrar, Straus and Giroux, 1984), 301.

13. Kaufman, 48, 49.

14. Ibid., 49.

15. Ibid., 27.

16. See Ellen White, *Christ's Object Lessons* (Washington, D.C.: Review and Herald, 1941), 150, 151.

17. See ibid., 151.

18. See ibid., 152.

19. Ibid., 158.

20. Luke 18:14, RSV.

Chapter 17

Who's in Control— You or Your Feelings?

For thirty-five years, when anyone asked me how I felt about something, I told them what I *thought*. I actually believed they were soliciting my point of view. So I said, "I feel that . . ." and proceeded to expound on my convictions. I didn't know the difference between a thought and a feeling. The best I could do when asked how I felt was to say something like, "I'm tired, and I have a headache." That was as close as I could come to describing my feelings. I could tell people what I *thought*; I could describe *physical* sensations; and I could "act out" or express feelings through passive-aggressive behavior. But I could not *experience* my emotions or express them verbally.

I knew the intellectual meaning of the word *feelings*, but I had absolutely no idea what a feeling felt like. I was out of touch with the sensory meaning of the word. Shame had wrapped itself around my feelings and encapsulated them. It had cut me off from my emotional self. Yet, ironically, my disowned feelings controlled me. People *act* out what they don't *speak* out. As the saying goes, we don't get mad; we just get even. What we don't *talk out* with our friends and family, we *take out* on them (or ourselves)!

How do you feel about your feelings?

Many people grow up believing that because feelings are somewhat fickle, they are not to be trusted at all. While it is true that emotions are subject to change and should not be the *only* resource we draw upon in defining reality, they are a viable and valuable source of information. Feelings, in and of themselves, are not wrong, but they can be used inappropriately. It is important to distinguish between our emotions and the fault of wrongly using them.[1]

How do *you* feel about your feelings? What are your preconceived notions about emotions? Are you afraid of them? Do you consider them bad, wrong, evil? Do you think it's sinful, foolish, or weak to express feelings?

I interviewed a number of young adults to see how they felt about their feelings. "I didn't think feelings were necessarily right or wrong," said one. "I just thought they were unimportant. I was taught to ignore them."

A graduate student told me he grew up with the attitude that showing feelings was a sign of weakness. "I thought men who acted emotional were sissies," he said. "I considered crying immature." He subscribed to the John Wayne theory: men should be strong, silent, stoical. And people who suffer in silence are to be admired.

Some people said they learned to control or curtail their expression of feelings in order to avoid negative social consequences. "It wasn't smart to let anyone know when I felt hurt or embarrassed as a child," said an attractive salesclerk. "My dad told me that people would dislike me if I talked about my feelings and my personal life. He said to keep my mouth shut."

Many individuals said their families treated feelings as a moral issue—they were judged to be right or wrong. "My grandmother said it was a sin to be discouraged or depressed," recounted a professional musician. "Christians were supposed to be happy all the time."

The most frequently reported feeling about feelings was guilt and shame. "My Sabbath School teacher said it was wrong to be angry. Expressing negative feelings to our parents was disrespectful—a violation of the commandment to honor your father and your mother," said a Christian athlete.

A minister's daughter said, "I was taught that perfect love casts out fear, so if I really trusted God, I wouldn't be afraid. Whenever I felt scared or anxious, I condemned myself, because it meant there must be something wrong with my spiritual life.

If I felt anything but happy, joyful feelings, I felt guilty."

Whether their attitudes about feelings were an outgrowth of cultural or religious values, whether they were based on spoken or unspoken injunctions, the outcome was the same: denial, repression, and a disowning of the emotional self. None of them realized that in denying themselves the right to their emotions, they were denying an essential part of their identity.

Three men in therapy

Charles was a late-stage workaholic pastor. At the age of forty-seven, he had come to a complete standstill. Along with his many accomplishments, he had achieved total burnout. "I couldn't function any longer. I went to the office, but I couldn't do anything except stare at my desk. I couldn't write letters. I couldn't read my Bible. I didn't even want to answer the phone. That's how depressed I was.

"One day my wife said she thought I deserved to feel better; she said she would support me in getting professional help. I was desperate enough to do almost anything. I arranged to go into an inpatient treatment facility to address my workaholism and compulsive care giving. When I arrived and was asked to tell why I had come to treatment and how I felt, I said I didn't feel anything. I was numb. I felt like I had a block of solid concrete from my neck to my navel."

Geoffrey was a middle-aged college professor with two failed marriages behind him and nothing to look forward to but years of boredom and loneliness. He had every reason to value himself in terms of his achievements, but he had never been able to sustain even a minimal level of self-esteem. In his early life, he had suffered severe verbal/emotional abuse at the hands of an alcoholic father. He had a shame core that wouldn't quit. No matter what he accomplished academically, he couldn't achieve enough to neutralize the shame.

He knew he didn't want to feel that way the rest of his life, so he went into codependency treatment. In therapy, one of his assignments was to do an exercise that would allow him to get in touch with his own preciousness. In the process, he pictured himself at five years of age. Hugging his adult frame with his arms, he rocked back and forth and cried out in pain and anguish. Then he crooned to that lonely little boy. "I love you, I love you." He did what he dared not do as a child—feel his feelings. His grieving was forty-five years overdue.

Larry, a fifty-something male, had a similar reaction when he addressed a major childhood loss: his mother's death. After her premature death when he was just a toddler, his father had disappeared for several years, leaving Larry and his siblings with the grandmother. When the father returned to reclaim his children, he had a new wife. No one ever told Larry face to face what happened to his mother.

In therapy, with the support of caring peers, Larry pictured the house he lived in when his mother died and imagined how he must have felt. He saw himself sitting on the porch, wondering what happened to his mother and wishing she were there to hold him and talk with him. He recalled the bouquet of roses he put on her grave when he graduated from academy. He realized how bereft he had been of human sympathy and understanding from the time of her death until the present. And he wept tears that had been waiting almost fifty years to be shed.

Each of these men was a high-achieving professional who was masking his personal pain and shame with workaholism, perfectionism, and other addictive behaviors. None were able to communicate openly or get close to their families, and they were lonely, unhappy people. But they wanted to change and were willing to go to any lengths to do so. They didn't want to repeat the sins of their fathers. In therapy they regained a God-given part of themselves that had been lost to them in childhood—their emotions.

An invaluable gift

I believe that our emotions are a gift from God, equivalent in kind and value to our five senses, without which we would be genuinely handicapped. Our physical senses serve two purposes: they allow us to experience pleasure, and they permit us to protect ourselves. Without them, we would be unable to enjoy the fun, flavor, excitement, sights, sounds, and smells of a day at the beach, a backyard barbecue, or a hike in the mountains. We would be unresponsive to the glory of a sunrise or the grandeur of a symphony. We would be insensitive to the beauties of life.

And we would be unaware of impending danger. My sense of touch tells me when I'm sitting too close to a hot stove. An unpleasant or bitter taste warns me not to swallow a harmful substance. And my senses of sight and hearing steer me out of the path of oncoming traffic when I'm walking along a country road. When I hear an approaching vehicle, I distance myself from it. Thus my physical senses guide me in setting boundaries in the interest of self-protection.

People can function without all their senses, but they are handicapped. They cannot experience the full range of pleasurable feelings or benefit from the protective value of the missing sense or senses.

I believe God gave us five *emotional* senses that function much as our *physical* senses do. They hold the same potential for self-protection and God-ordained pleasure.

Demystifying our emotions

Some of the misconceptions among Christians that cause us to deny our feelings are that emotions are dangerous, untrustworthy; feelings are bad or sinful; the display of feelings is a sign of weakness, immaturity, and craziness. Worst of all is the notion that to express certain feelings shows a lack of faith in God.

Many adult/children of abuse who attempt to express their feelings to others are told that their feelings are wrong. They're reminded that they shouldn't let their feelings get the better of them. They're told that they are "too sensitive."

While it is certainly true that feelings can create problems if they are not managed in healthy ways, I question the wisdom of throwing the baby out with the bathwater and denying the emotional side of one's nature completely. To deny the feeling self—to deny one's fear or pain or anger—is to cut oneself off from the sensory data needed to practice healthy self-care within our social environment.

We can't protect ourselves if we are "senseless." Senses are about feelings, not about thoughts! In my opinion, the ability to be *sensible* (wise) is directly connected to the ability to feel one's feelings, not just the ability to reason. In the book *Kids Who Carry Our Pain*, Robert Hemfelt and Paul Warren suggest that many people suppress anger to their great detriment. "Anger serves us well when it fuels change for the better," they maintain. This, I believe, is true of all feelings.

I do not consider the expression of feelings a moral matter. Feelings are neither good nor bad, right nor wrong. They should no more be subjected to moral judgment than our senses of sight, taste, touch, hearing, and smell. As a pastor friend of mine put it, "Feelings are morally neutral." While it is true that any of our physical or emotional senses can be perverted, it is also true that they are vital to our survival. They must be respected, appreciated, and managed in appropriate ways. No one can afford to be without them!

The purpose of our senses

The physical senses put us in touch with what is going on *outside* ourselves, in the material realm, so that we can experience joy and exercise caution. The emotional senses act similarly. They put us in touch with what is going on *inside* ourselves, in the spiritual realm, and allow us to connect with what is going on inside others in order to enjoy intimate relationships and protect our best interests.

Both physically and emotionally, our senses give us readouts of data essential to the safeguarding of our health and safety. They track the status of the internal and external environment. They provide information to guide us in determining how we should relate to our surroundings. In the physical realm, for instance, if a campfire is too hot, I move back. If smoke gets in my eyes and makes me uncomfortable, I change my position. If the fire is warm and cozy, I settle down and enjoy it. My physical feelings allow me to set boundaries—to move closer to or farther away from the fire.

Similarly, if my behavior makes me feel emotionally satisfied, happy, content, and guilt free, I keep doing it. But when I feel hurt, sad, or ashamed, I am aware that I need to make a change—move away from or directly confront the behavior, the person, or the situation making me uncomfortable. I need to alter my position, just as I do when smoke gets in my eyes—only the change of position is social rather than geographical.

The five emotional senses

Being in touch with my emotional senses is critical to my ability to make value judgments about my own behavior and set healthy boundaries with others. Setting boundaries involves creating distance when necessary, clarifying expectations, describing my needs, and establishing limits. If I am not in touch with my feelings, I cannot do these things. I won't know when I'm standing too close to a hot stove (or a toxic person).

God didn't give us negative feelings just so we could feel awful. He gifted us with feelings so we could be aware when it is time to make choices and changes that will improve our lives. Our emotional senses notify us when we need to do something to take care of ourselves in a responsible fashion. In order to relieve feelings of guilt and shame, we may need to stop doing something we know is wrong or make amends. We may need to stop accepting another person's unacceptable behavior in order to feel unafraid.

The five basic emotional senses are *glad* (happy), *sad* (hurt), *mad* (angry), *bad* (guilty or ashamed), and *afraid*. Each of these feelings serves a useful purpose. Even the feelings we consider negative contain a potentially positive blessing: anger gives motivation, energy (adrenalin), and strength. Healthy shame and guilt give us humility, accountability, and the incentive to make amends. Pain and hurt give us sensitivity, empathy, and understanding. Pain also allows us to grow and solve problems. Fear gives us discernment—the wisdom to exercise caution and good judgment. The ability to feel is a gift of God.

Fear of feelings

Perhaps our greatest paranoia about feelings is the fear that we will lose control. We don't want to "lose it," because we're afraid we'll do something dumb or undignified or worse yet, something to upset God. We might faint in terror, turn scarlet with embarrassment, look ugly when we cry, or do something "inappropriate." For that reason, we keep a tight grip on our emotions. In order to avoid these responses, we deny or bury (repress) our feelings entirely.

Unfortunately, buried feelings don't stay where they're put. Dr. Hemfelt likens repressed feelings to a toxic waste dump. He refers to the infamous Love Canal in New York State. Feelings don't go away just because we bury them, he says. Sooner or later, they "seep to the surface or percolate down into the water supply and poison the whole place."[2]

Buried feelings rise to the surface when least expected or desired. The result? We find ourselves behaving strangely around people who have hurt us. We can't tell brother so-and-so that we feel sad, bad, mad, or afraid of him. We don't want to face him and admit our "evil" feelings, nor do we want to offend him. So we gossip about him instead. Or we reject him out of hand. We wouldn't think of getting mad. We just get even.

It is not *expressed* feelings that govern us. It is *repressed* feelings. When we repress our feelings, we give them the power to control us. On the unconscious level, they are more toxic. When people express them simply and candidly, feelings lose their power to control. Repressed feelings explode; they flare out of control. Appropriately expressed feelings are manageable.

For a Christian to be concerned about being governed by his feelings is legitimate. What we don't understand is that our feelings are more likely to govern us when we stuff them down inside than when we let them out in healthy ways. Repressed feelings are like a pile of flammable junk in the basement. The slightest spark will set it afire. When we hide our feelings in the basement, we never know when they will explode. Again, *expressed* feelings don't govern us; *repressed* feelings do.

I think that's what the Bible means when it says Christians shouldn't let the sun set on their anger. We need to process our feelings responsibly (recognize, own, label, and express them) on a *daily* basis and not keep them hidden away where they can be ignited at a moment's notice.

How to honor your feelings honorably

Normal, healthy people are in touch with their emotions to

the extent that they recognize feelings within a short time of their onset. They are acute to their own pain, sadness, anger, fear, etc. Once they recognize a feeling, they use it constructively to motivate change making and boundary setting. And when the feeling has served its purpose—provided the necessary data and energy—they let it go.

The process is simple. First, one becomes aware of the physical sensations that accompany an emotion: a knot in the stomach, a tightening of the chest, a rigid jaw, clenched teeth, sweaty palms, burning cheeks, etc. Other cues are anxiety, negative self-talk, avoidance or distancing maneuvers (the inability to look at or be close to someone), defensiveness, and a sudden, unexplained sense of numbness or feeling "shut down."

These physical and emotional clues indicate that something is going on that needs attention. Often, we recognize that we're feeling "upset" or "frustrated," but we never nail down our feelings specifically enough to do anything about them except complain.

Emotional blockage

Frequently one's ability to identify feelings has been shut down for so long that it takes a concerted effort to get the emotional system functioning again. Therapy may be required to revive atrophied feelings. Children who grow up in painful conditions are forced to abandon the emotional part of themselves. They disown their feelings and lose the ability to express them. This connection must be restored. They must regain their ability to feel their feelings if they are to become socially functional. They need to come alive again.

In order to come alive, it may be necessary to exhume long-repressed feelings briefly, examine the pain of the past, and affirm its legitimacy. It is possible to process backlogged feelings in nondestructive ways. If one has become emotionally constipated (pardon the analogy) as a result of stuffing feelings for years and years, the blockage must be removed before the system can become functional again.

There are many safe places where this can be done: in group therapy, at twelve-step meetings, etc. Twelve-step programs are not meant to be a place for in-depth therapy, but they do provide a place to externalize the trauma verbally and to examine present behavior. Through instruction, discussion, and modeling, members of these groups gradually develop the ability to express their emotions more effectively.

Getting in touch

When my emotional senses signal me that something is wrong, I first identify the feeling itself. I label it and describe it to myself: "My heart is beating rapidly, and I'm feeling anxious." Then I accept and affirm the feeling. "I am afraid. The fear is mine. No one else made me feel the way I do. I am responsible. It's my job to take care of it." Next, I express my feeling simply and directly to someone—either to the party involved or to a sponsor or counselor: "I'm feeling threatened, hurt, scared, jealous, angry." This cuts the negative feeling in half. Now I'm prepared to take action, to set boundaries, etc. With practice, this process can be accomplished in five or ten minutes, start to finish, although in early recovery it may take anywhere from two to twenty-four hours or more.

Leslie Anne was a world-class care giver, a ready and willing doormat. When one of her colleagues telephoned early one morning and manipulated her into assuming some of his responsibilities, Leslie Anne didn't even realize what he had done to her. Half an hour later a feeling of anxiety came over her. It took another ten minutes for her to make the connection between her feeling and the event, but she finally recognized the source of her discomfort and decided to do something about it.

She was angry that she had allowed herself to be manipulated. She really didn't want to do what she had agreed to do, but she was afraid to alienate her colleague or jeopardize their relationship. However, she made a choice to take care of herself and be honest with him. She decided to tell him that she had changed her mind. She called the gentleman, who also happened to be in a recovery program, and told him frankly how she felt. He was very respectful. Their working relationship improved, and their friendship remained intact. This is a simple illustration of the part the emotional senses play in boundary setting.

The consequence of disowning feelings

Repressed feelings always take their toll: They express themselves obliquely and hurt people as a result; they create internal stress and pressure, which has potential medical consequences; and they set people up to anesthetize themselves with addictions. Anger, for example, leaks out in the form of passive-aggressive behavior—sarcasm, gossip, contemptuous looks, forgetfulness, argumentativeness, tardiness, procrastination, rejection, isolation. The medical consequences of repressing feelings include all of the stress-related illnesses as well as serious psychiatric disorders.

When we honor our physical senses and respect the messages they send us, we are able to take care of ourselves physically and experience the pleasures that God meant for us to have. Our physical senses make this possible.

When we honor our *emotional* senses and respect the messages *they* send us, we are able to take care of ourselves spiritually, socially, and emotionally. We experience the intimacy and meaningful, loving relationships that God intended us to enjoy.

---

1. Robert Hemfelt and Paul Warren, *Kids Who Carry Our Pain* (Carmel, N.Y.: Guideposts, 1990), 171.

2. Ibid., 156.

Chapter 18

Do Christians Have to Be Boundary-less to Be Selfless?

He was a handsome little fellow, one of the cutest two-year-olds I've ever seen—blond haired, blue eyed, and dimpled. But something wasn't quite right. Close up, he looked eighty years old—burdened, troubled, worried, and worn out. And it was no wonder. His parents were fighting a losing battle to save their marriage. The father was an alcoholic who was desperately struggling to stay sober. Although he was not drinking, he manifested all the other attitudes and behaviors of an alcoholic. In A.A. circles, he would be called a "dry drunk." He was tense, irritable, avoidant, irresponsible, isolated, and depressed. He was abusing his family by neglect. And his wife was severely codependent.

Both came from dysfunctional families. Both were earnest, sincere Christians who were powerless and didn't realize it. They were both trying to beat historical odds that they didn't even know existed. They were exhausted, disillusioned, ready to quit. Their anguish was written all over their precious little boy's face. I've seen many children in the same condition: a darling little girl patting her mother's leg saying, "Mommy, don't cry." A five-year-old worrying about her parents' financial problems and giving them pennies out of her piggy bank to "help." Sensitive children soak up their parents' distress like sponges and then try to solve their problems. We call them worried children.

Worried children

Children are easily overwhelmed by their parents' personal concerns. When a child hears his mother and father worrying out loud and sees the stressed looks on their faces, he absorbs their anxiety. This occurs in Christian families as well as alcoholic families. But Christian homes exhibit some unique variations.

Fear of damnation. Children who hear their parents obsessing about eternal life become anxious about their own salvation. They're terrified of being "lost." Sensing their parents' intensity, they take on the burden of their own sins and, in some cases, the sins of the rest of the family. The child who tries to "save" an unconverted parent is a classic example. Such children live in fear. Many children of fundamentalistic parents have nightmares about the judgment and an unreasoning dread of the second coming. This is not normal or healthy for young children. Nor is it God's will. Children should not have to assume the burdens of their parents socially, financially, *or* spiritually.

Pressure to be like Jesus. One of the gospel songs I learned in childhood went like this: "Be like Jesus,/this my song,/in the home and in the throng;/Be like Jesus all day long!/I would be like Jesus."[1] Maybe it was just my filter system, but the message I got was that since Jesus was perfect, *I* had to be perfect.

Trying to imitate Christ is a tall order for a small child. I could never make it a whole day without sinning. In due time, I was told that my righteousness was as filthy rags and that I could depend on Christ's righteousness to cover my flaws. But it was almost too late. I had gained a different impression first, and it did not dislodge itself easily.

It is a violation of a child's developmental process to demand perfection of him. Society allows children twenty-one years to grow up. That's about how long it takes *under the best of conditions*. God allows even longer. He gives His children a lifetime to achieve full Christian maturity (the process we call sanctification).

Pressure to be selfless. But in our idealism, we expect our children to be fully mature and totally unselfish by the time they are six or seven. We won't let them be self-centered for a second. It is possible, however, for a parent to promote unselfishness to the point that he fails to teach his children another important lesson: healthy self-care. It is possible to try so hard to make them selfless that we render them boundary-less.

That's what I did to my kids.

Having failed to learn boundary setting myself as a child, I entered adulthood with nonexistent boundaries. Then I married a man who was similarly handicapped. That was a sure-fire formula for disaster!

In our attempt to be good Christians, we tried to be all things to all people. We never said No to anyone, because we didn't want to be selfish. We didn't love our neighbors *as* ourselves. We loved our neighbors *instead* of ourselves. Our home, our guest room, our pantry, our bank account, our car, our personal attention were available to anyone any time. We were determined to be like Jesus, and He was the unwearied servant of mankind.[2] He gave all He had. We tried to do the same. We meant well, but we hurt ourselves and our family immeasurably.

Premature altruism. When our children were young, my husband and I expected them to share their personal possessions with others, but we did not teach them to set appropriate limits. We didn't even tell them it was OK to set limits. We couldn't model healthy boundary setting because *we* didn't have boundaries.

We insisted that they share their belongings with strangers whether they wanted to or not. And the strangers were usually *our* guests—children of *our* friends or parishioners, not *theirs*. We expected our sons to "cheerfully" allow visitors to play with their things and not murmur a word of complaint if their room was ransacked and their toys left damaged or broken. Even if our guests' children left the playroom in shambles, we said nothing.

I believe that was abusive. We expected our children to give up what they had not yet received—their exclusive "place" in life and their rights as individuals. They couldn't gain a sense of identity because they had to keep passing out parts of themselves to other people at our insistence.

A child's space and his belongings are an expression of who he is. These things are an almost sacred symbol of his uniqueness and individuality. But in our house, nothing belonged to our sons, not even their parents—certainly not themselves. We expected altruistic behavior of them before they were developmentally capable of it. We demanded that they share with others and be selfless before they even *had* a self!

One of the songs we teach children in Sabbath School is about sharing: "I have two dollies and I am glad/You have no dollies and that's too bad/ I'll share my dollies 'cause I love you/ And that's what Jesus wants me to do."[3] The adult leader chooses a child to act out the sharing role while the other children sing. At the critical moment, he is supposed to give one of two identical toys to another child.

More often than not, we have to physically force the little one to give up the extra toy. If he doesn't go along with the plan, if he protests or clings stubbornly to the dolly or truck, we shame him, or, worse yet, grab it away from him: "You have to give it to Johnny, or Jesus will be sad. If you aren't nice, you can't come up front again."

I am aware that Jesus was unselfish. Even when He was young, He denied Himself in order to give to others.[4] But to *overemphasize* His example as a mandate for fallible young children is unrealistic. Demanding this kind of unselfishness of a child without taking into consideration his developmental level is a disservice to the child *and* to the Lord.

I believe that God meant children to have a lifetime in which to grow up and become fully mature. To rush them, to try to telescope the maturing process into less time, is to abuse them. To put a suit and tie on a tiny child and then take him to church and expect him to sit still for an hour and a half is unrealistic. It's also unrealistic to demand that he put his shiny quarter in the offering plate when he wants to keep it for himself. Even if we succeed in getting the quarter into the offering plate, I'm not sure we have taught him unselfishness. We may have taught him the opposite.

When unselfishness is selfish

Even a viable concept like self-sacrifice can be skewed. How many goodhearted Christians are overcommitted, overextended, always magnanimous, but utterly exhausted? They give and give and give. They're so busy taking care of others that they don't take care of themselves. Where did they learn to abandon their own needs so mindlessly? And is their behavior a sign of sanctification or a mark of misguided zeal?

Swiss Christian psychiatrist Paul Tournier says, "We have all seen . . . men and women who have never grown up because they have been repressed by a religious upbringing and have been trained since infancy in systematic renunciation."[5] Such individuals are the epitome of selflessness, but their unselfishness is not always what it appears to be. "Contrary to what those who have been brought up in this doctrine of self-abnegation think, a certain more or less conscious egoism always lurks behind the pleasure one derives from devoting oneself to others."[6] Self*less*ness can be sel*fish*ness when the person serving others is trying to get his identity and self-esteem from giving.

Parents who try too hard to teach their children selflessness may be robbing them of the right and ability to set functional boundaries and practice healthy self-care. *Thus deprived, such children grow up to become spiritual self-abusers.*

For Christians, this problem hinges at a very basic level on two apparently conflicting beliefs: the gospel of self-realization and the gospel of self-renunciation. The conflict between these two ideas has placed psychology and religion at odds for decades. The principles of self-assertion and self-denial are seen as opposites and mutually exclusive by many believers.[7] They reject either religion or psychology because they cannot harmonize the two principles, each of which seems equally viable.

Is it egocentric and therefore evil to have wants and wishes? If we do nice things for ourselves, are we being selfish? Is it un-Christian to protect our interests? Must we give and give and give with never a thought of self?

Psychology suggests that people need a place of belonging, a home, a source of security—a fundamental sense of identity. Religion suggests that people cast away their earthly symbols of security and be free of attachment. Are these two concepts really at odds with each other? Are they as incompatible as they appear to be?

In his book, *A Place for You*, Dr. Tournier asserts that the disparity is more apparent than real. The principles of self-assertion and self-denial are not mutually exclusive.[8] Self-*fulfillment* and self-*denial* are but two movements of a single process, movements that are successive and complementary. They are two sides of the same coin.[9]

Using the scriptural account of Abraham as an example, Dr. Tournier suggests that the renunciation of self must be preceded by the assertion of self. Abraham was a very successful, very wealthy man. He lived in the most highly civilized culture of his time. He had a large household with many servants. Before Abraham was asked to surrender all, he was given all. He was not asked to detach from what he did not have. He was not expected to deny self before he had found self.[10] People who have never had a place of their own don't have a place to leave. If they have never received, they have nothing to give.

Finding our place, leaving our place, receiving, giving—these things occur in natural rhythm. They are complementary alternations. As Tournier puts it, "There is a time when the buds burst into leaf, and a time when the leaves fall. But only those that have grown in spring can fall in the autumn."[11] Only the person who has flourished emotionally as a child is fully prepared to deny himself or herself as an adult.

Jesus had a secure place in His childhood. He had parents who loved, guided, and affirmed Him. His father "initiated Him into the ritual duties which formed such a solid framework for the life of the Jews of His day."[12] His childish needs were fulfilled.

Dr. Tournier postulates that if an individual's family is healthy and his parents united, successful detachment can occur. But when his home has *not* acted as a real place, when it has *not* been healthy, then detachment becomes impossible. "He who does not attach himself properly at the time for attachment cannot detach himself properly at the time for detachment. . . . One can abandon only what one has got."[13]

It would be absurd, says Tournier, to urge detachment on a man who had never received the thing in question. How much more absurd to urge it on a young child whose childhood needs have not been met! Unfortunately, this is often done. "A man who is the victim of this denial hears renunciation being preached as if it were meant for him, when he cannot renounce because he has not received."[14]

We must develop self before we can deny self. We must find a place before we can renounce it. This renunciation, it seems to me, is a process for mature Christians, *not something to be imposed on the young.* In Tournier's words, "It is necessary first to be a child, to know to the full that protected and pampered place which is childhood, before being able to leave 'childish things.' "[15]

A child cannot give up his selfishness until he has expressed it in living.[16] Before anyone is able to freely give, before he can act with unselfishness, he must first define his boundaries, defend them, and establish himself as an individual.

---

1. James Rowe and B. D. Ackley, "I Would Be Like Jesus," *Gospel Melodies and Evangelistic Hymns* (Washington, D.C.: Review and Herald, 1940), 12.

2. See Ellen White, *The Ministry of Healing* (Mountain View, Calif.: Pacific Press, 1942), 17.

3. Myrtle Creasman, "Sharing Song," *Story Hour Songs* (Nashville: Broadman Press, 1943).

4. See Ellen White, *The Desire of Ages* (Mountain View, Calif.: Pacific Press, 1940), 87.

5. Paul Tournier, *A Place for You* (New York: Harper & Row, 1968), 91.

6. Ibid., 108, 109.

7. Donald Sloat, *The Dangers of Growing Up in a Christian Home* (Nashville: Thomas Nelson, 1986), 141.

8. Tournier, 93.

9. Ibid., 101.

10. Ibid., 88, 89.

11. Ibid., 99.

12. Ibid., 96.

13. Ibid., 98, 99.

14. Ibid., 99.

15. Ibid., 103.

16. Ibid., 108.

Chapter 19

What We Didn't Learn in Kindergarten

The process of securing the self is an elegant one, but I don't think it's terribly difficult, at least not as difficult as I tried to make it. Ideally, it occurs within the nourishing atmosphere of a healthy family where children are given the opportunity to gain self-confidence and social competence. "The adults of the family teach the younger members the skills they need in order to 'do life,' " says Janet Woititz.[1]

While growing up, children should come to experience their own preciousness on a deep, internal level. Ideally, they should gather self-esteem and self-respect from their families. They should gain a feeling of significance, a sense of mattering. They also need to learn certain skills, such as how to take care of themselves physically and emotionally, how to get their needs met in healthy ways, and how to act with moderation.[2] When this happens they grow into adulthood knowing, valuing, and liking themselves reasonably well most of the time.

Unfortunately, few people, Christian or otherwise, have this kind of upbringing. Through no fault of their own, they fail to receive the skills and knowledge they need to live happy, serene lives. Why? Because they don't have a teacher! Parents can't teach children what *they* don't know. They can't give what they weren't given.

Imagine a parent trying to tutor his child in algebra or calculus. Could he do it? Only if he were a mathematician. Parents who are socially or emotionally handicapped can't bequeath high-level social skills to their children. Only healthy parents can parent in a healthy fashion.

Teaching children to love and care for themselves and to relate effectively to other people is not a priority in dysfunctional families. While a parent is busy being sick, the child does not get his basic needs met. If he has no one to guide him, he doesn't learn to take care of himself in a healthy manner. Life skills training is simply not on the agenda.

Back to school

Most of us didn't learn everything we needed to know in kindergarten. Or in college. We didn't learn how to do life. Now we have to catch up. But learning in adulthood what we should have learned in childhood can be difficult as well as embarrassing.

As a young person, I didn't have the skills necessary to relate to myself and other people functionally. Vaguely aware of this deficit, I began to search for home remedies to fix my low self-esteem and social inadequacy. In the process, I bought every self-help book on the market. Twenty years later I found a clue in one of those books: A person doesn't have to love and esteem himself *in order* to take care of himself. He comes to love and esteem himself *as a result* of taking care of himself! Self-esteem is the *effect* of healthy self-care, not the *cause*.

I assumed that the reason I didn't take proper care of myself was that I didn't have enough self-esteem. But I couldn't gain self-esteem because I wasn't treating myself respectfully. Talk about a Catch-22! If only I could learn to love myself as Jesus loved me, I thought, *then* I would treat myself better. I even beat myself up for not having enough faith to internalize God's love! If He loved me enough to send His Son to die for me, I *should* love and esteem myself. Shame on me for not accepting His grace!

Now I knew that I didn't have to wait for the mercurial love of self before beginning to practice healthy self-care. Twelve-step groups suggested I *act as if*. "Fake it till you make it," they said. I wasn't even sure how to fake it. I didn't know where to begin making changes. Something was definitely missing. I couldn't *think* myself into a new way of *acting*. I would have to *act* myself into a new way of *thinking*.

The missing element was boundaries. I couldn't take care of myself because I didn't have boundaries. I lacked boundaries for two reasons: I had never learned the art of boundary setting, and I didn't have access to my feelings, which prevented me from recognizing when I had been violated and responding in my own best interests.

Our feelings or *emotional senses* are like the electric eye on a burglar alarm. They tell us when our boundaries have been crossed. Because I was emotionally shut down, I was unaware of where my boundaries were or when they had been crossed. Thus I was unable to defend them. I had no idea when someone was trespassing or "walking all over me." I didn't even know I *had* boundaries, much less that they had been stepped on! Even if I had known my boundaries were being violated, I didn't think it was OK to feel hurt. If I felt offended, I told myself I was just being too sensitive!

Before I could practice healthy self-care and thereby enhance my self-esteem, I had to reactivate my emotional senses. I had to regain the ability to feel my pain. Then I had to give myself the right to protect myself from injury. Finally, I had to learn how to set boundaries and defend them in healthy ways.

What is a boundary?

Like the concept of *feelings*, the concept of *boundaries* was foreign to me. Beyond the grammatical meaning of the word, I could not relate to it any more than I could have related to a Latin term. I had no context of personal experience within which to place it. I wouldn't have known a boundary if I had tripped over one!

I had to begin in kindergarten. My teacher was Pia Mellody. Her definition of a boundary was understandable: A boundary is the means by which we protect ourselves without offending others.[3] I could grasp that.

I eventually came to think of my boundary as the invisible line around my body and spirit that allows me to protect myself, maintain my self-esteem, and refrain from offending others. The boundary is made up of my sense of self, of worth, of strength, of identity, and of respect for my own rights. It is the means by which I create and communicate to others a clear sense of what I want and need from them. In other words, my boundary is an intangible barrier between myself and others beyond which I will not go and behind which they are not permitted to come.[4]

It is important to make my boundaries visible and my wants and needs known in order to play fair in relationships. My friends and family will not know where my boundaries are unless I tell them, and vice versa. Giving one another this information is an act of mutual respect. Because I couldn't express my feelings and needs, people had to guess where I stood. They couldn't help but trespass on me, because my boundaries were invisible. I was abused by default. People didn't mean to hurt me, but they couldn't aim at an unseen goal!

A place kicker can't score a field goal if he doesn't know where the goal posts are. A relationship with no boundaries (goal posts) becomes a comedy of errors. Everyone tries to manipulate everyone else into meeting his or her needs without anyone expressing their expectations. Everyone wants to win the game, but no one knows the rules. No wonder everybody loses!

Battered boundaries

American poet Robert Bly speaks poignantly of people's boundaries being invaded: "A grown man six feet tall will allow another person to cross his boundaries, enter his psychic house, verbally abuse him, carry away his treasures, and slam the door behind; the invaded man will stand there with an ingratiating, confused smile on his face."[5]

This occurs initially, Bly says, when children are physically or emotionally abused by adults. He calls the defenders of a child's boundaries his *warriors*. When a child is abused, his warriors collapse, go into a trance, or die.[6] "If a grown-up moves to hit a child, or stuff food into the child's mouth, there is no defense— it happens. If the grown-up decides to shout, and penetrate the child's auditory boundaries by sheer violence, it happens. Most parents invade the child's territory whenever they wish."[7]

Bly suggests that every child lives deep inside his or her own psychic house and that he deserves the right of sovereignty inside that house. But if an adult decides to cross the child's physical or sexual boundaries, there is nothing the child can do to protect himself. And when he is thus invaded, something within him dies.

Bly adds movingly, "The child, so full of expectation of blessing whenever he or she is around an adult, stiffens with shock and falls into the timeless fossilized confusion of shame. What is worse, one sexual invasion, or one beating, usually leads to another, and the warriors, if revived, die again."[8] When this individual is thirty years old, "he will still feel unprotected, and be unable to defend himself from other people enraged at their own unprotection."[9] *Abusers are people enraged at their own unprotection.*

Notice the quandary of the victim: " 'I am a victim,' he says over and over; and he is. But that very identification with victimhood keeps the soul house open and available for still more invasions."[10] The victim is left handicapped. He either has no boundaries, badly damaged boundaries, or impenetrable walls instead of boundaries.[11]

It is with such a legacy that most children of addiction and abuse approach adult relationships. Not only do they lack boundaries, but they have also been stripped of the *right* to protect themselves.

Our inalienable rights

The ability to set boundaries begins with the deep belief that one has the *right* to do so. It is *not* selfish to have needs and wants and to practice healthy self-care. If I were to knit a sweater for a friend and then discover that she was using it as a dust rag, I would be hurt and angry. Honoring God's handiwork— treating myself with respect and expecting others to do the same—is the *least* I can do to show my gratitude for the gift of life. Boundary setting is the means for accomplishing this. It is the basis of healthy self-care. Pia Mellody has identified four basic premises upon which boundary setting is built.[12]

- Physically, each of us has the right to determine when,

where, how, and who touches us and how close they will come to us.
- Sexually, we have the right to determine with whom, where, when, and how we wish to be sexual.
- Emotionally, we have the right to evaluate messages expressed by others about ourselves before we take them in. Anything another person says or does to us at any given moment is more about that person and his history than it is about us.
- Intellectually, we have the right to think and believe as we wish, knowing that we are accountable for the consequences.

The function of a boundary is to protect one's body, thinking, and feelings from invasion. It is also a means of monitoring the appropriateness of one's behavior toward others.[13] Everyone has boundaries, but many are unaware of their presence. If we are out of touch with our feelings, we literally don't know where we stand. If we can't *feel,* we can't know when we're being stepped on. And if we don't know we're being stepped on, we can't act to protect ourselves.

There are several reasons why an adult may find himself with damaged boundaries.

- He may be codependent—that is, he was abused or neglected in childhood.
- His major care givers may have expected him to be selfless; he was not allowed to express wants and needs.
- He may not have been taught to identify, label, and express his feelings.
- One of his parents may have been dominant and the other a martyr, a doormat, or a victim.
- Both of his parents may have failed to protect *themselves* effectively and thus modeled boundary-lessness.
- His parents may have failed to protect him.

Establishing boundaries
Boundary setting is a skill that takes time to develop. Some

boundaries can be established on the basis of one's existing values and beliefs—the social, cultural, and religious "absolutes" that a person has assessed and deemed appropriate for himself. These constitute what I call *preset boundaries*. You may decide that you will not use alcohol or cigarettes or permit their use in your home or car. You may decide that you won't borrow or lend money or cosign loans, etc. I find it helpful to examine my values and list my existing boundaries on paper periodically. This reinforces them in my mind and helps me to act with resolve in letting others know where I stand.

If you have not had healthy values modeled to you in childhood, you cannot assume that your preset boundaries are functional.

Janet Woititz and Alan Garner suggest people assess their boundaries. There are three ways to do this. The first is to examine your relationships to see whether or not you are getting a fair exchange. "People exchange cash, goods, services, and sentiments. Out of a misplaced sense of loyalty, adult children often give and give and give, even when they're not getting. . . . Be loyal to others, but set reasonable limits to your loyalty. If the rewards of a personal or business relationship don't match the costs, you need to renegotiate the terms of the relationship."[14]

The second approach is to look around for clues to normal behavior. Do your neighbors allow people to borrow their lawn mowers? Do they let them send their children over to "play" every day? Do they work overtime every weekend, accept more responsibility than they can handle, allow their grown children to take advantage of them, etc.?

Finally, ask someone whose judgment you respect, as long as that person doesn't have a vested interest in your decision. If he or she has something to gain by advising you one way or the other, that's not the person to consult. Then ask yourself, "Is what I am about to do or is the boundary I am about to set what I would advise another person to do?"[15]

Basing your boundaries on your existing value system works quite well when the issues are clear-cut. But in the complex realm of relationships, it is not always so simple. Sometimes we have to rely on instinct to let us know when a boundary has been crossed. The individual who has lost touch with his feelings in the experience of childhood deprivation and abuse may find this almost impossible. Only those who are well connected to their feelings "sense it" when their boundaries are being violated. Our feelings act as an alarm system. They send sensory warning messages when the invisible line of our boundaries has been crossed.

At first it may take anywhere from a few minutes to a few hours for one to become aware that his alarm system has been activated. Feelings that have been dormant for years do not reawaken instantly. Initially, a person may be oblivious to his pain when someone steps on his toes. He may even apologize for having his foot in the way! He has no idea that he has been trespassed upon. Only if and when he experiences the pain will he know that he has been violated. His emotional senses are the crucial variable. They send a distress signal from his foot to his brain, whereupon he says, "Ouch." Saying "ouch" is an elementary form of boundary setting. It needs to be followed with a statement like, "Please get off my foot."

Some of us may not know where our boundaries are until we feel the pain of being trampled on. If we lack access to our emotional senses, we will not know when we have been hurt nor will we act to protect ourselves from further injury. That's why we feel so vulnerable, so unsafe. Having been hurt again and again, we tell ourselves we will never trust another soul, never make ourselves vulnerable again.

The fact is that people are fallible and will disappoint us repeatedly. The problem is not our inability to trust *them*. It is our inability to trust *ourselves* to act in our own best interests. Once we can count on ourselves to set boundaries and represent our rights, we no longer feel exposed and unprotected. We are empowered. The other person's trustworthiness does not guarantee our emotional safety. Our own boundaries do.

How to say "Ouch!"

If you are in touch with your feelings, they will signal you when you have been offended or abused. The first clue is an unpleasant physical sensation—like butterflies in the stomach.

With practice, you will begin to recognize these sensations and connect them with the feelings they represent: anxiety, hurt, anger, resentment, or fear. The presence of one of these sensations warns you that there is a problem needing attention. Your boundaries have been crossed. You have been violated, controlled, manipulated, or used. Now it's your responsibility to take action, for your own sake as well as for the offender's sake. The offender has no way of knowing he is "out of bounds" if he doesn't know where your boundaries are. It's your job to let people know your wants, needs, and preferences. When you are hurt, you have to say "Ouch."

After-the-fact boundaries. An honest statement of your feelings is a gentle way of letting someone know when you have been offended. This is what I call an after-the-fact boundary: "When such and such happened, I felt so and so." Telling another person how you feel is a gracious and courteous act, because he no longer has to try to figure out where you stand.

My husband and I had a chance to practice this recently. He answered a phone call from a mutual friend while I stood nearby. In the midst of their conversation, without the caller's asking and without my offering, he handed me the phone and said, "Here, say Hi to so-and-so." Although the caller was a good friend, I really didn't care to talk just then. Because I felt that I didn't have a choice, I reluctantly complied. But I was upset. Afterward I said, "When you handed me the phone without asking first, I felt controlled and angry."

The difficult thing for most of us is to hear what is said without feeling obligated to defend, explain, argue, or apologize. What I told my husband was simply a statement of my feelings, a description of my reality. It was not about him. He listened openly, because he knew my statement was a reflection of me, not an attack on him. Thus, he gained information about my preferences. That's all. He learned how his behavior impacted me in that instance, but he was not obligated to apologize or change.

Before-the-fact boundaries. The second level of boundary setting is what I call a before-the-fact boundary. It differs from the after-the-fact boundary only in the timing and in the addition of a statement of need: "When such and such happens, I feel so-and-so, and I need [or want] such and such." Once again, the other person is only expected to listen, nothing more.

A few minutes after I hung up from the unwelcome phone call, I realized that this kind of thing had happened before more than once. Each time, I had grown a little more angry, but my husband had no idea what was going on inside me. When I became aware of the anger, I knew I had to set a boundary. This is what I said: "I just realized that you have urged me to talk to people on the phone like that before without asking me first. I know you didn't mean to offend me, but I need to ask you not to do that again." Thus I created a before-the-fact boundary that will apply should such a circumstance occur again. If my husband forgets, I will simply state the boundary again. If he ignores my boundary after I have reminded him, I will move to a higher level of boundary setting.

The more my husband and I practice boundary setting, the more aware we are of each other's wants and wishes and the more we are able to treat one another with respect. We don't have to guess anymore, nor do we have to manipulate and control. When we see one another as individuals with boundaries, we value each other and our relationship more.

Candy had been working on boundaries for several weeks in her therapy group. She needed to ask her father for some money, but she was reluctant to approach him. She was afraid that when she asked him, he would go on and on about his financial problems and thus shame her for asking. In the past when she had expressed a need, he often overwhelmed her with a recital of his financial problems, and she ended up feeling ashamed for having needs. She didn't want that to happen again.

With the help of her group, Candy prepared a before-the-fact boundary statement: "Dad, in the past when I have asked you for money, you've given me a long explanation of why you can't afford to give it to me, and by the time you're done, I feel hurt and angry. I'm about to ask you for some money, and I'm very willing to accept either a Yes or No answer, but I don't want to hear a recital of all your financial woes." Her father was very respectful of her request. As a result, she relaxed and had a long talk with him, the best conversation they had had in years.

Contingency boundaries. The next level of boundary setting is the contingency boundary. In addition to the "when/I feel" statement and "and I need" statement, it includes an "if/then" contingency statement. The contingency statement suggests what you will do if your boundary is violated.[16] It should be expressed in a factual, nonthreatening manner: "When you make fun of me, I feel hurt. I need you to stop making fun of me and treat me respectfully. If you keep teasing me unkindly, I will have to distance myself from you."

A contingency statement about the unwelcome telephone call would be, "If you urge me again to talk to a caller on the phone without giving me a choice, I will not come to the phone." Before I create a contingency boundary, I must be prepared to follow through, which would be difficult in this case because *I* might be embarrassed.

Spur-of-the-moment boundaries. Once a person's emotional sensory system is working again, he can set boundaries almost instantly. When he feels uncomfortable with someone's suggestions or behavior, he can "just say No." He will be immediately aware of his discomfort (fear, anger, guilt, anxiety, or pain) and recognize that he needs to set a boundary to protect himself. For instance, if a friend invites him to do something he doesn't enjoy, he'll say, "I would rather not." If someone begins to gossip, he will let that person know he feels uneasy talking about another person when he's not there. If a friend insists on driving while intoxicated, he will choose to ride with someone else.

Buying time. When one is faced with a situation he hasn't thought through in advance and doesn't want to decide on the spur of the moment, he can buy some time: "I'll have to think about it. I'll give you my decision tomorrow." Buying time is a legitimate way to set boundaries when cornered. If a person in a managerial role is asked by an employee to make an exception to policy, he can say, "I'll give it some thought and consult with so-and-so. Check with me on Friday."

Laser-beam boundaries. I didn't recognize this kind of boundary until someone zapped me with one. What the person said to me was so clear, direct, and powerful that I dubbed it a "laser beam" boundary. I was expounding about my work to one of my adult sons. Since he has endured my work addiction all his life, he wasn't particularly interested in my obsession. He had the courage to stop me midsentence with the words, "Mom, I don't want to hear about it." He wasn't rude or unkind, but he was definite. I winced and shut my mouth. The pain was adequate to keep me from doing it again.

Broken-record technique. If a person with whom I set a boundary argues or otherwise tries to dissuade me, I use the "broken record" technique. It works well with people who won't take No for an answer. The idea is to calmly repeat your statement of refusal over and over like a broken record until the other party gives up.

If a friend asks to borrow your car and you say No, but he proceeds to give you 101 reasons why you should let him use it, after each of his remarks, just repeat the line, "No, I don't lend my car." Don't explain or respond to his arguments, or you will give him material for further argument. He learns that all he has to do to bulldoze your boundary is litigate. Don't argue. Just repeat your original statement over and over.[17]

Lack of boundaries

Woititz and Garner identify several ways of knowing when one's boundaries are missing. If you feel beaten down, angry, depressed, violated, used, or overworked, your boundaries are not in good shape.[18] If you are easily influenced or swayed, you probably lack boundaries. If you find yourself unable to say No, if you are easily taken advantage of, or if you are embarrassed by other people's behavior, you lack boundaries. If you take on other people's feelings, shame, or responsibilities, you have a boundary problem.

If you share confidences inappropriately, if you bulldoze others, if you demand instead of asking, if you shame people who displease you, if you blame others for your feelings, if you expect to be taken care of, if you humiliate people, if you treat them patronizingly, if you act superior, if you insist on dictating what others think or feel, you lack boundaries. You need to contain yourself within your own space.

In adult relationships, the lack of boundaries renders a person unable to take care of himself *and* unable to keep from offending others.[19] He has a tendency to absorb other people's feelings, beliefs, thoughts, and values. He then bases his choices on what they think or want instead of what he believes and wants. Or he pushes his feelings, thoughts, and values off on other people and demands that they agree with him. He blames others for the way he feels and allows them to determine what he thinks. A person who lacks boundaries is quite readily persuaded to violate his own values. At the same time, he is blithely unaware of how his feelings, thoughts, and actions affect others. He offends or abuses them intellectually and spiritually.

An individual who lacks boundaries may be unaware when others are physically or sexually inappropriate with him. If someone violates him, he is unable to move away or to act in his own defense.[20] And he is likely to offend others sexually and physically.

Jesus set boundaries

The Gospels contain numerous examples of boundary setting. Jesus set boundaries, even with His own parents![21] When His mother attempted to dominate and control Him, He told her not to tell Him what to do.[22] When Peter tried to manage His behavior, Jesus set a laser beam boundary: "Get away from me, Satan! You are an obstacle in my way."[23]

When the disciples tried to take control and deter the children from coming to Him, Jesus brought them up short with the words: "Forbid them not!"[24] When they criticized the woman who anointed His feet with expensive perfume, He drew a clear boundary: "Why are you bothering this woman? It is a fine and beautiful thing that she has done for me."[25] He rebuked the moneychangers,[26] called the church officials hypocrites,[27] and put the Pharisees in their place on numerous occasions.[28]

Boundary setting affords us an opportunity to define ourselves more clearly in our own eyes and in the eyes of others. The simple act of examining our values, our wants and wishes, our needs and preferences reveals much about who we are. It casts our identity in a clearer light. The act of taking care of ourselves increases self-esteem. And telling others what we want and need makes it easier for them to relate to us.

Boundary setting is not a matter of selfishness, self-centeredness, or ingratitude. When people define, describe, and defend their boundaries, they are being mature adults who are aware that they are responsible for their own well-being and who know that it is their job to take care of themselves. Boundary setting is not an attempt to control other people. It is simply a way of saying, "I matter, and you matter too."

One's self-respect does not depend on how others react to his boundaries. It comes from knowing who he is and demonstrating to others what is important to him. It comes from knowing that he cares enough about himself to take care of himself.

----

1. Janet Woititz and Alan Garner, *Lifeskills for Adult Children* (Deerfield Beach, Fla.: Health Communications, 1990), vii.

2. Pia Mellody, "Codependence: An Overview," videotape from Mellody Enterprises, Wickenburg, Ariz., 1989.

3. Pia Mellody, "Overview of Codependency," audiotape from Mellody Enterprises, Wickenburg, Ariz., 1988.

4. Woititz and Garner, 86.

5. Robert Bly, *Iron John* (New York: Addison-Wesley, 1990), 146.

6. Ibid., 147.

7. Ibid.

8. Ibid., 147, 148.

9. Ibid.

10. Ibid., 149.

11. Mellody, "Codependence: An Overview."

12. Ibid.

13. Ibid.

14. Woititz and Garner, 87.

15. Ibid., 87, 88.

16. Ibid., 96

17. Ibid., 93.

18. Ibid., 86.

19. Mellody, "Codependence: An Overview."

20. Ibid.

21. Luke 2:49.

22. John 2:4.

23. Matthew 16:23, TEV.

24. Matthew 19:14.

25. Matthew 26:10, TEV.

26. Matthew 21:12, 13.

27. Luke 13:15

28. Matthew 9:11-13; 12:2-8; John 8:3-7.

Chapter 20

Can the Church Be a Dysfunctional Family?

Can the church be anything *but* a dysfunctional family? Given the fact that every member is a fallible human being and most of us are codependent, how can it be anything else? Much as we might wish it were otherwise, the emotional baggage we bring with us from childhood affects all our adult relationships. Codependents act out immature coping skills wherever they are— at home, at the office, on the highway, in church. Any group of people (school faculty, construction crew, committee, team, board, or church) can fall into dysfunctional patterns of behavior.

If one is a victim, abuser, martyr, manipulator, or controller at home, he will be the same at church. People do not leave their maladaptive behaviors behind when they step across the hallowed threshold. In the church setting, we often see domination on the part of a few, ongoing power struggles, and political posturing. This leads to a loss of unity and an eroding of spirituality. Apathy and personal discouragement follow. Members are critical, hypervigilant, and controlling on the one hand, or withdrawn, suspicious, and distrustful on the other.

Fractured fellowship

I've seen small churches in which the entire membership was caught up in a self-defeating cycle of codependent behavior. The system was so shut down that the whole congregation appeared to be clinically depressed. Church members are shattered by shame when a brother betrays his beliefs and commits a crime that brings reproach on the congregation. They are overwhelmed with grief when someone forsakes their fellowship and denies the faith. They're immobilized by unexpressed feelings of anger when misunderstandings arise among them. They're separated from one another by secrets they are afraid to share or sins they are loathe to confess.

In a family system—which is precisely what the church is— failure to process (discuss and resolve) problems shuts the system down. Each member closes himself off from the others in order to hide his feelings. Unspoken feelings create invisible barriers. Unresolved issues alienate member from member.

Many have the idea that talking about such problems makes them worse. That is a legitimate concern. Most people lack the skill and ability to express feelings and settle differences in a healthy manner, so talking about problems *can* do more harm than good. But it is possible to learn boundary-setting skills, and with healthier boundaries come healthier relationships.

Wounded saints

I have seen Christians mortally wounded by their brethren. I've witnessed grief and loss beyond description. I've seen church after church fractured by petty disputes. Sadly, the pall of depression and shame lingers over a discordant congregation long after the original schism is forgotten.

Congregations divide into factions over the color scheme for redecorating the church, over building programs and plans, over changes in the order of service, over the choice of church officers, the selection of a pastor, the budget, matters of church discipline, standards and rules, ad infinitum and ad nauseam. Many of these disputes could be prevented if personal boundaries were respected and healthy detachment practiced.

Boundary violations in the church setting

I believe that most internal warfare and bloodshed in churches is caused by a lack of boundaries. Many Adventists work, go to school, worship, and socialize with the same people. This is a major overlapping of boundaries. When boundaries are thus blurred, people feel free to mind each other's business, arbitrate each other's beliefs, monitor and control each other's

202 NEVER GOOD ENOUGH

behavior, and take each other's moral inventories with no sense
of the inappropriateness and offensiveness of such behavior.

The kinds of violations common to the church setting include:

- Enmeshment—members interfering in one another's per-
  sonal lives.
- Spiritual abuse—people playing God.
- Violation of anonymity—gossiping in the name of Christian
  concern.
- Control—telling others what their Christian duty is.
- Manipulation—refusing to let a fellow member say No.
- Taking advantage of others—expecting them to take church
  responsibilities without asking them in advance.
- Unhealthy care giving.
- Intellectual abuse—forcing others to agree with one's be-
  liefs.
- Shaming.
- Dishonesty—not being candid about feelings, breaking
  confidentiality.

Functional vs. dysfunctional families

In dysfunctional families, there is a lack of healthy separation
between members. Everybody minds everybody else's business.
Boundaries are nonexistent. The uniqueness of the individual
is not respected. All are expected—yea, required—to reflect the
values of the group. Individual rights, tastes, feelings, needs,
opinions, and goals are not honored. In functional families, by
contrast, the individual is permitted to be unique.

In dysfunctional families, the individual exists for the sake of
the system, not the system for the sake of the individual. Yet
the Bible says that God's system and the principles that govern
it were made for the individual. The individual was not created
for the sake of the institution (see Mark 2:27). God intended
that systems serve the people within them, not the other way
around. Functional systems support the needs of the individual.

Dysfunctional systems are characterized by denial and delusion. Overwhelming weaknesses and flaws may permeate the
system, but everyone within it insists that everything is fine.

Anything negative that happens is kept a secret. There is a great deal of censorship. In healthy, functional systems, people face reality rather than denying it.

In functional families, there is an abundance of nurturance, unconditional love, acceptance, freedom, and fun. Mistakes are treated as learning opportunities, and forgiveness is readily available. People are flexible. In dysfunctional systems, acceptance and approval are conditional—they must be earned. Failure is met with shaming and punishment. People in dysfunctional systems are not as forgiving as God is.[1]

An addictive society/an addictive church

Addictive thinking and behavior exist on every level of society—individual, familial, organizational, national, and global. Anne Wilson Schaef, author, therapist, and an astute social commentator, postulates that all institutions are affected by the addictive process. "Society itself operates addictively," she says. "Its institutions perpetuate the addictive process."[2] Given who we are, it couldn't be otherwise.

Some of the dysfunctional characteristics that carry over from families into church organizations are delusion and denial (having our heads in the sand), grandiosity (having an overinflated sense of our own importance), and arrogance (believing that we know best). Other symptoms that appear in the church setting are obsessive thinking about moral issues and the mission of the church and preoccupation with control. There is a need to maintain the status quo. Perfectionism and judgmentalism are characteristic of addictive systems, as are repression of feelings, secret keeping, and indirect communication.[3]

Addictive individuals and organizations tend to define their value on the basis of how others perceive them. In order to control their image, they demand rigid adherence to set forms and rituals. Outward appearances must be maintained at all costs. Image management is a major concern.[4] There is a tendency to avoid self-assessment. Criticism is viewed as an attack. The church or institution operates as a closed system, isolating itself and relating only to those who think as it does. Divergent ideas are disallowed. In short, the entire system is regulated by an

addictive thinking process. Such a system has all the characteristics of the individual addict.[5] Organizations are considered
addictive any time they manifest one or more of the following
traits:

- When a person in a key administrative position is an alcoholic, workaholic, etc.
- When the members or employees are actively codependent.
- When the constituency uses the goals and mission of the
organization as a drug.
- When dysfunctional patterns of interaction characterize
the political structure of the organization.[6]

The administrators are addicts. In assessing the addictions
of key leaders in an organization, the full range of dependency
disorders must be considered: chemical dependence, compulsive
eating, workaholism, and addictions to excitement, power,
money, status, beliefs, etc.

Aimee was the daughter of a workaholic pastor. She remem-
bers her home life as extremely chaotic. Her father was rarely
there, and when he was, he was always tired, always overextended, always irritable. His mood swings paralleled those of
an alcoholic. Like the family of an alcoholic, everyone around
him—his wife and children, his secretary, and his colleagues—
walked on eggshells.

His obsession with work created pressure on everyone. He had
little respect for anyone who was not willing to suffer for Christ.
His church members felt uneasy and guilty in his presence. No
matter what they did, it was never enough. His family and staff
tolerated his abuse and enabled his inappropriate actions, which
they excused on the basis of his dedication. He was an active
addict, and his entire organization was affected.[7]

The members are codependent. When the people within an
organization are codependent, the whole organization becomes
dysfunctional. Members *enable* dysfunction—that is, they support irresponsible, inappropriate, or addictive behavior on the
part of others. Because they don't want to rock the boat, they
ignore the addict, make excuses, cover up, bail him out, accept

his rationalizations, or project the blame for his actions on someone else. They exhaust themselves trying to compensate for his weaknesses and attempting to control him.

Sometimes church agencies help people in a shaming fashion. They minister in a degrading manner. They decide what the recipients of their help need and how they should be cared for without asking them what *they* think they need or helping them achieve it for themselves. This kind of caretaking is oppressive, abusive, and very codependent.[8]

The institution is a drug. Another form of organizational addiction involves the institution itself becoming the drug of choice. In this case, employees or adherents are obsessed with the organization and its cause. This "includes addiction to the mission of the organization or addiction to the promise of the organization," according to Schaef.[9] "A person addicted to the promise of the organization is willing to endure any amount of bad experiences to hold onto that promise, which can be any-thing from 'life everlasting' to a sense of belonging to a commu-nity or being accepted."[10]

The rules are dysfunctional. When an organization operates its business practices and policies by dysfunctional rules, it is acting addictively. When leaders deny the existence of problems and refuse to face issues and discuss them candidly, when they triangulate (communicate indirectly), keep secrets, send double messages, lobby and play power games, manipulate and control, they are communicating dysfunctionally. If leaders place unre-alistic expectations or demands for perfection on themselves and their workers, if they do not treat their employees equally and show respect to all, they are acting addictively.

When an organization is operating by dysfunctional rules, there is an incongruity between what it says it believes and what it actually does. In other words, it does not practice what it preaches. "Its personnel practices, its emphasis on control, and how it interprets and works with power can all reveal signs of addiction," says Dr. Schaef.[11]

Addiction culminates in spiritual bankruptcy. If an addictive organization is to survive as an entity, it must confront its addic-tive patterns and seek wellness.

Roles played in dysfunctional organizations

Family systems theorists have identified various roles played in dysfunctional families (the hero, the superachiever, the troublemaker, clown, mascot, responsible one, little parent, scapegoat, etc.). There are parallels in the church.

The hero. An individual who has grown up in a chaotic family system knows what to do in times of crisis. Accustomed to living on the edge, he has quick reflexes. He is at his best under stress. When life gets boring, he creates a crisis in order to showcase his talents. At the critical moment, he overinflates himself so he will be big enough, strong enough, and wise enough to manage.

The colossal care giver. This individual is a master at moving the cushions around so no one ever has to hit bottom (suffer the consequences of his actions). The care giver deprives people of the opportunity to learn from their mistakes. He does things for others that they *should* do for themselves. He gives without being asked. He gives in order to get.

There is a distinct difference between healthy and unhealthy care giving. To care for another in a healthy way is to show respectful concern for him by sharing one's own experience, strength, and hope *without violating his boundaries* and *only when asked.* A healthy giver gives without ulterior motive and with no strings attached.

Lisa and Tom were the only young professionals in their church. They were natural leaders. New pastors quickly recognized in them the most reliable members of the congregation. Lisa was the unofficial church hostess. Their children grew up watching people come and go, staying out of the way while their mother frantically prepared for bake sales and entertained visiting preachers. Of course, the children were expected to pitch in and help whenever she was overtaxed.

When Lisa and Tom's youngest child was in treatment for alcoholism, he made one of the most poignant remarks I've ever heard: "All my life I had the Bible served to me for breakfast, lunch, and dinner. I've seen the church walk all over my parents. We did everything for the church, but the church never did anything for us. I hate the church, and I hate God. He *used* my parents."

The imperfect perfectionist. Perfectionism is an insidious form of addiction that threads its way from one generation to the next, creating pain, isolation, and loneliness. Perfectionists cannot tolerate their own flaws and mistakes, nor can they accept the imperfections of others. They won't allow themselves to be human. As Pia Mellody says, "Anyone trying to be perfect is in an active state of delusion. He is busy being sick."[12] No other addiction isolates its victims so completely. I believe perfectionists are the loneliest people in the world. An alcoholic can always find someone to drink with. But people scatter when a perfectionist comes near, because they feel defective in his presence.

The compulsive do-gooder. Some people find it easier to give to others than to give to their own families. They avoid their pain and problems by concentrating on other people's pain and problems. The compulsive do-gooder espouses causes, collects cripples, and all but kills himself trying to save the world. After all, if he doesn't, who will?

The heresy hunter. There are those who feel called of God to monitor the moral standards of the church and the immoral behavior and questionable beliefs of its members. Says Archibald Hart, "Every church I have ever known has its 'heresy hunters'—those members who feel a self-imposed responsibility to keep the faith 'pure.' They are on guard for any hint of heresy (as defined by them) and will jump down others' throats or go for the jugular at the slightest provocation."[13] They cause more headaches and ulcers for pastors than anything else. And all the while, they believe they are the agents of God, keeping apostasy at bay.[14]

The suspicious saint. Some Christians distrust anyone and anything that is not officially approved by the church. They are convinced that all other institutions and agencies are of the devil and that people will be led astray if they go anywhere near them. As one of the elect, the suspicious saint is determined not to be deceived. Neither he nor his church is perfect, but his denial and delusion keep him from recognizing that fact. He has no use for any individual or institution that does not meet his standards. While his prudence may be valid, he carries it to the point of paranoia.

The scapegoat. This person is the carrier of the congregation's shame. He is at the bottom of the church's pecking order. His sinfulness is just pronounced enough that others can use him to distract themselves from their own defects of character. Their sins are equally grave, but his are more noticeable. Various individuals and groups in the church become scapegoats: the young, the liberals, the conservatives, the wealthy, single parents, pastor's wives, etc. When we need someone to criticize, they are handy.

The politician. Boundary violations between various departments and administrative levels of a church organization are not uncommon. People in church leadership fall into the same traps politicians fall into. They become prey to their own need for control and lust for power. In order to maintain their status, they act the part of people pleasers and approval seekers. They violate personal and departmental boundaries within the organization in order to establish control.

Taking moral inventory

There are legitimate gifts within the body of Christ. Carrying out a God-given assignment is not wrong. Exercising one's spiritual gifts is not wrong. Standing up for one's convictions is not wrong. But the faithful need to face their codependent tendencies. If we continue to use church and church organizations as a drug, there will be consequences.

In the interest of soul searching, there are two questions that every Christian should ask himself: Am I healthy enough to hear the call of the Holy Spirit and not confuse it with the unconscious urgings of my own codependency? And am I free enough from addictive symptoms to act in the spirit of Christ rather than on the basis of compulsion as I seek to fulfill my Christian calling? If not, I am in danger of perverting God's call and harming myself and others.

Addictive organizations can recover, but, like any other addict, they often have to hit bottom first. The alternative is intervention. Intervention provides an opportunity for concerned people to confront an addiction before it reaches its lowest point. It makes it possible for active addiction and codependence on an organizational level to be intercepted. The church can recognize its dysfunctional patterns and intervene before greater losses occur. Not until we accept this responsibility will we recover.

My husband and I set out years ago to create a ministry of reconciliation for young Adventist addicts and alcoholics. As noble as our motives were, we created an organization that was shot through with addiction because we were codependent. Over a period of time, we attracted more than one codependent employee and conspired together to create a dysfunctional family.

Somehow, the ministry survived. We did the best we could to make our work a success, but while we were trying harder and harder and praying harder and longer, we were getting sicker and sicker. We didn't know how to take care of ourselves or relate to each other in healthy ways. It was not until we reached the point of burnout that we confronted our own symptoms, as individuals and as an organization.

One at a time, our staff members went through therapy and joined twelve-step programs appropriate to their issues. That was just the beginning. As an institution, we had to change our policies and stop abusing ourselves. We were working far too hard. We were paying our staff far too little. We were keeping secrets and hiding our feelings from each other. We were triangulating, talking behind each other's backs, violating each other's boundaries, and confusing our roles.

In order to recover, we had to clarify our roles and responsibilities, set boundaries, and learn to communicate. We hired trainers who could teach us these skills. We set up weekly "processing" meetings in order to confront each other directly with our feelings and concerns. What has this accomplished?

I can only speak for myself. My personal recovery has given me self-esteem, the ability to accept my imperfections, the ability to practice healthy self-care, the ability to set boundaries, and the ability to practice moderation. Working in an organization where the entire staff is in recovery is very gratifying. I no longer live in pain, fear, and stress.

There are anxious moments and angry moments and sad

moments. But that's just what they are—*moments*, not hours or weeks or months. As a group, we are no longer stuck in our old self-defeating patterns of behavior. We know what to do when problems arise. Now that we have learned to communicate in healthy ways, we don't wait for our weekly processing meeting to clear the air. We do it on an ongoing basis. I feel free to express my opinions and feelings to anyone at any time.

I am extremely grateful, not only for the presence of the Holy Spirit among us and the calling God has placed upon us, but also for the serenity that has become ours through the gift of individual and organizational recovery from addiction and co-dependence. I believe this kind of fellowship is available to the members of every Christian organization that is willing to go to any lengths to achieve it.

---

1. Fred Downing, "The Family Disease Workshop," videotape from Paradox Productions, 1984.

2. Anne Wilson Schaef, "Is the Church an Addictive Organization?" *The Christian Century*, 3-10 January 1990, 18.

3. Ibid., 20.

4. Ibid., 19.

5. Ibid., 18.

6. Ibid., 18-20.

7. Ibid., 19.

8. Ibid., 18, 19.

9. Ibid., 20.

10. Ibid.

11. Ibid.

12. Pia Mellody, "Overview of Codependency," audiotape from Mellody Enterprises, Wickenburg, Ariz., 1988.

13. Archibald Hart, *Healing Life's Hidden Addictions* (Ann Arbor, Mich.: Servant Publications, 1990), 139.

14. Ibid., 141.

Part 4:
Thrice Born: Recovery From Codependence

Chapter 21

Pardon, Your Symptoms Are Showing

A few years ago, I found one of the best commentaries on codependent behavior I've ever seen in one of the least likely places—an airline magazine. It was a watch advertisement.

The scene is an airport runway at dawn. The aura is hazy and mysterious. Two men are standing near a small plane. They're wearing trenchcoats and looking highly suspicious. One of the men says, "My first mission was a tough one. A diplomatic problem in Moscow. I was briefed on the tarmac in Amsterdam. It was wet, windy, and daybreak. To my surprise, it was Davis who briefed me. He was a leader at this game. He'd been in and out of Cuba three times. And not for cigars.

"He told me the problem, and, eyeing my lone raincoat, left me with, 'By the way, it's twelve below zero in Moscow.' I had to respond, 'Let me tackle the diplomatic problem first. *I'll fix the weather later.*' "[1]

Mission impossible

Trying to do the impossible is the theme of the codependent's life. In order to satisfy his own unmet needs, he is compelled to control people, to manage circumstances—to "fix the weather." He wants to make everything nice for everyone. Why? So they will be pleased with him.

The official definition of codependence reflects this clearly:

"Codependence is a pattern of painful dependence on compulsive behavior and on approval to find safety, self-worth, and identity."[2]

Because the codependent was emotionally shortchanged in childhood, he is forever searching for that which he did not receive. He is an approval seeker. His self-worth is determined by what other people think of him. If they don't think what he wants them to think and say what he wants to hear and do what he wants them to do, he won't be OK. Because his good feelings are based on their opinion of him, he finds it necessary to control what they think.

He doesn't realize that it's impossible to control *anyone's* thoughts or behavior, least of all his own. Because he doesn't know he can't fix the weather, he makes a valiant attempt. He is like the person described in A.A. literature as the "actor who wants to run the whole show; is forever trying to arrange the lights, the ballet, the scenery and the rest of the players in his own way. If his arrangements would only stay put, if only people would do as he wished, the show would be great. Everybody, including himself, would be pleased. Life would be wonderful."[3]

When he doesn't get what he wants, the codependent digs his heels in a little deeper. He moves from one adaptive behavior to another in an effort to make things turn out the way he wants them to. He tries care giving, hoping that if he meets other people's needs, they will meet his. It worked fairly well once before; perhaps it will work again. In this endeavor, he is able to use his survival skills to great advantage. But there are so many needy people! He shifts into hyperdrive. Because he sees himself as taking care of everyone else, he has no idea that he is really controlling them to get his needs met.

In this process, he becomes a major people pleaser. Because he believes he won't be anybody until somebody loves him, he's got to make everyone love and appreciate him. He anticipates their wants and needs. He masters the art of making them happy. Everyone's wish is his command.

If he is in a relationship with someone who is an active addict, he controls by enabling. Most of his enabling is done out of a sincere desire to help his loved one. But his efforts are doomed to fail because no one can "save" an addict. With failure comes even lower self-esteem.

Another of the codependent's maneuvers is manipulation—getting others to do what he wants without their being aware of it. His manipulation can range from hinting and nagging to raging and weeping. He makes other people feel responsible for his physical and emotional ills. He sets them up to take care of him—to do his business. He takes without asking, which is extremely manipulative, whether the thing taken is a tangible item like a shirt or an intangible item like sympathy.

He whines, complains, shames, and scolds anyone who doesn't follow his script. "Why did you do it that way?" "Why don't you do it this way?" "Why didn't you listen to me?" He doesn't hear his *whys* as whining, but they are. He appeals to people's sympathy: "If you knew what I've been through, you wouldn't treat me this way." He blames: "My dad was an alcoholic, so you have to make allowances for me," or "My parents neglected me; therefore, you have to attend to my every need." He conveys the impression that it's your job to make him happy.

When shaming and blaming don't work, he moves on to demanding and commanding. He gives up on subtlety and takes direct control. He hands out orders. He becomes dictatorial and coercive. Perhaps if he acts powerful enough, people will succumb. If he is aggressive enough, he will make his point. If he is big enough (overinflated enough), no one will question him. Or if he is intellectual enough, he will win his case. He merely needs to sharpen his arguments, add a proof text or two, be a little more convincing. Thus he controls others by intimidation.

When every ploy has failed and he is completely exhausted, he sinks into self-pity. He retreats to lick his wounds. He isolates periodically to recoup his energy for another round. Meanwhile, he controls by obsessing, which is a way of managing the universe within the confines of his mind. He ruminates on his problems and mentally massages them over and over.

Throughout the entire process, he smiles incessantly and tries to look as if he's got it all together. When he has had time to reconnoiter, he sets out to repeat the cycle. He keeps doing the same thing over and over again, expecting different results, hoping it will work next time if he just does it a little better.

When his efforts to validate his worth by care giving, controlling, working, earning money, maintaining a relationship, raising children, making it to the top, managing his body image, establishing his position in society, or gaining God's approval fail, he considers his failure a crime punishable by death. He is likely at this point to attempt suicide.

Defining the problem

The defeated codependent has no idea that he is not a bad person who needs to get good, but rather a sick person who needs to get well. He has no idea that throughout his whole life he has been trying to do a grown-up's job with the coping skills of a small child. He has never learned to do life! No one taught him. He needs someone to take him by the hand and compassionately remind him that he is expecting mature behavior of an immature child. He needs to be told that he is not a failure.

He is, rather, a very brave, very persistent little kid who is anything *but* a failure, anything but a quitter. True, he needs guidance and direction, but it's OK to ask for it. Admitting that he doesn't know how to do it doesn't mean he's a failure. He can quit pretending, stop trying, let go, and accept defeat: "Only through utter defeat are we able to take our first steps toward liberation and strength. Our admissions of personal powerlessness finally turn out to be firm bedrock upon which happy and purposeful lives may be built."[4]

Some experts refer to codependence as a disease of relationships. If this is true, then the relationship that is most pathological is one's own relationship with himself. "The problem," says Pia Mellody, "is that who *you* are is unknown to you."[5]

Children who have been robbed of the opportunity to grow and mature never move beyond adolescence developmentally. According to Erickson's formulation of the Eight Stages of Man, the key task of adolescence is *identity development*. Because children of dysfunctional families are developmentally frozen at the point in their lives when their trauma became overwhelming (somewhere in early or middle childhood), they never complete adolescence and thus lack a well-formed identity.[6]

Erikson suggests that the primary task of early *adulthood* is intimacy. A person's ability to be intimate is based on his awareness of self (his identity). Adult/children lack identity because they are stuck in childhood, unable to move into adolescence. A codependent's capacity to be intimate is sabotaged from day one because he has not completed the identity stage of human development.

If I don't have an identity, I can't bring myself to the party. If I've been cut off from essential parts of my being, how can I be present in a relationship? If I don't know who I am, how can I tell you who I am? If I don't have a self, how can I give of myself to another? And if I can't present a reasonably mature, reasonably authentic self to my fellows, how can I expect to find intimacy?

The codependent in relationships

As I have indicated, codependents play childhood roles that become their undoing in adulthood. Some of these roles have been identified by Earnie Larsen.[7] I present them here with my own modifications.

The care giver and the baby. Many adult care givers played the hero role in childhood, and they still get their self-esteem from taking care of people. They have an almost inborn sense of obligation. They feel they must earn the right to exist. Care givers attract needy, helpless people and form permanent relationships with them.

Babies, on the other hand, grow up believing that if they don't want to do anything, they really don't have to—somebody else will. They have an inborn sense of entitlement. In adulthood, the baby is attracted to people who will take care of or parent him/her. Care givers marry babies. They go out of their way to find each other.

The victim and the abuser. Victims come in two forms: the martyr and the people pleaser. People pleasers get their self-esteem from making other people happy. They have an inborn gift of adaptability. They adjust to whatever the situation demands. They never defend their rights; in fact, they have no rights to defend. The people pleaser's greatest fear is abandonment, and he will do anything to avoid it.

Martyrs get their self-esteem from self-sacrifice. According to Larsen, martyrs glory in pain and disappointment and take pride in being able to endure more than anyone else.[8]

The abuser learns early in life that whenever something isn't going his way, all he has to do is get verbally or physically violent. Abusers get their self-esteem from intimidating and controlling others. They rarely apologize or offer encouragement. Of course, they marry people pleasers and martyrs.

The pressure cooker and the deadpan. The deadpan guards his self-esteem by avoiding emotional reaction. He keeps his cool while everyone around him goes crazy, and then he stands back and feels superior. He prides himself in not caring and in not being affected by "normal" feelings.

The pressure cooker is the counterpart to the deadpan. While the deadpan is busy avoiding emotional responsibility, the pressure cooker is internalizing the deadpan's unexpressed feelings (which he *assumes* are his feelings—mind reading is one of his talents). When he gets overwhelmed, he blows up. He is actually carrying both his own and his partner's feelings. When he explodes, his even-tempered partner feels superior because she doesn't stoop to such "childish" behavior.

The pursuer and the avoider. This dyad involves a "tap dancer" with a love addict in hot pursuit. The pursuer is willing to do anything to gain the eternal love of the noncommittal partner. And the tap dancer is carefully cataloging his partner's faults so he will have an excuse to leave whenever he wants to, blaming his departure on a flaw in the other, who dutifully carries the guilt. Many married couples do this dance within their relationship, one seeking affirmation and affection and the other withholding warmth and intimacy.

The perfectionist and the slob. The perfectionist measures his worth by the quality of his performance. His self-image is based on being perfect. He is never satisfied with himself or anyone else. This means that almost anyone will do as a partner, because no matter how good the partner is, the perfectionist will consider that person a slob in order to maintain his own illusion of superiority.

Sick attracts sick

Based on the above systems, it would appear that almost all relationships are dysfunctional. In the words of the inimitable Earnie Larsen, "Sick attracts sick and healthy attracts healthy."[9] Sick does not attract healthy.

Unwittingly, codependents choose partners whose symptoms are the perfect counterpart of their own. Then they proceed to make beautiful music together. Would that it were so! Instead, they enmesh like gears and grind away, thus enabling each other to grow sicker and sicker! All the while, each blames the other for his or her faults. Many relationships are more about addiction and codependence than they are about love. Yet there is hope for any relationship, if the partners are willing to take responsibility for recovery.

One expert says that addictive diseases have the power of death over their victims.[10] I believe that is correct. The tragedy is not so much that people die physically from these diseases. The tragedy is that they only half-live. Recovery is a process of growing up, of coming alive again—the rebirth spoken of in Scripture! Perhaps "becoming as little children" is our acceptance of an unchangeable reality: we are all immature children in adult bodies. And we must be changed, born again.

That's what recovery is all about!

---

1. Bulova watch advertisement, *Korean Airlines Magazine*, April 1990.

2. Panel of experts, First National Conference on Codependency, Scottsdale, Ariz., August 1989.

3. *Alcoholics Anonymous*, 3rd ed. (New York: Alcoholics Anonymous World Services, Inc., 1976), 60, 61.

4. *Twelve Steps and Twelve Traditions* (New York: The A.A. Grapevine, Inc./Alcoholics Anonymous World Services, Inc., 1953), 21.

5. Pia Mellody, "Codependence: An Overview," videotape from Mellody Enterprises, Wickenburg, Ariz., 1989.

6. Ibid.

7. Earnie Larsen, "Life Beyond Addiction: Identifying Self-Defeating Learned Behaviors," videotape from Fuller Video, Minneapolis, Minn.

8. Ibid.

9. Ibid.

10. Fred Downing, "The Family Disease Workshop," videotape from Paradox Productions, 1984.

Chapter 22

Sanctified White-Knuckling

Christians who want to minister to alcoholics often make the mistake of assuming that the alcoholic's problem is lack of willpower. If he would just make up his mind to, he could quit. Since his willpower is obviously so weak, the well-meaning Christian volunteers to play bodyguard—to stand between the alcoholic and the liquor store and keep him from drinking. This is codependent care giving at its best.

Pastor Wheeler came to prayer meeting with just such a plan. A member of his church had telephoned to ask for help in overcoming his alcohol problem. The earnest clergyman was eager to be of service. He humbly solicited the prayers of the saints and proceeded to tell them all about the young man's problem (with no thought of the fact that he was violating his anonymity).

The pastor had given him a number of Bible texts that promised victory. He had introduced him to the Highest Power, Jesus Christ. He had gone to the young man's house and helped him get rid of his booze. Then he had set up a schedule to keep him busy so he wouldn't be tempted to drink. He intended to meet with him every morning for prayer, drive him to work, and pick him up after work so he wouldn't stop off at the bar.

The pastor asked those assembled to join him in claiming victory for the youth. Several members offered to assist in guarding him from evil. If enough people were willing to help, they could see that he was never left alone. Neither the pastor nor the members realized that they were unwittingly enabling the alcoholic. They were deluding themselves *and him* into thinking they could control his drinking and manage his life. That they meant well is undebatable. They simply did not know that they did not know how to help him.

Sincere Christians trying to minister to alcoholics and addicts are prone to oversimplify the problem. They think that special prayer, Bible study, a healthful diet, exercise, faith in God, etc., will cure alcoholism. Unfortunately, this kind of program will turn the alcoholic into a sanctified white-knuckler at best or push him toward suicide at worst.

When an alcoholic is "white-knuckling" it, he is controlling his drinking by chaining himself to the bedstead or hanging onto the arms of a chair until his knuckles turn white. *Sanctified* white-knuckling is basically the same thing, only the white-knuckler does it with a Bible under his arm. I do not say this irreverently.

The issue is that—converted or not—the drinker is codependent. He is irritable, irresponsible, insecure, immature. He has not dealt with the developmental deficits that set him up to drink or drug in the first place. The fact that he has accepted Christ does not compensate for his developmental deficits. Although abstinent, he is still immature. Take away the alcohol, and you have a dry drunk, with or without a Bible under his arm.

Many of the church's alcoholic "converts" end up sober but miserable while doggedly struggling to live happy, victorious Christian lives. They use religion like a drug—to mask their deeper problems. This is not likely to work. When the "born-again" alcoholic rebounds from his initial religious high, he will experience a painful low or depression that is very likely to precipitate relapse.

The alcoholic with a painful family history is rarely delivered of the dysfunctional attitudes, beliefs, and behaviors learned in childhood as readily as he is relieved of the urge to drink. It is fairly easy to put a cork in the bottle. But if his learned self-defeating behaviors are not addressed therapeutically, the addiction will return sooner or later, though perhaps in another form.

Codependence is not usually healed instantly. Conversion is

not a cure-all. The scars created in childhood remain. As indicated earlier, the hurt and damage of years gone by is not automatically voided when one is born again. Conversion does not cancel the consequences of childhood trauma and restore deficits in emotional development.

Years ago, when we first started working with addicts, we received applications for employment from several alcoholics who had experienced miracle cures—instant deliverance from the desire to drink. They were excited about their healing and anxious to help others like themselves. Invariably, we found them to be childish, immature, demanding, and irresponsible. They were sincere Christians, but they had never grown up. Their conversion may have removed their craving for alcohol, but it did not cure their immaturity.

Abstinence vs. sobriety

Glenn was a recovering Christian alcoholic from the Midwest. He and his wife had been clean and sober for some time. They had accepted Christ as their Saviour six years before and had not had a drink or drug since. They felt grateful for their sobriety and were quick to give God the glory. But they were not at all serene, and their four children looked absolutely miserable. Glenn described his situation in these words: "I feel as if I have been sitting on the lid of a garbage can with my alcoholism inside trying to get out. It's all I can do to keep the lid on. It takes all my energy just to keep from drinking. I want relief. I'm going to my first A.A. meeting tonight."

The newly converted alcoholic can't help but manifest addictive patterns of thought and behavior—"stinking thinking"—because in spite of his rebirth he is still an immature child in an adult body. He needs to grow up. A complete change is necessary. This doesn't happen randomly, magically, or even miraculously. It must be addressed specifically through therapy and twelve-step programs. Until he gets help, the alcoholic may practice abstinence; but sobriety, in the truest sense of the word, will elude him.

In his book *Dying for a Drink*, Dr. Anderson Spickard tells the story of a church revival during which the town drunk got saved. He became the personification of divine grace to the community, a testimony to the miracle-working power of God. He was "exhibit A" of what the church can do.

About a year after his conversion, the poor man had a slip and got drunk. His church was devastated. In their eagerness to salvage him, they offered him the standard solutions: study the Bible, go to prayer meeting, witness, etc. He followed their suggestions and didn't drink again—for three months. Then he had another slip.

Once more, he regained his sobriety and practiced abstinence for a period of time. Then he relapsed again. Gradually, as his relapses recurred, he moved from the front pew to the back of the church. Shame separated him from his brethren. One evening, in desperation, he came to a revival meeting, only to leave before it was over, commenting to someone on his way out the door, "There's only one way I'm ever going to quit drinking." And he went home, sealed the garage shut, got into his car, and started the engine.

Try harder, pray longer

The advice most well-meaning Christians offer for recovery from sin and addiction is to try harder to do the right thing. As already suggested, this kind of advice is based on the assumption that the alcoholic has willpower. He doesn't. His will was damaged or broken long ago, probably even before he picked up his first drink or drug.

When Christians counsel an addict to exercise his willpower, they're defeating their own purpose. As Gerald May points out, "Addiction is not something we can simply take care of by applying the proper remedy, for it is in the very nature of addiction to feed on our attempts to master it."[1] When the addict's attempts to master it fail, his faith in church and God may be badly shaken. Many a desperate alcoholic has prayed earnestly and tried harder and harder, only to fail and fail again.

A profound testimony to this effect came from a respected professional who is a recovering alcoholic. "I'm a third-generation Adventist," he said, "and I'm a third-generation alcoholic. You'll never know how hard I tried to quit drinking. When that didn't

222 NEVER GOOD ENOUGH

work, I *really* tried. And I drank again. Then I *really, really* tried. . . . But I drank again. Then I *really, really, really* tried."

When an addict or alcoholic exhausts the church's resources (prayer, claiming promises, exercising the will, giving his heart to the Lord, being filled with the Spirit, anointing and prayer, etc.) and nothing works, he comes to the conclusion that if God can't give him victory as he has been led to believe, then something must be terribly wrong with God, something must be terribly wrong with him, or those church members didn't know what they were talking about. In any case, it's hopeless.

Within a period of three months, I heard the tragic stories of three addicts from Adventist backgrounds who died by suicide while they were using the try-harder, pray-longer method. Each believed what the church had taught him—that if you pray earnestly enough and try hard enough, you will gain the victory.

Two of the three committed suicide the day after taking communion. They participated in one of the highest sacraments of the church, only to be overwhelmed with the compulsion to drink a few hours later. In despair, they decided that the only way to get right with God and stay right with Him was to repent and then kill themselves before they had a chance to sin again.

The church did its best, but it wasn't enough. I am not suggesting that God failed. Nor do I believe that those who lost their lives failed. They simply were not given the right kind of help at the right time. If anything, the *system* failed. Why? Because we were blind and did not see.

Perhaps these tragedies could be prevented if we in the church would humble ourselves and recognize that we don't have a corner on curing alcoholics. We don't have all the answers. Withdrawal from mind-altering substances creates a physical and emotional crisis—a kind of toxic psychosis—that laypeople are not equipped to deal with.

Addicts and alcoholics in withdrawal and early recovery need the guidance of physicians and other professionals as well as the support of recovering addicts who have been through what they're going through. For us as Christians to assume that we know the best way to cure alcoholics is a mark of our arrogance and a clear demonstration of our own addictive thinking.

Marsha was reared in a physically abusive home. She was battered by her churchgoing parents, who subjected their children routinely to abject abuse. Needless to say, she had trouble reconciling her parents' profession of faith with their behavior toward her.

In high school, she started drinking and drugging. Then she met a young Seventh-day Adventist boy who became her knight in shining armor. They married hastily. After their marriage, she was baptized into the church. It was quite an adjustment for Marsha, but she wanted to be able to worship with her husband and willingly swore off alcohol and drugs in order to become a member. In spite of her decision, however, the urge to drink and drug didn't disappear. She went to the pastor for help. Would it be OK for her to go to Alcoholics Anonymous? she asked.

It was his opinion, he said, that going to A.A. would be a violation of the text, "In Christ all things are made new." He had heard that A.A. members identify themselves as alcoholics and consider alcoholism an incurable disease. That, he believed, was a negation of the power of God. He advised her to depend completely on the Lord and get more involved in the church instead of going to A.A.

Ten years later, Marsha's drinking and drug use had escalated out of control. She and her husband were divorced. Her children had been removed from her custody because she was abusing them physically. And she was hospitalized for attempted suicide.

The caring church

I have mentioned four individuals whose addictions ended in tragedy. In each case, the help of the church was enlisted. And the church cared. But it wasn't enough to prevent the tragedy that ensued. These stories might have ended differently if the sufferers had been placed in a treatment center or gone to A.A. meetings. But lacking a knowledgeable network of Christians who could refer them to this kind of help, they lost everything.

In each case, the churches exhausted their repertoire of resources and never suggested professional care, with one exception. In that case, a church member suggested the addict seek professional treatment. But the addict, who was a physician, felt he could manage his own withdrawal. His refusal to accept help cost him his life.

Contrast such tragic loss with the case of a small church in Texas. In order to foster church growth, the pastor held a Revelation Seminar. A young couple read an announcement about the meetings and decided to attend. They were impressed with the message and the warmth and kindness of the church members. At the conclusion of the seminar, they accepted Christ and were baptized.

They failed to mention to their newfound church family that both of them had been deeply involved in drugs. They were sure that becoming Christians would relieve them of their addictions, and for a time it did. But after a while, the young man resumed his drug use. Noticing that he had stopped coming to church, one of the elders invited him to dinner and asked him what was wrong. Carlos told the truth. He was back on drugs.

Realizing that Carlos had a problem he wasn't qualified to handle, the elder called a treatment center and asked for advice. He was encouraged to bring the young man in for an assessment, and when it was determined that professional treatment would be necessary, the church raised the money to pay for it.

As soon as Carlos was admitted, the pastor and elder contacted his counselors to see if there was anything else they could do. When they were asked to participate in Alanon Family Groups in their local area so that they could relate to Carlos in a healthy way when he returned home, they did so willingly.

When Carlos's wife was invited to attend Family Week at the treatment center, the church covered her travel expenses. They sent cards and letters of encouragement. Throughout the months following his rehabilitation, the church offered support and nurturance—all under the guidance of professionals.

This is what I consider competent caring. The church had a knowledgeable network of members who were willing to refer people in trouble to agencies where they could be served appropriately. They didn't attempt to directly rescue Carlos or be his savior themselves. But by accessing viable resources, they were instrumental in saving his life.

Those who long to manifest the character of Christ to a dying world need a thorough understanding of addiction and compulsion if they are to offer viable support to the chemically dependent. As Ellen White puts it in *The Desire of Ages*, "The Saviour gave His precious life in order to establish a church *capable of caring* for sorrowful, tempted souls."[2]

God *has* provided the answer to addiction, and the principles *are* scriptural! But the practical implementation of those principles has been accomplished by people who were probably better prepared to put them to use than most Christians are: a group of alcoholics in Akron, Ohio, in 1935.

I believe that the members of Alcoholics Anonymous understand alcoholism *and* sin better than we do. They consider alcoholism a spiritual disease that requires a spiritual remedy. Their application of spiritual principles is so far beyond the practical Christianity of the average churchgoer that there is no comparison. We can learn from them if we are willing. But we may have to face our own addictions, admit our ignorance, and surrender our arrogance in order to become teachable.

----

1. Gerald G. May, *Addiction and Grace* (San Francisco: Harper & Row, 1988), 4.
2. Ellen White, *The Desire of Ages* (Mountain View, Calif.: Pacific Press, 1940), 640, emphasis supplied.

Chapter 23

Healing for Adult/Children of Pharisees and Publicans

Many children of fundamentalistic families have serious misconceptions of God. Yet their only hope for lasting recovery from addiction and codependence is first, to accept their powerlessness; second, to believe that a power greater than themselves can restore them to sanity; and third, to turn their will and their lives over to the care of God as they understand Him. Herein lies the problem: Turning one's will and life over to the care of God is difficult for people whose understanding of Him is actually a *misunderstanding*, as is the case with many adult/children of dysfunctional Christian homes.

The courage to change

Janelle's lineage was impeccable. Her great-grandparents were missionaries, and her grandfather was a preacher. Her mother was a conscientious Seventh-day Adventist until Janelle was four years old. Then everything changed. Her mother ran off with another man, and her father remarried and moved away. Janelle and her brother went to live with their grandparents. Whether their grandfather developed a mental disorder in his old age that would explain his subsequent behavior or whether he was a closet sex addict is unknown, but, in any case, he committed incest with Janelle.

As is often true with sexually abused children, the victim absorbed the perpetrator's shame. Janelle's grandfather acted shamelessly, and she bore his shame even though she had done no wrong. For years, she carried it deep within her. In order to medicate her pain and shame, she did what children who have been rendered precociously sexual do: she became a sex/love/relationship addict herself.

At fifteen, she was drawn to a teenage boy who seemed to love her. She got pregnant, and they were married before Janelle was sixteen. After the birth of their son, Janelle and her husband partied quite a bit, but eventually Janelle settled down and went back to church. Her husband continued to drink and drug. Feeling abandoned, Janelle drew closer and closer to God and church. Confident that Jesus was coming soon, she was determined to be ready for His return.

Divorced by this time, Janelle was a lonely young woman. In spite of her religious convictions, she became involved with a married man at church and began a secret affair. She would sneak away to spend time with him and then, crushed with guilt, promise herself never to see him again. But, try as she might, she could not stop. Her guilt was profound. In terms of values, she professed a high level of conservatism, which she was violating in her personal life. She was living two lives, and it became more and more difficult for her to hide her behavior from the people at church.

One weekend, hardly knowing where she was going, she stumbled into a Christian twelve-step group, where she was introduced to the possibility of recovery. She felt enormous relief. She started going to A.A. and CoDa (Codependence Anonymous) meetings. She explored the steps in the light of her beliefs and found them sound. She concluded that the principles of the twelve-step programs were harmonious with hers, although the groups used nonspecific terminology in referring to matters of God and faith.

Ultimately, Janelle admitted herself to a treatment program for dependency disorders, where she specifically addressed her relationship problem as an addictive disease and admitted that she was powerless over sex and alcohol. Because she had been sober for several years, Janelle did not realize that she was, in fact, an alcoholic.

She faced the full range of addictions and compulsions that were destroying her life. She realized that she could not find freedom through her religious beliefs alone. She had tried that, without success. She accepted the fact that if Bible study, prayer, a careful diet, hard work, and fellowship with loving Christians was going to get her sober, it would have done so by now. To her great relief, she discovered that with therapy and the support of twelve-step groups *plus* her church affiliation, she could keep her addictions in remission. Gradually her compulsions diminished. Today, by the grace of God, she is rejoicing in the Lord *and* in recovery—one day at a time.

What it takes

The process of recovery from codependence involves four things: therapeutic help to externalize long-repressed feelings; a maturing process that addresses developmental issues; an ongoing support system; and a spiritual awakening.

Therapy. The codependent's interests are best served if, at some point, he does therapeutic work. He needs to get rid of his backlog of pain and set his emotional system to functioning again. This gives him a real jump-start on recovery. In therapy, he can study the negative patterns in his family history and learn how he is contributing to their repetition in the present. Thus he will become aware of what specific attitudes, beliefs, and behaviors he needs to adjust in order to go about changing.

Codependents are out of touch with their feelings. They need to reconnect with their emotions and learn to experience and express them in healthy ways. They need to establish boundaries and learn to defend themselves. They are focused on people and things outside themselves. They need to learn to nurture and care for themselves. They need to identify normal human needs and give themselves permission to have needs and wants. And they need to learn how to take responsibility for getting their needs met appropriately.

Codependents cannot sustain appropriate levels of self-esteem. They need to develop identity and ego strength. They need to learn how to be interdependent as opposed to antidependent or codependent (being dependent on one relationship).[1]

Codepends don't have a database for normal behavior. They tend to act in the extreme. Without guidance, they will continue swinging from one extreme to the other. They need help in finding and practicing moderation. They need to examine their family system and social system for self-defeating messages and rethink their self-imposed rules and requirements. Much of their pain comes from unreasonable expectations. They try too hard to do the right thing, then get discouraged and give up. These critical lessons can be learned in therapy. The time, expense, and effort required are well spent—an investment in *life*.

Growing up. The second task of recovery is to find a family of choice within which the codependent can find nurturance and reparenting—people who will guide him through the process of maturation. His lack of development is an issue that must be specifically addressed. He cannot wish or pray himself to maturity.

The best person to serve the surrogate parent role is a sponsor. Sponsorship is provided in twelve-step groups. The sponsor and family of choice (recovering peers) are vital to the codependent's maturing process. They will love him until he can love himself. He will learn from them what is normal. They will give him the guidance he missed as a child.

The key is to find nurturance. Children from dysfunctional families live in an atmosphere of high stress and low nurturance. They need low stress and high nurturance in order to grow up. As the saying goes, it's never too late to have a happy childhood. Where recovery is concerned, the codependent must make it his job to find a family of choice who can give him the nurturance and guidance he needs.

Support system. The third component of recovery is a support system. One's support system must be carefully selected. The addict/codependent must find people who are qualified to address the specifics involved in his particular addiction. Such support is available in meetings like Codependence Anonymous; Sexaholics Anonymous, Sex/Love Addicts Anonymous, and CoSa or S-Anon (for people affected by someone else's sexual addiction); Incest Survivors Anonymous; Alcoholics Anonymous;

Narcotics Anonymous; Alanon or Naranon (for those affected by someone's chemical dependence); Emotions Anonymous; Gamblers Anonymous; Workaholics Anonymous; ACOA (for adult/children of alcoholic or dysfunctional families); Overeaters Anonymous, etc.

In most communities, information about these groups can be obtained through Alcoholics Anonymous, through a local hospital or drug treatment center, and through physicians and counselors. A list of addresses and phone numbers for the national headquarters of these organizations is provided in the Appendix.

The recovering person's relationship to his church is an important issue also. The spiritual guidance and support of fellow believers can be a real blessing. It is worthwhile to maintain these relationships if possible. For one who has suffered a great deal of spiritual abuse, however, this may be difficult. When the codependent has progressed to the point that he has developed good boundaries and feels he is ready, a reconciliation with his religious heritage is desirable.

Church relationships do not duplicate or replace twelve-step groups. The recovering Christian needs both. Many individuals find God for the first time in twelve-step programs and then rush into church affiliation, replacing their twelve-step association with church activities. This may or may not work, in terms of the person's staying sober from his primary addiction. Without the support and guidance of twelve-step programs, he will remain at a disadvantage emotionally and socially.

Some churches offer twelve-step study groups during Sabbath School. These are not official twelve-step meetings (unless they are based on the twelve traditions of A.A.), but they can be a meaningful option for church members who need ongoing support. Many are glad to find such meetings available at church on Sabbath morning. It is wonderful to be able to celebrate one's recovery and his love for God and Scripture at the same time.

Spiritual awakening. Because of the nature of addictive diseases, I believe the most effective way for any addict to achieve a healthy recovery and a genuine spiritual awakening is through the twelve-step program of Alcoholics Anonymous and related groups. These steps encompass the gospel as most Christians understand it. In fact, they promote Christian principles in a more explicit and practical way than most of us have previously known.

My personal Christian experience, prior to my affiliation with twelve-step programs, was basically composed of the third step (conversion) and the twelfth step (witnessing). I tried to hang a heavy disease on these two steps. I've had much greater success in my Christian life and in my recovery since I learned to practice all twelve steps.

The practical principles taught in twelve-step programs have been extremely useful to me. Being able to discuss ideas like *detachment, powerlessness, anonymity, acceptance, humility, honesty, open-mindedness,* and *willingness* at twelve-step meetings has been very helpful to me. As a result, I have found greater intimacy with God and my friends and family. That is a spiritual awakening at its best.

Preserve life

Many Christians are afraid to access professional services and twelve-step groups. They know they are in deep difficulty with their addictions and compulsions—they may even realize they're dying. But they are afraid their beliefs will be compromised if they reach out for help.

This is an issue of priorities. I heard recently of a newborn child who had been taken to the hospital with a dangerously low hemoglobin count. A diagnosis had not yet been made, but there was a possibility that the baby would need a transfusion. His parents were afraid to consent to a transfusion because of the risk of AIDS. When they asked a nurse friend for advice, she told them this: "Preserve life. There may be risks, but the risk of not giving the baby the transfusion is greater than the risk of giving it. Your first concern is to preserve life."

I received a call some months ago from a man who had heard me on a radio talk show. He was dying of codependence and wanted to speak to a Christian counselor. He told me he needed professional help but was afraid to go to a treatment center or twelve-step group because he was not sure what level of spirituality he would find there. Whatever level of spirituality *he* was at, he was dying! I told him to preserve life.

When someone is actively suicidal, when he is on the verge of major loss, when his health or the well-being of his family is at stake, preserve life! Worry about theology later. I understand the fear many Christians have. But I do believe God's healing power is present in any place where viable efforts are being made to preserve life.

The twelve steps to life

There's a line in the foreword to the *Twelve Steps and Twelve Traditions* (the official handbook of Alcoholics Anonymous) that suggests that the steps are a group of principles—spiritual in their nature. If practiced as a way of life, it says, these steps can expel obsession and enable people with compulsions and addictions to become happily and usefully whole.[2] The twelve steps are parallel to the gospel as I understand it.

Step one—Acknowledging our need. "We admitted we were powerless over [alcohol, sex, tobacco, etc.], that our lives had become unmanageable." Deliverance from compulsivity and restoration to intimacy with God and those we love begins with acknowledging our need of help. When one has tried as hard as he can for as long as he can and his best efforts have failed, he is ready to take this step. It is painful to admit defeat, but it is also a relief. One's admission of personal powerlessness is the foundation upon which recovery is built.

Step two—Faith. "Came to believe that a power greater than ourselves could restore us to sanity." Having admitted defeat, having recognized his powerlessness, the addict has no alternative but to place his faith in a Power greater than himself. His thinking is dominated by a lifetime of dysfunctional attitudes and beliefs. He can't trust his own "board of directors." He must seek a Power outside himself and greater than himself if he is to recover.

Step three—Surrender. "Made a decision to turn our will and our lives over to the care of God as we understood Him." This step suggests that the addict/alcoholic/codependent make a decision to turn his will and his life over to the care of God as he understands Him. Most professing Christians can relate to this step very well in theory. We cut our eyeteeth on phrases like "surrender of the will." But we are past masters at going through the motions of surrender and then acting as if we were in control.

The first three steps are summarized beautifully in *The Desire of Ages*: "The Lord can do nothing toward the *recovery* of man until, convinced of his own weakness, and stripped of all self-sufficiency, he yields himself to the control of God. . . . From the soul that feels his need, nothing is withheld."[3]

Step four—Soul searching. "Made a searching and fearless moral inventory of ourselves." Until now, he may have been convinced that his troubles were caused by other people or circumstances. Now he takes an honest look at his assets and liabilities. His compulsivity has kept him from seeing the truth about himself. If his life is to change, that change must begin with a realistic self-appraisal. The fourth step promotes self-knowledge. It cuts through denial and delusion and arrives at the truth. The purpose of such self-examination is to identify any aspects of one's behavior that might interfere with recovery.

Step five—Confession. "Admitted to God, to ourselves, and to another human being the exact nature of our wrongs." In this step the addict lets go of the secrets that have kept him sick. He reveals the truth about himself, exposes the darkest areas of his life, and in so doing, discovers that he is still loved and accepted. Admitting one's deficiencies to another human being is a humbling experience, but very beneficial. The fifth step gives one a sense of belonging he may have never felt before. It allows him to burn the bridges between his old, sick behavior and a new way of life.

Step six—Willingness. "Were entirely ready to have God remove all these defects of character." Having completed his moral inventory, the recovering Christian is acutely aware of his defects of character, no longer in generic terms, but in specific detail. He recognizes how he has been at fault in many past life situations and what his negative patterns of behavior are. When he admits these flaws aloud to another human being, he can no longer deny their existence. He thus makes himself accountable.

As willing as he may be to change, though, he is still powerless.

His character defects are an intrinsic part of his defense system. They have served a purpose. At a given point, they kept him alive. Giving up these defenses leaves the codependent feeling exposed, vulnerable. The only thing more painful and difficult than giving them up is keeping them.

Step seven—Transformation. "Humbly asked Him to remove our shortcomings." If one is not humble before he begins this step, he will be before he finishes. Having asked God to remove his defects of character, his behavior seems to get *worse* instead of better. How can this be? It only *seems* worse because he is more aware than he was before. He is thoroughly disgusted by his behavior. His sense of powerlessness is heightened. Now he knows for certain that he is beyond human aid!

Step eight—Contrition. Steps eight and nine are among the most important. Step eight says, "Made a list of all persons we had harmed, and became willing to make amends to them all." It is almost impossible, before step eight, for the addict to acknowledge the enormity of his crimes. However, at this point, his denial and delusion have dropped away. He has recognized his excuses and rationalizations for what they are. He can admit the harm he has done without hating himself. He has cast aside the habit of holding grudges and blaming others. He is prepared to be honest and humble as he approaches the ninth step.

Step nine—Restitution/reconciliation. It's time to put the past to rest. Step nine reads, "Made direct amends to such people except when to do so would injure them or others." Making amends is much more than just delivering a casual apology. We literally "mend" or set right the wrong we have done. We are prepared to accept the consequences of our actions, to pay the price, to make restitution. Says Bill Wilson, the founding member of Alcoholics Anonymous: "The readiness to take full consequences of our past acts, and to take responsibility for the well-being of others at the same time, is the very spirit of Step Nine."[4]

Step ten—Accountability. "Continued to take personal inventory, and when we were wrong, promptly admitted it." This is an instant awareness and a willing admission of our wrongdoing, along with a correcting of our errors—immediately. We are no longer afraid to make mistakes. Being human, we will err.

As long as we remain willing to admit our faults and correct them promptly, we can risk being imperfect. This is a great relief!

Step eleven—Prayer and meditation. "Sought through prayer and meditation to improve our conscious contact with God as we understood Him, praying only for a knowledge of His will for us and the power to carry that out." The combination of self-examination, meditation, and prayer creates an unshakable foundation for life.[5] The soul-searching involved in the earlier steps has shown up the negative side of our natures. "Meditation is our step out into the sun."[6] And what a glorious step it is!

In praying, we simply ask God that throughout that day He place within us the best understanding of His will that He can, and that He grant us the grace by which to carry out His will. Other than that, we ask for nothing.

Step twelve—Witnessing. "Having had a spiritual awakening as a result of these steps, we tried to carry this message to alcoholics, and to practice these principles in all our affairs." Step twelve assures us that, as a result of practicing the other eleven steps, we will experience a spiritual awakening. Some who are unfamiliar with the program of Alcoholics Anonymous hesitate to involve themselves in twelve-step organizations because they believe the groups' use of the term *Higher Power* is too nebulous. Actually, the flexibility that A.A. practices in defining God is one of the strongest points of the program.

Those who have experienced spiritual abuse face major barriers in achieving a positive concept of God. They have grave doubts about Him. They no longer believe in Him. They don't trust Him. To be receptive to God as they previously understood Him is virtually impossible. Such individuals often find it necessary to simply find *a* power outside themselves. Unless they find such a power, they will be limited to their own mental resources; and as long as they consult themselves alone, they will receive skewed information.

Many such individuals use the group itself as a higher power—not as a supreme being, but as an alternative to their own distorted thinking. They do not consider the group a divine entity, but rather a source of wisdom and guidance that is more trustworthy than their own thinking. The Bible supports this in teaching that there is "wisdom in the counsel of numbers."

Generally, according to A.A. literature, by the time a recovering person reaches step twelve, whatever his history and whatever his doubts, he will "love God and call Him by name."[7] He then achieves great satisfaction in carrying A.A.'s message to other suffering people, in sharing his own experience, strength, and hope. "This is Twelfth Step work in the very best sense of the word. 'Freely ye have received; freely give.' "[8]

The process of recovery from codependence and other compulsions usually requires three to five years. From the very beginning, there is significant relief. Life keeps getting better and better, one day at a time. But it must be emphasized that the process is just that: a process, *not an event*. There are no home remedies. Reading a book will not bring healing. Knowledge, according to Terry Kellogg, only makes one a more informed prisoner. As addicts, we are beyond human aid. But, by the grace of God and with the help of other people, recovery is possible.

---

1. Pia Mellody, "Overview of Codependency," audiotape from Mellody Enterprises, Wickenberg, Ariz., 1988.

2. *Twelve Steps and Twelve Traditions* (New York: The A.A. Grapevine, Inc./ Alcoholics Anonymous World Services, Inc., 1953), 15.

3. Ellen White, *The Desire of Ages* (Mountain View, Calif.: Pacific Press, 1940), 300, emphasis supplied.

4. *Twelve Steps and Twelve Traditions*, 87.

5. Ibid., 98.

6. Ibid.

7. Ibid., 109.

8. Ibid., 110.

Chapter 24

When the Holy Spirit Came to Akron

One fateful day in 1935, a desperate alcoholic from New York City was inexorably drawn toward a hotel barroom in Akron, Ohio, when his feet turned instead to a church directory in the lobby. These few steps, not too dramatic in themselves, led to the formation of a movement that has become the means of saving millions of alcoholics all over the world.

Frantic with the realization that he was about to get drunk again after nearly three months of sobriety, Bill Wilson, a stockbroker who was in Akron on business, called an Episcopal minister on the phone. He reasoned that he might be able to keep himself from drinking if only he could talk to another drunk. He called the minister for a "referral."

Wilson had joined an "Oxford Group" in New York because he had been inspired by the example of an alcoholic friend who had gotten sober by getting "religious." (The Oxford Group was a Christian revival organization that specialized in helping people with "unwholesome" lifestyles.[1]) He immediately had a spiritual experience. The miracle occurred during his final stay on a drunk ward in the hospital. He was a regular patient at the hospital, and he was tired of it. So in desperation he cried out, "God, I'm willing to do anything—*anything*!"[2]

In his own words, "I humbly offered myself to God, as I then understood Him, to do with me as He would. I placed myself under His care and direction. I admitted for the first time that of myself I was nothing; that without Him I was lost. I ruthlessly faced my sins and became willing to have my new-found Friend take them away, root and branch. I have not had a drink since."³

Immediately Bill went to work helping other drunks. Although strikingly unsuccessful in his efforts, Wilson *himself* managed to stay dry. In the process, he came to appreciate the powerful potential of one drunk talking to another, which became the basis for A.A.'s ongoing "twelfth-step work," or "carrying the message."

But on that fateful Saturday in Akron, Wilson was intent on only one thing: saving himself. A stranger to the community, he fled the sound of laughter coming from the bar in the Mayflower Hotel and began what has become part of A.A.'s unwritten tradition: "Before you pick up a drink, pick up the phone."

The Episcopal minister gave Bill the telephone numbers of about ten Oxford Group members in Akron. The last call he made netted the desired result. He was told to call a woman by the name of Henrietta Seiberling. To her, Bill introduced himself with these words: "I'm from the Oxford Group, and I'm a rum hound from New York."⁴

Mrs. Seiberling became the link between Bill Wilson and the man who was to become the co-founder of Alcoholics Anonymous, Dr. Robert Holbrook Smith. On the verge of professional ruin because of his drinking, Dr. Smith was Henrietta's "pet project." Having failed until now to help him, she saw the call from Bill Wilson as an opportunity to try once again to straighten out the good doctor, whose practice and reputation were being rapidly ruined by his out-of-control drinking. Convinced that Divine Providence had sent the New Yorker to help Dr. Bob, Henrietta hosted their first meeting on May 11, 1935.

Smith was not pleased by her invitation, but he condescended to allow Bill fifteen minutes of his time. The two men went into Henrietta's library and spent almost six hours in conversation. There, quite accidentally, they stumbled upon the time-honored formula that has proven successful as a means of healing from that day till this: the process of one person telling his story to another with honesty and candor. They shared the fellowship of common suffering.

Bill Wilson had a long and painful drinking history, as did Dr. Bob. Both men had enormous potential in terms of talent and training, but neither had achieved the greatness to which he aspired. And both had sacrificed their vocational, financial, and social status to alcohol. Each of them were "absolutely licked," as they later described it.

Bill was relieved of the compulsion to drink by a combination of three things: a personal spiritual experience obtained through his contact with the Oxford Groups, the medical help of a neurologist at Towns Hospital from whom he learned the grave nature of alcoholism, and his own ministry to alcoholics like himself. Wilson joined his personal testimony together with the best medical knowledge and the most effective spiritual approaches then available. With this combination he created a system that is still widely acknowledged by people of science and religion as one of the most powerful social forces in human history, one that has brought renewed life to more people than any other.

The Oxford Groups of Bill Wilson's time, and from thence the early support groups that he and Dr. Bob formed, operated in the style and manner of New Testament Christians. Their goal was spiritual renewal. They reached out to those who were broken in spirit. Their key principles were surrender, restitution, and sharing.[5]

Their base of operations was private homes, where they met together to pray, study, and share personal experiences. The simple tenets of the Oxford Groups were complete deflation of false pride, dependence on a Higher Power for guidance, soul-searching, confession, restitution, and ministry to other suffering persons.[6]

Once he had been rescued from the gutter, Wilson launched a crusade to rescue others like himself. He was determined to "save every alcoholic in sight."[7] He set out with evangelistic fervor to feed and house as many as possible at his home in Brooklyn. But he met with little success. The drunks he tried to save didn't appreciate his high-pressure tactics. Bill simply overdid it, as he reported later: "Lois and I continued to find that if we permitted alcoholics to become too dependent on us they were apt to stay drunk."[8] The fact that he became codependent to his first converts is not surprising, since anyone with an addictive personality tends to overdo whatever he does.

In Akron, Bill spent almost a month in continuous dialogue with Dr. Bob, until he, too, gained sobriety. Then, together they canvassed Akron hospitals for other alcoholics with whom they could share their secret. One of their candidates was a lawyer who was a violent, late-stage alcoholic. He became their first convert and the third alcoholic to join their association, counting themselves. That is how Alcoholics Anonymous began. In its first four years it attracted only a hundred members, but it grew to over 150,000 within twenty years, to over a million within forty years, and to more than two million today (1993). Bill and Bob literally lighted "the spark that was to flare into the first A.A. group."[9]

Initially, the fellowship met in private homes, where the wives of alcoholics waited patiently while their husbands stood over the "new recruit" kneeling in the bedroom above, listening to his "litany of drunken sins and his plea for redemption."[10] The early members shared what they had with one another, much as the early Christians of Acts 1 to 3.

Eventually the A.A. groups departed from the Oxford movement because of its aggressive tactics. Wilson had learned through painful experience that drinkers did not yield to pressure in any form. They had to be led, not pushed.[11] Wilson was also concerned about the political bent of the Oxford movement, which proved ultimately to be its undoing. He was wise. Distancing A.A. from religious and political movements and taking a position of neutrality made the program palatable to more people. He widened the gateway "so that all who suffer might pass through."[12]

However, the Oxford movement did create the spiritual climate in which A.A. managed to survive and grow.[13] As Wilson himself stated, "Early A.A. got its ideas of self-examination, acknowledgment of character defects, restitution for harm done, and working with others straight from the Oxford Groups."[14] It was a valuable heritage.

Bill Wilson's viability is questioned in some religious quarters because he was imperfect. He was described in one recent Christian publication as "unredeemed," a judgmental term which both surprised and distressed me. Today Wilson would probably be diagnosed as an alcoholic and a victim of mild chronic depression, and he would certainly be considered codependent. Wilson himself alluded to codependent behavior in an article published in the *Grapevine* (an A.A. periodical) in 1958, although he did not label it *codependence*.

In that article, entitled "Emotional Sobriety," he made reference to the lack of real maturity and balance and the adolescent urges that he considered characteristic of alcoholics. For all practical purposes, he was describing codependence. "Since A.A. began," he said, "I've taken immense wallops in all these areas because of my failure to grow up emotionally and spiritually."[15] This certainly fits our understanding of codependence. The symptoms of codependence are described but unlabeled on page 53 of the *Twelve Steps and Twelve Traditions*.

Bill admitted that he had a "basic flaw," which he called "dependence—almost absolute dependence—on people or circumstances to supply me with prestige, security, and the like."[16] Bill was probably what we would call a relationship addict, an approval seeker, a controller and manipulator—in other words, a codependent.

Even in his weakness, however, Bill was an effective witness to other alcoholics. As one of them stated: "As a failed human being, I couldn't stand it if I thought Bill hadn't failed. I couldn't live up to a perfect example."[17] Herein lies an important principle: People "buy" the message best from those they perceive to be like themselves.

Perhaps that is why some Christians have a favorite Bible character—they identify with his weaknesses. Many heroes of Scripture that we hold up as models of inspiration were fallible human beings who were grave sinners. Please note that I am not putting Wilson on a par with the authors of the Bible. Like Wilson, however, many of them would qualify for the diagnosis of codependence. Yet we do not question their contribution to the Faith. Nor can I find it within myself to question Wilson's.

Composing the Twelve Steps

With wisdom, tact, insight, and (I believe) the guidance of

the Holy Spirit, Bill began formulating the Twelve Steps in 1938. They were drawn from the original core beliefs of the Oxford program: "Unconditional surrender of the human will to the will of God; taking a personal moral inventory; confessing ('sharing') before other members; making amends to people whom a member had harmed, and working with others who needed help, willingly and without thought of financial reward."[18]

Until 1938, A.A.'s version of these principles read: "(1) We admitted that we were licked, that we were powerless over alcohol. (2) We made a moral inventory of our defects or sins. (3) We confessed or shared our shortcomings with another person in confidence. (4) We made restitution to all those we had harmed by our drinking. (5) We tried to help other alcoholics, with no thought of reward in money or prestige. And (6) we prayed to whatever God we thought there was for power to practice these precepts."[19]

In order to make them more explicit, Wilson decided to expand the six principles. He did not want to leave a "single loophole through which the rationalizing alcoholic could wiggle out."[20] Not knowing how many steps he would create, Bill prayed for guidance and began to write. When finished, he numbered his new version of the steps and was gratified to discover that they totalled the same number as the number of Christ's apostles.[21]

Wilson's wording of the steps has been altered very little, although they were passed around among the existing membership for some time and debated over hotly before they were published. In the end, a few minor changes were made in order to avoid offending agnostics, atheists, Catholics, or Episcopalians.[22]

Keeping their primary purpose ever in mind (to minister to the greatest number of alcoholics possible), Bill and his cohorts used language that would be acceptable to a wide range of people from a variety of backgrounds. This, it seems to me, makes great good sense. Bill deliberately used generic spiritual language rather than religious or psychological terms in order to strike a balance that would open A.A. up to anyone who needed help.[23]

This may be one of the most effective features of the program of Alcoholics Anonymous. There is no dogma. A.A. membership is available to anyone who has an honest desire to stop drinking. Perhaps the fellowship of the church would be more appealing to non-Christians if we would realize that the desire to stop sinning ("go and sin no more") is the only qualification for membership in God's family!

Bill's purpose in writing the steps and the "Big Book" was to show other alcoholics precisely how they (the first hundred or so alcoholics) recovered.[24] In so doing, he followed the advice of his beloved peer, Dr. Bob, who said, "Let's not louse this thing up, Bill, let's keep it simple."

By way of testimony, a prominent minister wrote these words about the steps: "I became aware of the true significance of the Twelve Steps, not as stages to sobriety, but rather as directives to living. They became a way of life—guidelines to a good life, a full life, a wholesome life, a well balanced life, a mature life, a healthy life, and, therefore, a happy life."[25]

When I first became involved in twelve-step programs, I felt uneasy. My religious background was such that I was actually a trifle paranoid. I was afraid my faith would be compromised. This is embarrassing to admit, but it is true. However, after careful study, I became convinced that the twelve steps were synonymous with the principles of Scripture that I had always valued. I found that the practice of the steps enhanced my Christian experience.

Before long I noticed that going to twelve-step groups seemed to meet a need within me that my church affiliation did not. I assumed (incorrectly) that something was wrong either with my church or with me. Eventually I realized that nothing was wrong with either of us. It is just not possible for anyone to get all of his needs met in one place, nor is it necessary. Much as I appreciate one supermarket for the quality of its produce and another for its lower prices, I value the contributions that both church and twelve-step programs have made to my sanity, my serenity, and my salvation.

In church, I find people whose beliefs and doctrines are the same as mine. Our view of the future is similar. We share a common hope and a common heritage. This is reassuring. I enjoy discussing doctrines and reminiscing about the pioneers of the church, among them my grandparents. It is meaningful to belong to a group of people with common goals, a common mission, shared traditions, rituals, and sacraments.

Both in church *and* in twelve-step meetings, I find genuine fellowship. I am very comfortable with the basic Christian principles practiced in both places. And I am inspired by the dedication of the people who are involved in both groups. I admire their willingness to go to any lengths to achieve their life-saving objectives.

Just as there are certain blessings that are unique to my church affiliation, I find unique blessings in twelve-step groups. I appreciate the fact that they practice simple, specific spiritual principles in a strategic manner. The concreteness and simplicity of the twelve steps appeal to me. I am especially grateful for the unwritten rule of twelve-step fellowships that directs each person to do his own moral inventory and no one else's.

I consider the tradition of anonymity that disallows the practice of gossip and criticism to be one of the strongest and most winsome features of the whole program. Another outstanding feature of twelve-step groups is their noncondemning spirit, whereby even those who fail are encouraged to "keep coming back" because "it gets better." The concept that the growth of any twelve-step organization is based on the principle of attraction rather than promotion is also a unique and valuable feature.

Not unlike many glorious movements in the history of the church, the A.A. movement began with a group of committed people who had a vision. As Bill Wilson said in one of his final addresses to the thousands of alcoholics attending A.A.'s twentieth anniversary convention, "It has become almost literally true that where two or three of us are gathered together in His name, there a group will form."[26] And, not unlike the humble beginnings of many Christian organizations that have been enormously successful, "What once looked like a mighty poor acorn has produced a great oak."[27]

How can we say anything but "Praise the Lord"?

1. Robert Hemfelt and Richard Fowler, *Serenity: A Companion for Twelve Step Recovery* (Nashville: Thomas Nelson Inc., 1990), 16.

2. *Alcoholics Anonymous Comes of Age* (New York: Alcoholics Anonymous World Services Inc., 1957), 63.

3. *Alcoholics Anonymous*, 3rd ed. (New York: Alcoholics Anonymous World Services Inc., 1976), 13.

4. Nan Robertson, *Getting Better, Inside Alcoholics Anonymous* (New York: William Morrow and Co., 1988), 31.

5. Hemfelt and Fowler, 17.

6. Ibid., 19.

7. Robertson, 45.

8. *A.A. Comes of Age*, 74.

9. *Alcoholics Anonymous*, xv.

10. Robertson, 21.

11. *A.A. Comes of Age*, 74.

12. Ibid., 167.

13. Ibid., 40.

14. Ibid., 39.

15. Bill Wilson, "The Next Frontier: Emotional Sobriety," *The A.A. Grapevine*, January 1958.

16. Ibid.

17. Robertson, 36.

18. Robertson, 58.

19. *A.A. Comes of Age*, 160.

20. Ibid.

21. Ibid.

22. Robertson, 70.

23. *A.A. Comes of Age*, 17.

24. *Alcoholics Anonymous*, xiii.

25. *Emotions Anonymous* (St. Paul: Emotions Anonymous International, 1978), 13.

26. *A.A. Comes of Age*, 82.

27. Ibid., 88.

Chapter 25

Rejoicing in the Lord *and* in Recovery

In examining my history, I can see signs of codependence as far back as early childhood. My first noticeable symptoms were rescuing and caretaking. I was a competent care giver by the time I started school, when I began consciously defending the "underdog" (classmates being picked on by peers). I have always been attracted to such people, which is a clear indication of how I viewed myself.

I began to feel "less-than" when I was in the first grade. I was the youngest child in my classroom, and I compared myself unfavorably to my schoolmates. I couldn't do what was expected of me. I wept over my assignments, and I was anxious all the time. It was too much for a child who was barely five years old, but I didn't give up. I tried harder.

By the time I was in the third grade, I had forged ahead of my peers. For this reason, my parents and teacher made a well-intended decision to advance me to the fifth grade, thinking they were doing me a favor. They didn't know that in so doing they were abusing me socially and intellectually.

Now I was almost *two* years younger than the other students in my class. This remained true for the rest of my educational experience, and I always felt inadequate and isolated. Being a tiny eight-year-old in the fifth grade, I was inept at athletics and was always picked last for team sports. I had to find a way to compensate in order to feel worthwhile. I chose the ego booster that was most readily available: achievement.

When I got A's, my parents were pleased. Their pride in my

accomplishments made me feel good. The strokes I received encouraged me to take on more difficult academic challenges. I began to drive myself. When I was praised for my achievements, I got a shot of self-esteem. When that "fix" wore off, I began striving for another impossible goal. That has been the story of my life.

I graduated from the eighth grade when I was barely twelve and went to boarding academy. Once again, I struggled to find acceptance among my peers. After my sophomore year in academy, I started taking college classes. When I enrolled in Emmanuel Missionary College two years later, I registered as a sophomore. First semester, I took an upper division religion class that was so philosophical I couldn't wrap my sixteen-year-old mind around it. I dropped the class and was depressed for the rest of the school year because I felt that I had failed. Two years later I received my B.A. degree.

Barely nineteen and afraid to face life on my own, I married a young man who was an achievement addict like myself and the adult/child of a dysfunctional family as well. Our wedding was on graduation day—not a day or even a week later.

By now my drivenness was apparent. Within a week, I started graduate school. For the next several years, I rushed from one project to another, fighting to find meaning and self-esteem, never quite satisfied, always pushing myself to achieve one more thing. For some time, this behavior was gratifying. As long as I got my "fix," I was satisfied.

Our eldest son was born when I was twenty-one, and within a short time I was back in school, working a part-time job, being a full-time mother, and supporting my husband in his pastoral ministry. Not six months after our second son was born, it all caught up with me. I began to experience severe mood swings— the inevitable consequence of behavior in the extreme.

Depression was stalking me, and I was on the run. I might as well have been a heroin addict. I had to find a way to stave off the depression. But my "drug" had to be socially acceptable. So I plunged into church work. I would be the best pastor's wife anyone had ever met.

Totally unaware of what I was doing, I slid into compulsive

care giving. I found satisfaction and stimulation in trying to fix everyone around me—first our parishioners, then our friends, relatives,and neighbors. Before long, I was dependent on helping people. It gave me a feeling of significance and self-esteem. I had to earn my right to exist by being needed. I was on shaky ground.

Eventually, the depression caught up with me. Now what was I to do? I had run out of acceptable addictions. The only possibilities that remained were unacceptable to me or to the church. Should I compromise my values in order to find relief? I couldn't do *that*! What would people *think*? There were no more options. So I turned to God and begged Him to save me.

In so doing, I rolled into another addiction—religion (though I don't believe religion was the problem. The real problem was my dependent nature). In any case, I experienced a profound conversion. I could not have been more powerless, nor could I have been more sincere. I recognized my need, but I still did not recognize my compulsive nature.

In spite of my pathological reasons for seeking Him, God drew near to me. I'm so grateful that He doesn't expect people to have pure motives when they approach Him! I sought Him with all my heart, and I found Him. To this day I treasure that experience and thank God for my salvation. I walked and talked with Jesus. I was filled with the Holy Spirit. I felt complete. But, alas, because I had an addictive personality, everything I touched turned into an addiction, including my Christian experience.

For years, I had used compulsive overachieving and care giving to repair my damaged integrity. And they worked. Then I used people—my husband, my children, our church members, the people I was helping. But I ended up depressed again. So I turned to religion. I couldn't get enough of it. No amount of reading and study could save me from my pain. I memorized Scripture. I read commentaries and other inspirational literature. I devoured self-help books of all kinds, hoping to heal myself.

No matter what I did, I could not satisfy the ravenous beast within, the insatiable neediness. I had grown up in a world that demanded more than I could give. Nothing I did was ever enough. In this setting, I had internalized my own taskmaster. I was my own worst enemy. I beat myself up constantly with overwork and unrealistic expectations. With every success came greater feelings of inferiority and inadequacy. I had created a god who could not be pleased and who would not be appeased. But without that god's approval, I could not survive. This is the dilemma of all addiction. The addict makes someone or something into a god with an insatiable appetite, a god that he cannot satisfy.

Of course, my family was affected by my behavior. By the time I was thirty-eight years old, I was in the fourth stage of workaholism. I was using religion and perfectionism just to feel normal. Nothing felt good anymore. I was empty, bankrupt. I wasn't even sure I wanted to go on living. I had abused myself mercilessly trying to be the perfect student, the perfect pastor's wife, the perfect mother, the perfect Christian, the perfect teacher, the perfect counselor.

At forty-four, I was so burnt out professionally and personally that I was immobilized. I was offending and alienating my family, my friends, my colleagues, and my clients. I was trying so hard to "save" them that I was controlling compulsively, to everyone's detriment, particularly my own.

When I didn't have the strength to run any longer, depression overwhelmed me. I was, as the prophet phrased it in Lamentations, "without strength before the pursuer."[1] Now in the fourth and final stage of addiction to work, religion, perfectionism, and care giving, I felt that God had left me "sick and desolate the whole day through." Jeremiah's description of the plight of Jerusalem is an excellent definition of my addiction in its final stages: "He wove my sins into ropes to hitch me to a yoke of slavery. He sapped my strength and gave me to my enemies."[2]

My valued relationships had suffered enormously. My husband and children were in distress. They hadn't abandoned me yet, but it was only a matter of time. I was getting harder and harder to live with. I was on the verge of losing everything—my family, my career, my sanity, and my life.

Then one of the most precious people in the world to me said, "Mom, you need help." The next day, I went into a treatment program for codependence. I had to admit I couldn't do it alone—I had to surrender. I was an addictions counselor in absolute denial about my own addiction. I didn't know I was out of control until my son confronted me.

My codependence was not caused by the alcoholics I lived and worked with. I chose to live and work with addicts because I was codependent, as are 80 percent of the people in helping professions. I didn't have a drinking problem. I had a *living* problem. I could no longer relate to anyone without manipulating and controlling, without caretaking and enabling. I had to manage and fix other people in order to feel OK myself.

I expected my family (both my biological and church family) to meet my emotional needs in return for my care giving and kindness. I made them responsible for my well-being. And when they failed to give me what I wanted on my terms, I became angry and avoidant. I am arrogant and grandiose, just like an alcoholic, but I have never taken my first drink. The only difference between me and a drug addict is that the addict medicates his pain with chemicals, and I medicate mine with people and projects.

I was totally exhausted. Thanks to God, professional treatment, and twelve-step programs, I have been restored to sanity, serenity, and salvation—one day at a time. My program has not only given me life, but a quality of life I never dreamed possible. Through twelve-step programs, I have found the freedom to love and accept myself and others. In God, I have placed my trust and my hope for tomorrow.

As I have noted before, the story of the prodigal son is a classic example of addiction. Why the boy was inclined to addictive attitudes and thoughts, I do not know. The father is presented in Scripture as an ideal parent. Maybe that was not always the case. Perhaps he mellowed out (recovered from his own addictions) in his old age. He doubtless made mistakes in rearing his sons. I have wondered more than once why he chose to "enable" his younger son by giving him his fortune on demand.

Perhaps, like us, the father was fallible. Or perhaps, like our heavenly Father, he simply gave his son what any loving father would give—freedom. In any case, the son went off to a far country and spent his fortune overnight.[3] After a period of wallowing in the gutter, he realized that he was licked, came to his senses, and took twelve steps to recovery. (1) He admitted he was powerless and that his life was unmanageable: "I am starving to death."[4] (2) He recognized that he needed help, that he couldn't do it alone: "I will arise and go to my father."[5] (3) He turned his will and his life over to his father, (4) did a moral inventory, and (5) admitted in the presence of God and another person that he had done wrong: "I have sinned against heaven and against you. I am no longer worthy to be called your son; make me like one of your hired men."[6]

At this point he is interrupted by his father's jubilance. The transformation of steps 6 through 9 occurs almost instantly when he confesses his unworthiness to his father and the father covers him with his own garments, thus restoring him to a place of honor in the family. I have no trouble believing that this young man continued to learn from his mistakes (10), that he maintained contact with his heavenly Father (11), and that he shared his experience, strength, and hope with others as time went on (12).

The prodigal son was actually very fortunate. It didn't take long for him to hit bottom. Many addicts don't crash until they are thirty or forty years old. Those with chemical dependency seem to hit bottom sooner, sometimes in their twenties. They're the lucky ones, really. People with "clean" addictions usually suffer a great deal longer.

As is always the case when one person in an addictive family begins to recover, the status quo is disturbed. Other family members are thrown off balance. They can no longer focus their attention on the "sick" person and blame him for their problems. They, too, must make changes if their relationship is to survive.

The prodigal's older brother was in just such a position. He was so incensed by his brother's restoration to full sonship that he refused to speak to him.[7] When his father invited him to join the festivities, he complained bitterly. He was attached (bound, addicted) to his brother by his own resentment—more attached, in fact, than the prodigal had ever been to his self-defeating lifestyle.

In the attitude of the older brother I see my own attitude as well as that of many other Christians. We have a shaming, disdainful, unforgiving spirit toward addicts and alcoholics. We do not realize that we are equally sick. We do not know that our righteousness is as filthy rags. We actually think that our "faithfulness" qualifies us for some kind of special treatment, like the resentful vineyard workers in Matthew 20:1-15. We want the privileges of the kingdom to be ours exclusively because we have worked so hard to earn them. But it will not be so.

If you believe, as I do, in the second coming of Christ, you will be interested in this description of the alcoholic's place in the kingdom of God: "Those whom Christ has forgiven most will love Him most. These are they who in the final day will stand nearest to His throne."[8]

For some reason, I picture this as an A.A. meeting—one that I hope to attend. Both the pretentious sibling (the codependent) and the prodigal son (the alcoholic) were welcomed by the father. They were celebrated: " 'My son,' the father answered, 'you are always here with me, and everything I have is yours.' "[9] For that I am forever grateful.

God, grant me the serenity to accept the people I cannot change, the courage to change the person I can, and the wisdom to know that person is me! Amen.

---

1. Lamentations 1:6.
2. Lamentations 1:13,14, TLB.
3. Luke 15:13, 14.
4. Luke 15:17, NIV.
5. Luke 15:18, RSV.
6. Luke 15:18, 19, NIV.
7. See Luke 15:25-30.
8. Ellen White, *The Ministry of Healing* (Mountain View, Calif.: Pacific Press, 1942), 182.
9. Luke 15:31, TEV.

Appendix

Twelve-Step Recovery Organizations

Alcoholics Anonymous World Services
Box 459, Grand Central Station
New York, NY 10163
(212) 870-3400

Al-Anon/Alateen Family Groups, Inc.
Box 182, Madison Square Station
New York, NY 10159
(800) 356-9996

Narcotics Anonymous
P.O. Box 9999
Van Nuys, CA 91409
(818) 780-3951

Nar-Anon Family Group Headquarters, Inc.
P.O. Box 2562
Palos Verdes, CA 90274
(310) 547-5800

Emotions Anonymous International Services
P.O. Box 4245
St. Paul, MN 55104
(612) 647-9712

Co-Dependents Anonymous, Inc.
P.O. Box 33577
Phoenix, AZ 85067-3577
(602) 277-7991

Adult Children of Alcoholics
P.O. Box 3216
Torrance, CA 90510
(310) 534-1815

Overeaters Anonymous, Inc.
P.O. Box 92870
Los Angeles, CA 90009
(213) 936-6252

Gamblers Anonymous
P.O. Box 17173
Los Angeles, CA 90017
(213) 386-8789

Sexaholics Anonymous
P.O. Box 300
Simi Valley, CA 93062
(805) 581-3343

S-Anon International Family Groups
P.O. Box 5117
Sherman Oaks, CA 91413
(818) 990-6910

Sex & Love Addicts Anonymous
P.O. Box 119, New Town Branch
Boston, MA 02258
(617) 332-1845

Co-Sex & Love Addicts Anonymous
Program Wide Services
P.O. Box 614
Brookline, MA 02146-9998

Sex Addicts Anonymous
P.O. Box 3038
Minneapolis, MN 55403
(612) 339-0217

Codependents of Sex Addicts (CoSA)
P.O. Box 14537
Minneapolis, MN 55414
(612) 537-6904

Incest Survivors Anonymous
P.O. Box 5613
Long Beach, CA 90805-0613

Survivors of Incest Anonymous
P.O. Box 21817
Baltimore, MD 21222
(410) 282-3400

Workaholics Anonymous
P.O. Box 661501
Los Angeles, CA 90066
(310) 859-5804

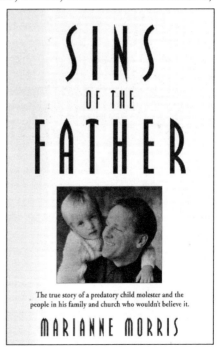